Social Psychology for Foundation Year

Introducing students to topical issues and controversies drawn from specific areas of social psychology, *Social Psychology for Foundation Year* answers a series of contemporary questions and debates by bringing together current theories and studies from a number of areas within the field.

Aimed primarily at students starting out on their degree journey, this book demonstrates how psychological research can help us understand our social world. Exploring topics from the Obama effect to groupthink, from what makes a good leader to the role of social identity in riots, it demonstrates how theories and studies contribute to our understanding of human behaviour. It embraces both established theories and recent empirical evidence to enable readers to see how research is linked to practical application in psychology and empowers readers to develop a greater understanding of why we do the things we do.

Social Psychology for Foundation Year is a key textbook for both foundation year and introductory psychology courses and will be of interest to anyone wanting to delve into topical issues in contemporary psychology.

Wendy Garnham is Professor of Psychology and Director of Student Experience for the Central Foundation Years, University of Sussex, UK. As co-founder of the Active Learning Network, Wendy has experience of teaching across the educational spectrum from reception to postgraduate level, including leading a further education psychology department to Grade 1 status and leading a sixth form before returning to Higher Education. Wendy has won several awards for innovative teaching, including a National Teaching Fellowship in 2020, was part of a Foundation Year team awarded both a CATE award in 2019 and a Pearson award for Outstanding Student Support in 2023.

John Drury is Professor of Social Psychology at the University of Sussex, UK. His research focuses on collective behaviour, including in emergencies and disasters, riots, protests, and social movements, as well as at ceremonies, music, and sports events. He has published over 100 peer-reviewed journal articles on these and other topics. He teaches crowd psychology to the UK Fire and Rescue Service and to crowd safety managers around the world. As part of the response to the COVID-19 pandemic, he participated in the UK government SAGE behavioural science subgroup SPI-B and is a member of Independent SAGE. He is a former editor of the *British Journal of Social Psychology*.

Social Psychology for Foundation Year

Key Ideas for Foundation Courses

Wendy Garnham
with guest chapter by John Drury

LONDON AND NEW YORK

Cover image: Getty Images © bauhaus1000

First published 2025
by Routledge
4 Park Square, Milton Park, Abingdon, Oxon OX14 4RN

and by Routledge
605 Third Avenue, New York, NY 10158

Routledge is an imprint of the Taylor & Francis Group, an informa business

© 2025 Wendy Garnham

The right of Wendy Garnham to be identified as author of this work has been asserted in accordance with sections 77 and 78 of the Copyright, Designs and Patents Act 1988.

All rights reserved. No part of this book may be reprinted or reproduced or utilised in any form or by any electronic, mechanical, or other means, now known or hereafter invented, including photocopying and recording, or in any information storage or retrieval system, without permission in writing from the publishers.

Trademark notice: Product or corporate names may be trademarks or registered trademarks, and are used only for identification and explanation without intent to infringe.

British Library Cataloguing-in-Publication Data
A catalogue record for this book is available from the British Library

Library of Congress Cataloging-in-Publication Data
Names: Garnham, Wendy, author. | Drury, John (Social psychologist), author.
Title: Social psychology for foundation year : key ideas for foundation courses / Wendy Garnham, with guest chapter by John Drury.
Description: Abingdon, Oxon ; New York, NY : Routledge, [2025] | Includes bibliographical references and index. | Identifiers:
LCCN 2023059064 (print) | LCCN 2023059065 (ebook) |
ISBN 9781032499574 (hardback) | ISBN 9781032499567 (paperback) | ISBN 9781003396208 (ebook)
Subjects: LCSH: Social psychology.
Classification: LCC HM1033 .G37 2025 (print) | LCC HM1033 (ebook) | DDC 302--dc23/eng/20220716
LC record available at https://lccn.loc.gov/2023059064
LC ebook record available at https://lccn.loc.gov/2023059065

ISBN: 978-1-032-49957-4 (hbk)
ISBN: 978-1-032-49956-7 (pbk)
ISBN: 978-1-003-39620-8 (ebk)

DOI: 10.4324/9781003396208

Typeset in Times New Roman
by KnowledgeWorks Global Ltd.

Access the Support Material: www.routledge.com/9781032499567

Contents

Preface vii
Acknowledgements ix

CHAPTER 1   Do you really know yourself? 1
CHAPTER 2   The psychology of physical attraction 23
CHAPTER 3   Do we only help others to benefit ourselves? 55
CHAPTER 4   Why do we want to be the same as everyone else?
            Or do we? 85
CHAPTER 5   The art of persuasion 101
CHAPTER 6   Seeing the social world through biased eyes 123
CHAPTER 7   Is a pub the best place to visit on a hot day? 147
CHAPTER 8   Soft drinks, President Obama and the reduction
            of prejudice 183
CHAPTER 9   Do groups make the best decisions? 205
CHAPTER 10 Guest Chapter: How does collective violence spread? 227
            JOHN DRURY
CHAPTER 11 What makes a good leader? 243

Index 259

Preface

This book is intended to entice readers into the fascinating world of Social Psychology, to inspire, enthuse, and hopefully encourage readers to want to find out more and continue their exploration of this subject. If it manages to succeed in any one of these aims, that is a good thing because this is very much a foundation, a diving board into a broad and vast field of research which we only scratch the surface of here.

Included in this book are a series of snapshots of how psychologists have tried to understand the way we behave in our social world. For example, do other people know us better than we know ourselves? Does familiarity breed liking when it comes to relationships? You will find out why it is important to consider the knowledge of everyone in your group when problem-solving, how doctors may succumb to the availability heuristic and how to win the hearts of well-educated individuals in appeals. You'll find out what the boomerang effect is, how anchoring and adjustment might be something to watch out for if you're bargaining and why fairy tales might not be the sweet and pleasant stories we think they are.

The aim of this book is to enable readers not only to immerse themselves in topical and often controversial debates but also to develop a critical awareness of alternative viewpoints, methodological weaknesses or theoretical short-comings. As you read the chapters, do try to link what you read to your own experience. Question the theories, think about the implications of this research, and perhaps even plan how you might address these issues in your own research going forward.

Enjoy!

Acknowledgements

I would like to thank the Routledge team for their help and support in getting this book published. Your professionalism and encouragement are much valued and appreciated. Thank you especially to Professor John Drury for sharing his ground-breaking research in Chapter 10. It means a lot to have your contribution to this book.

I am grateful to be able to work with some incredible colleagues in Foundation Year who are a constant source of inspiration, support, and positivity. Thank you to you all. My amazing students deserve a mention too – I hope this book helps and enthuses you as much as I intend it to.

And especially a big thank-you goes to my husband Alan, and our boys, Harry, George, Ben, Robin, and Tom for their constant support in everything and for always keeping me laughing. As Charlie Chaplin once said "A day without laughing is a day wasted" and you make sure I don't waste any!

I dedicate this book to my amazing parents, for making it all possible.

Chapter 1

Do you really know yourself?

Who knows you best? Yourself, right? Well, we like to think so for sure. In fact, psychology was initially founded on the idea of introspection, as described by William James (brother no less to Henry James, the famous novelist) who claimed:

introspective observation is what we have to rely on first and foremost and always.

(1890/1981, p. 185)

Introspection, according to Smithies (2012), describes a process of being able to look inwardly at our own minds and report what we find. We might be tempted to think that this process gives us unique access to our inner world and hence we come to know ourselves best. But is this right? A closer look at research in this area gives us a slightly different impression.

DO WE REALLY HAVE SUPERIOR ACCESS TO KNOWLEDGE ABOUT OURSELVES?

de Camp Wilson and Nisbett (1978) in a classic series of studies demonstrated that the idea of having exclusive introspective access to our thinking processes is erroneous. They conducted an experiment in a large store in a shopping centre. The researchers set up tables that displayed four identical nylon stocking pantyhose (you might be more familiar with the term "tights" nowadays!) on racks that were approximately three feet apart. A sign asked customers to make a judgement about which were the best quality. The position of the tights was counterbalanced. Rather intriguingly, the tights positioned furthest to the right were chosen as the best quality ones much more often than the rest and the further to the left the tights were displayed, the fewer times they were chosen. Positioning did seem to have an effect. When asked what determined their choice, participants pointed to features such as the elasticity or the sheerness but no one mentioned the position in the display. In fact, when asked if this could have influenced them, all but one participant flatly denied such a suggestion.

A similar picture was painted by Nisbett and Schachter (1966). In a study that would raise a few ethical eyebrows more recently, they asked university students to endure a series of electric shocks that increased in intensity as the experiment progressed. Before the experiment began, half of the students took a placebo pill that they were told could cause symptoms that were associated with those experienced when we are in shock, that is irregular breathing, heart palpitations, and butterflies in the stomach. Nisbett and Schachter found that those given the placebo pill were able to endure four times as much electric shock as those who were not. It is possible that they were attributing the symptoms they experienced to the placebo pill and not to the shock. However, when asked why they were able to ensure so much shock, the participants did not mention the placebo at all. When asked if this was a possibility, they argued that others may have been influenced by it but not them.

How about if you were asked to write an essay that argued for a point of view opposite to your own? Bem and McConnell (1970) asked psychology undergraduates to do just that. One group were given a choice about what to argue in their essay. The other group were given no choice and were asked to argue that they should have no choice at all in their curriculum, something which contradicted their own expressed attitude at the beginning of the study. When later asked about their attitudes to the topic of curriculum choice, those who had written an essay that conflicted with their initial views declared more agreement with this "new" view. When asked what their attitudes had been before they wrote the essays, many misremembered that they had always had the "new" attitudes.

All of these studies ask participants to reflect back and explain their behaviour but what if we ask participants to forecast how they might feel in the future? Sieff et al. (1999) asked individuals attending the Pittsburgh AIDS Task Force testing site to predict how they would feel five weeks after getting their HIV test results. Not surprisingly, the predictions were of misery if the news was bad and elation if the news was good. However, when they were actually asked, five weeks after receipt of the test results, those who received bad news were less distraught and those who received good news were less elated than expected. Their anticipated responses were much more extreme than the reality that occurred. It is no coincidence then that Wilson 2002 argues that we are strangers to ourselves.

Woodzicka and LaFrance (2001) asked female respondents to read a scenario in which interviewers asked an interviewee questions considered sexually harassing. The participants were then asked to imagine that they were in that position. How would they respond? Not surprisingly, 62% claimed they would ask the interviewer why the questions were being asked or would say the questions were inappropriate. A further 28% said they would leave the interview or rudely confront the interviewer. Twenty-seven percent expressed how angry they would feel. In a follow-up study, a new group of female participants were invited to participate in an interview designed to determine eligibility for a research assistant position. For half of the participants, interviews contained three "harassing" questions (e.g. Do people find you desirable?). For the other half, interviews contained three "control" questions (e.g. Do people find you morbid?). Did the actions of the harassed participants meet the imagined responses declared in the first study? No. All participants answered all questions. Few confronted the interviewers. In fact, 52% ignored the harassment completely. Thirty-six percent did ask why the question was being asked but 80% of those asking the question did so only after the interview had terminated. Whilst many of the participants in the first study imagined feeling angry, 40% of those in the second study reported feeling fearful. Only 16% reported feelings of anger.

You might be thinking that these instances are set in somewhat unusual situations. It isn't everyday that we go for a job interview, for example. Surely, in everyday situations, we are not so susceptible? Unfortunately, even here we find it difficult to predict our own behaviour. Think about how long it will take you to complete your next assignment. How long will you need to prepare it? According to Kruger and Evans (2004), chances are you will underestimate how long it will take. This is known as the planning fallacy (Kahneman & Tversky, 1977). Kruger and Evans asked undergraduate students to make predictions about everything from time taken to complete holiday shopping to formatting a document to preparing food. To prevent the planning fallacy they argued, we have to "unpack" a task into its subcomponents and this is something we rarely do. Table 1.1 shows the difference that "unpacking" can make to our predictions. We are still far from perfect but it does reduce the discrepancy between how long we think it will take and how long it actually does take.

■ **Table 1.1** Mean time predicted and taken to complete a document formatting task by packing condition.

	Predicted	Actual
Packed	17.3	39.7
Unpacked	28.3	38.0

Data taken from Kruger and Evans (2004).

Even when we are deliberately asked to reflect on our reasoning for a decision, we are not very good at it. In fact, introspection can actually impair our processing of information. Tordesillas and Chaiken (1999) reported that introspection caused a decline in the amount of information processed by college students when making decisions about course choices and Wilson and Schooler (1991) found that it led to decisions that contrasted more with expert opinion. When asked to rate a series of strawberry jam samples, the ratings of participants in the control condition (where participants were simply asked to state their preferences for the different jam samples) aligned with those of trained sensory experts. The ratings of those asked to think about the reasons why they liked or disliked the jams, in contrast, were quite different.

OBSESSED WITH THE SELF?

Given the controversy over whether we have superior access to the self, it is something of a paradox that we are increasingly obsessed with the self. Writing in 2009, Roy Baumeister claimed:

> *No topic is more interesting to people than people. For most people, moreover, the most interesting person is the self.*
>
> (p. 1)

And Twenge and Campbell (2009) have argued that we are experiencing a "narcissism epidemic", such is the focus on the self. Narcissism, they claim is:

> *... a very positive and inflated view of the self. People with high levels of narcissism – whom we refer to as "narcissists" think they are better than others in social status, good looks, intelligence, and creativity.*
>
> (p. 19)

In a meta-analysis of 85 studies, Twenge et al. (2008) suggested that students now endorse two more narcissistic items than students in the 1980s and this shift is so significant that the generation you represent is now a better predictor of narcissism than sex difference.

You only have to look at the rise in selfie-taking on social media to see how we have become increasingly obsessed with the self. Chae (2017), for example, points to data that suggests that in excess of 255 million photos had been hash tagged with #selfie on Instagram and Brandt (2014) reported Google statistics that suggested about 93 billion were taken every day! What makes this even more shocking is these statistics were taken only from Android phone users. According to Carpenter (2012) one of the best predictors of posting such content on social media is indeed narcissism.

If information is relevant to us, we remember it better (Rogers et al., 1977). We will remember what is said about us better than what was said about someone else even 2 days after the conversation has finished (Kahan & Johnson, 1992), and even just thinking about whether a word describes us helps us to remember it better (Kuiper, 1981). Mor et al. (2010) asked high school juniors to complete diary entries six times a day for three consecutive weekdays. As well as measures of self-focus, they were asked to document any thoughts in which they were engaged immediately before completing the diary. For females, 42% of the time, their

■ **Figure 1.1** Are we obsessed with the self?

thoughts were focused on the self. For males, the corresponding figure was 32%. Even if you look at the lyrics of popular songs, you will find a focus on the self. DeWall et al. (2011) reported a steady increase, for example, in the number of first-person singular pronouns in lyrics.

In fact, we are so obsessed with the self, that often we assume others are equally obsessed with us too. Gilovich et al. (2000), for example, talk of the "spotlight effect". This is where we believe that others are observing us more than they really are. Gilovich asked participants to wear a Barry Manilow t-shirt to a room where other participants were seated. When asked who would recall what t-shirt they wore, they thought many more would than was really the case.

It isn't just that we think others are observing us but actually that they can read our emotions, thoughts, and feelings more than they can too. Gilovich et al. (1998) called this the "illusion of transparency". We think of ourselves as being more "transparent" to others. Now imagine having to deliver a public speech. Savitsky and Gilovich (2003) found that participants who reported feeling nervous as they did so believed that they appeared nervous to others too. However, their expectations of how nervous they appeared did not match the ratings given by those in the audience. The good news is that when speakers were told about the illusion of transparency, they thought they appeared more relaxed to their audience and evaluated their own speeches more positively.

DO OTHERS KNOW US BETTER THAN WE KNOW OURSELVES?

There is good reason though as to why we might think that others are more concerned with us than they really are. As MacDonald and Ross (1999) report, others can often predict our behaviour better than we can. MacDonald and Ross compared the predictions of the longevity of dating relationships as made by students themselves, their parents, and room-mates. Students were significantly more optimistic about the enduring nature of their relationships than either their parents or room-mates but in terms of accuracy of prediction, the room-mates won (followed by parents).

Smith et al., in 2008, reported that spouses' ratings of an individual's negative affect and social behaviour are consistently associated with coronary artery disease but self-reports of the same things are not. Vazire (2010) reported that self-ratings of creativity were significantly more positive than those given by others and Fiedler et al. (2004) found that peers were better able to predict who remained on active duty in the military compared to self-report measures.

In three meta-analyses, Connelly and Ones (2010) reported that observer ratings of personality were strong predictors of behaviour. For example, in terms of academic achievement or job performance, the ratings of others were much more predictive than those given by the individual themselves. With the rise in Artificial Intelligence (AI), it may come as no surprise to find that computer-based models are even more accurate than our Facebook friends at making judgements of personality (Youyou et al., 2015)!

So, why is there a discrepancy? According to Vazire (2010), we tend to see ourselves much more favourably in our self-report. It would appear we have something of a blind spot when it comes to our failings. In a rather shocking study, Stewart (2005) demonstrated the implications of this for assessing responsibility in situations of car crashes. Car crash survivors who experienced crashes of greater severity were significantly more likely to see the "other" driver as more responsible rather than themselves. Where personal responsibility was acknowledged, weather and road conditions were blamed more often.

■ **Figure 1.2** Do we really know who we are?

MANAGING HOW OTHERS SEE US

It may come as no surprise then that we seem to be obsessed with finding out about our "self" from others. Cooley (1902) introduced the idea of the "looking glass self" to describe how we internalise other people's view of ourselves. To ensure that others have a positive view of ourselves, however, we often engage in behaviours that attempt to control their view of ourselves.

False modesty

Have you ever watched an awards ceremony on TV? If so, you may well have noticed the lengths that award winners go to, to thank those around them for contributing to their success. How sincere do you think these thanks are? Baumeister and Ilko (1995) describe this as potential "shallow gratitude". When we experience success, we tend to take credit for this ourselves but only privately. Publicly, we show a tendency to thank others. Baumeister and Ilko asked students to write two stories, one about a major success experience and one about a major failure experience. For half of the students, they were asked to write their name on the bottom of the page and were told that they would be expected to read their story aloud to a group who would be engaging in a discussion. This was the "public" condition. For the other half of the students, they were not told to write their names or read their stories aloud and were not expecting any group discussion. This was the "private" condition. Consistent with the shallow gratitude idea, those in the public condition were significantly more likely to acknowledge external help in achieving success. Privately, however, credit was instead directed to the self.

This is not an isolated example. Miller and Schlenker (1985) reported a similar finding when observing the actions of groups asked to work together on a "survival exercise". For half of the groups, they received feedback saying that on the basis of the decisions made by the group they would have only an 11% chance of survival. The other half of the groups received feedback saying that on the basis of their group's decisions, they would have a 91% chance of survival. Participants were then asked to complete a questionnaire which explored their thoughts about responsibility for the outcome, their own individual contribution, the role of luck, and task difficulty. For some, they were told they would be asked to share their questionnaire responses with the others. For some they were told their responses were confidential. Similar to Baumeister and Ilko's findings, participants claimed more responsibility for successful outcomes privately than they did publicly. When they knew that their questionnaire responses would be shared amongst group members, they claimed to have had less responsibility for successful outcomes than their peers.

Why might we be so tempted to do this? Perhaps we don't want to be disliked by others (Forsyth et al., 1981) or we fear provoking envy (e.g. Bedeian, 1995). Perhaps taking more credit for success ourselves is about ensuring we do not look conceited or arrogant in front of others (Weiner, 2005). In fact, Exline and Lobel (1999) claim that our concern with how others see us, particularly when successful, can pose a threat to our well-being. This is likely to be the case in situations where other people might feel uncomfortable as a result. For example, Exline and Lobel give the example of a student who outperforms a peer on a college test. They are, it is claimed, more likely to feel anxious about meeting that peer as a result. It is interesting to note that this self-serving bias does disappear when we are working with friends. In these cases, we are much more likely to see responsibility for both positive and negative outcomes as being shared. Amongst strangers, however, the bias comes into play in full force (Campbell et al., 2000).

False consensus effect

Not only do we want to be seen as nice, but we also want others to see us as being "similar". Time to introduce another paradox in our study of the self: although we like to think of ourselves as unique, we actually want others to see us as "one of the crowd". Ross et al. (1977) defined the false consensus effect as the tendency to:

> *... see their own behavioural choices and judgements as relatively common and appropriate to existing circumstances while viewing alternative responses as uncommon, deviant or inappropriate.*
>
> (p. 280)

That is, we believe that other people share our attitudes or behave similarly to us much more than is the case. Wolfson (2000) asked non-drug using students, cannabis-using students, and amphetamine-using students to estimate how prevalent cannabis and amphetamine use was amongst students more generally. The estimates of cannabis use given by cannabis users were significantly higher than those given by non-drug users. Similarly, the estimates of amphetamine use given by amphetamine users were significantly higher than those given by non-drug users. The tendency to overestimate behaviours similar to those they engaged in themselves was clearly demonstrated.

It works in other contexts too. Collisson et al. (2021) demonstrated false consensus effects in perceived celebrity popularity. Participants overestimated the percentage of other people who would identify the same celebrity as them, as their first, second, and third favourite. Koestner et al. (1995) demonstrated a similar effect in voting estimates in a Canadian Referendum. Those who were more emotionally involved in supporting a positive outcome gave significantly higher estimates of how many people would vote yes in the referendum. Monin and Norton (2003) even demonstrated this effect in a field study of water conservation. Students at Princeton University who took one or more showers during the period of a shower ban gave significantly higher estimates of how many other students took showers during this time period. Even when it comes to eating habits, the false consensus effect has a role to play. Eibach et al. (2003) reported a significant difference in the estimates given for how prevalent food advertisements were by those dieting and those not dieting. Those dieting tended to give much higher estimates, a finding that is not so surprising given that we know dieters tend to be more aware of external food cues (Baumeister et al., 1994).

The false consensus effect is a reminder that we like to think we have a lot of support for our ways of thinking or behaving. This can be especially useful for cases where we are not so successful or where we engage in behaviours that are not socially desirable. Failure, or at least the anticipation of it, leads us to our next example of how we manipulate the view that others may form of us, self-handicapping.

Self-handicapping

Imagine the view that others would have of us if we were seen to fail. Perhaps repeatedly. Well let's not dwell on that thought for too long! Thankfully, we have developed a way of protecting ourselves and presenting a more positive view to others. It is called self-handicapping, a term introduced originally by Berglas and Jones (1978). As much as we like to be humble and be modest about our successes, when it comes to failure, we like to look to external factors to explain them, thereby protecting the self. If there isn't an obvious candidate to pass the blame to, we create "handicaps" to enable us to overcome this.

Jones and Berglas (1978) point to a number of examples such as the tennis player who adjusts the strings on his tennis racket, a golfer who avoids taking lessons or the high school senior who limits his sleep the night before an exam. Where a bad shot is taken or an exam is failed, there is always an external factor to blame rather than the self. Rhodewalt et al. (1984) studied male swimmers from the Princeton University swimming team. Two weeks before the first competition of the season, they were asked to complete the Self-Handicapping Scale which includes items that assess any concerns about achievement as well as any tendencies to adopt self-handicapping behaviours. One day prior to the competition, they were then asked to complete a different questionnaire that probed their feelings about their practice, health, and preparation. Those who scored low on the self-handicapping scale tended to increase their effort before a competition but those who scored highly did not. Those who scored highly were more likely to see the conditions for performance as being less than ideal and to see themselves as being in poorer physical condition, all of which may well explain poorer outcomes, and thereby avoid lack of ability being seen as the cause.

One of the most heavily studied areas where self-handicapping occurs is the area of academic achievement. Imagine taking part in a test at a prestigious university. You are trying your best to answer what are actually insoluble problems. It's tough. Nonetheless, at the end of this first test, you are told that you had achieved one of the best scores. In the next stage of the study, you are told you will be asked to complete a second, similar test and will be given a choice of two drugs you could take. One, Actavil, is a drug that will improve your performance on the next part of the test. The

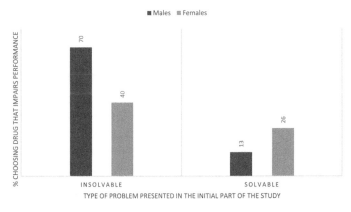

■ **Figure 1.3** Percentage choosing the drug that they believed would impair performance when initial problems were solvable or impossible to solve. Data taken from Berglas and Jones (1978).

other, Pandocrin, is a drug that will impair your performance. You can also choose what dosage to take of your chosen drug. Which would you choose and how much would you take? This was exactly the scenario that Berglas and Jones (1978) presented to their undergraduate students.

To the researchers' surprise, the majority of participants chose the drug that would impair their performance but only when the initial problems were-unsolvable. Why choose a drug that will inhibit performance? If they performed poorly then they could blame the drug rather than their ability. Urdan and Midgley (2001) suggest that handicapping may be related to avoidance of looking stupid in front of others. Again, we want to ensure that other people have a good impression of ourselves.

Can we all be better-than-average?

You may be getting the idea now that there is something of a paradox here. We look to other people to find out about ourselves but we are also keen to ensure that other people develop a good view of us as individuals. We need the input of others to bolster our self-image but we do everything we can to ensure that the input we receive aligns with our desire in terms of how we want to be seen. And believe it or not, how we want to be seen is usually as a better-than-average individual (Zell et al., 2020). This refers to:

> ... the tendency for people to perceive their abilities, attributes and personality traits as superior compared with their average peer.
>
> (Zell et al., 2020, p. 118)

In a meta-analysis of 124 articles, 291 samples, and more than 950,000 participants, the authors demonstrated the robustness of this effect. Cross (1977) studied university professors (and yes, I know I am opening up a whole can of worms here), but 94% rated themselves as better than the average professor. Svenson (1981) reported a staggering 90% of adult drivers believe they are above average in driving ability and Sedikides et al. (2014) demonstrated the effect on criminals. Prisoners rated themselves as better than the average prisoner in terms of positive personality traits such as honesty and kindness but also better than the average individual in the general population! In fact, Alicke et al. (2001) share findings which suggest we think we are better than we are even when provided with evidence that suggests other people also rate themselves as better than average.

What happens when we receive negative feedback or obtain information that is not consistent with this view? Thunström et al. (2016) suggest we engage in "strategic self-ignorance". When given the opportunity to see the calorie count of an unhealthy meal, many diners chose not to, opting to look at a blank piece of paper rather than the one that had the calorie count written on it. When an essay written by an African American student was criticised by a white student, who was aware of the race of the writer, negative criticism had little effect on self-esteem. The evaluation was instead attributed to racial prejudice (Crocker et al., 1991). It is interesting also to note that when positive feedback was obtained, and the white student was aware of the writer's race, this had a negative effect for the same reason. It is worth noting here, that if you receive negative feedback, chances are you will spend less time reading it anyway (Baumeister & Cairns, 1992).

And whilst we are on this topic, let me mention this – don't try to impress your room-mates by emphasising your personal good qualities and hiding the bad ones. If they perceive this to be a means of you trying to get them to like you, that will lead to them liking you less and reducing your self-esteem (Canevello & Crocker, 2011). And it is to self-esteem that we turn next.

WHAT HAPPENS IF WE THINK TOO HIGHLY OF OURSELVES?

Thinking positively of ourselves has been taken to indicate high levels of self-esteem. Self-esteem is defined as:

> *... a person's overall negative or positive self-evaluation or sense of worth.*
>
> (Myers et al., 2014, p. 64)

Baumeister (2022) points to historical views that low self-esteem was linked with high crime and violence rates, poor school outcomes, and unstable family relationships. Murray et al. (2002), for example, led participants to believe that their romantic partner had identified a flaw in the relationship. Those who reported low self-esteem tended to interpret this as a sign of reduced closeness and a waning of affection. Forrester et al. (2017) linked low self-esteem to non-suicidal self-injury and Salmela-Aro and Nurmi (2007) linked it to unemployment, feelings of exhaustion, and low levels of work satisfaction. Renzetti (1992) even suggested that it was a contributory factor in explaining the jealousy and possessiveness that led to domestic violence in some relationships. If you ever happen to go on a talent show, be aware that low self-esteem in your audience won't fair well. Van Dijk et al. (2012) reported that low self-esteem individuals are more likely to relish the misfortunes of others as a way of restoring their own sense of worth, a concept known as Schadenfreude. It really isn't looking great for individuals with low self-esteem is it. No wonder then that we engage so much effort into trying to ensure that the impression we give to others, which we then look to, to understand ourselves, is positive. In fact, Bushman et al. (2011) claim that a boost to self-esteem is preferred to pizza, sex, and beer in college students, it is that important! (Incidentally they even rated it as more welcome than seeing a best friend ….).

But as with many things in life, it is possible to have too much of a good thing. If we look at individuals with higher than average self-esteem, things do not look too rosy for them either. In fact, Baumeister et al. (2009) refer to this as "the dark side of self-esteem". Bushman and Baumeister (2002) suggest that this is linked with membership of teen gangs, with violent crime and with terrorism. On a less frightening note, it has also been linked with poor performance on examinations. Forsyth et al. (2007) sent all of their students who had received a poor grade in the mid-term assessment, a weekly email. For one-third of the students, the email contained both a review question and a message aimed at increasing their self-esteem. For one-third, their message was a reminder to take responsibility for their grades and the final third received no message at all. Unfortunately, the attempt to bolster self-esteem backfired and students performed worse in the final exam. The students were convinced to think well of themselves regardless of academic achievement. So maybe not all was lost.

Sticking with the theme of students and their experience of teaching, tutors beware! As much as you may find this hard to believe, evaluations of teaching are heavily influenced by self-esteem. As Vaillancourt (2013) discovered, give a high self-esteem student a bit of positive feedback and you can be assured your teaching will be evaluated favourably. However, give negative feedback to a high self-esteem student and chances are your teaching will receive significantly lower evaluations. According to Vaillancourt, poor evaluations are a form of aggressive behaviour motivated by the threat to self-esteem.

It also works with peers too. Bushman and Baumeister (1998) asked participants to write a paragraph which another student would evaluate. For half of the participants, their writing was evaluated positively with praise but for the other half, it was criticised. All participants were then invited to take part in a reaction time game with the evaluator. If the evaluator lost, the participant could deliver a noise of an intensity and duration of their choice. You can probably guess the ending to this sorry tale. Yes, those with the highest self-esteem delivered three times as much auditory intensity and duration to those who had criticized their work as those with lower self-esteem! Heatherton and Vohs (2000) reported something similar with their undergraduate participants. After self-esteem had been threatened by giving them the impression they had scored lower than expected on a test, high self-esteem individuals were rated as more antagonistic and unfriendly in a later conversation. Baumeister et al. (2000) do suggest that such occurrences are best described as cases of "threatened egotism" where individuals fiercely defend a highly superior view of themselves against someone who is trying to attack it. As with most things, a fine balance is perhaps the best option!

CULTURE MAKES A DIFFERENCE

It should be remembered that much of the research discussed so far is based on studies conducted in individualistic, western cultures. As Ma and Schoeneman (1997) point out, individualist views emphasise the private self more than collective identity. Value is attached to the idea of independence and personal goals dominate. In collectivist cultures, however, the self is defined in terms of relationships with others. Group goals dominate over personal goals and conformity to group norms are emphasised. Ma and Schoeneman asked participants to complete a shorter version of the Twenty Statements Test (Kuhn & McPartland, 1954). This involved answering the question "Who am I?" in a different way 15 times. Individuals from Kenyan Maasi tribal societies showed more collectivist responses than individuals from American colleges. Whilst 80% of the responses given by Maasi individuals were considered to be social, only 12% of those given by American individuals were. This is in line with the idea that individuals from collectivist cultures think of themselves as interdependent on their social groups as opposed to being independent (Gudykunst & Lee, 2003).

Time for a quick question: if there are four blue pens and one orange pen, and you were asked to choose one to use, which would you choose? Kim and Markus (1999) asked participants to make this decision. Seventy-seven percent of American students chose the orange one-Thirty-one percent of Asian students did so. This was the case even when the colour of the uncommon pen changed to green. Kim and Markus explain this in terms of the uniqueness of the uncommon pen. American, individualist culture emphasises uniqueness as a favoured quality. This difference is also seen in advertisements (Kim & Markus, 1999), in popular songs (Schoeneman, 1994) and even Facebook profile pictures (Huang & Park, 2013). When asked to watch an animation of an underwater scene, individuals from a collectivist culture such as Japan recall significantly more about the relationship between component parts of the scene than American individuals (Nisbett, 2004).

It is important to avoid hard distinctions however. As time changes, so do cultural norms. There is an indication that younger citizens in collectivist cultures are beginning to hold more individualistic ideas (Arora, 2005) and some researchers such as Oyserman et al. (2002) are reporting that African Americans are now the most individualist group in America.

REFERENCES

Alicke, M. D., Vredenburg, D. S., Hiatt, M., & Govorun, O. (2001). The "better than myself effect". *Motivation and Emotion, 25*, 7–22.

Arora, D. (2005). Foreign multinationals in India: Adapting to India's work culture and management practices. *Internationale Geschäftstätigkeiten in Asien: München und Mering, Rainer Hampp, Germany*, 1–37.

Baumeister, R. F. (Ed.). (2009). *The self in social psychology*. Psychology Press.

Baumeister, R. F. (2022). *The self explained: Why and how we become who we are*. Guilford.

Baumeister, R. F., Bushman, B. J., & Campbell, W. K. (2000). Self-esteem, narcissism, and aggression: Does violence result from low self-esteem or from threatened egotism? *Current Directions in Psychological Science, 9*(1), 26–29.

Baumeister, R. F., & Cairns, K. J. (1992). Repression and self-presentation: When audiences interfere with self-deceptive strategies. *Journal of Personality and Social Psychology, 62*(5), 851.

Baumeister, R. F., Heatherton, T. F., & Tice, D. M. (1994). *Losing control: How and why people fail at self-regulation*. Academic.

Baumeister, R. F., & Ilko, S. A. (1995). Shallow gratitude: Public and private acknowledgement of external help in accounts of success. *Basic and Applied Social Psychology, 16*(1–2), 191–209.

Baumeister, R. F., Smart, L., & Boden, J. M. (2009) Relation of threatened egotism to violence and aggression: The dark side of high self-esteem. In R.F. Baumeister (Ed.) *The self in social psychology*. Psychology Press.

Bedeian, A. G. (1995). Workplace envy. *Organizational Dynamics, 23*(4), 49–56.

Bem, D. J., & McConnell, H. K. (1970). Testing the self-perception explanation of dissonance phenomena: On the salience of premanipulation attitudes. *Journal of Personality and Social Psychology, 14*(1), 23.

Berglas, S., & Jones, E. E. (1978). Drug choice as a self-handicapping strategy in response to noncontingent success. *Journal of Personality and Social Psychology, 36*(4), 405.

Brandt, R. (2014). Google divulges numbers at I/O: 20 billion texts, 93 million selfies and more. *Silicon Valley Business Journal*, (June 25th). Retrieved from http://www.bizjournals.com/sanjose/news/2014/06/25/google-divulges-numbers-at-i-o-20-billion-texts-93.html

Bushman, B. J., & Baumeister, R. F. (1998). Threatened egotism, narcissism, self-esteem, and direct and displaced aggression: Does self-love or self-hate lead to violence? *Journal of Personality and Social Psychology, 75*(1), 219.

Bushman, B. J., & Baumeister, R. F. (2002). Does self-love or self-hate lead to violence? *Journal of Research in Personality, 36*(6), 543–545.

Bushman, B. J., Moeller, S. J., & Crocker, J. (2011). Sweets, sex, or self-esteem? Comparing the value of self-esteem boosts with other pleasant rewards. *Journal of Personality, 79*(5), 993–1012.

Campbell, W. K., Sedikides, C., Reeder, G. D., & Elliot, A. J. (2000). Among friends? An examination of friendship and the self-serving bias. *British Journal of Social Psychology, 39*(2), 229–239.

Canevello, A., & Crocker, J. (2011). Interpersonal goals and close relationship processes: Potential links to health. *Social and Personality Psychology Compass, 5*(6), 346–358.

Carpenter, C. J. (2012). Narcissism on Facebook: Self-promotional and anti-social behavior. *Personality and Individual Differences, 52*(4), 482–486.

Chae, J. (2017). Virtual makeover: Selfie-taking and social media use increase selfie-editing frequency through social comparison. *Computers in Human Behavior, 66*, 370–376.

Collisson, B., McCutcheon, L. E., Johnston, M., & Edman, J. (2021). How popular are pop stars? The false consensus of perceived celebrity popularity. *Psychology of Popular Media, 10*(1), 14.

Connelly, B. S., & Ones, D. S. (2010). Another perspective on personality: Meta-analytic integration of observers' accuracy and predictive validity. *Psychological Bulletin, 136*(6), 1092.

Cooley, C. H. (1902). Looking-glass self. *The Production of Reality: Essays and Readings on Social Interaction, 6*, 126–128.

Crocker, J., Voelkl, K., Testa, M., & Major, B. (1991). Social stigma: The affective consequences of attributional ambiguity. *Journal of Personality and Social Psychology, 60*(2), 218.

Cross, K. P. (1977). Not can, but will college teaching be improved? *New Directions for Higher Education, 1977*(17), 1–15.

de Camp Wilson, T., & Nisbett, R. E. (1978). The accuracy of verbal reports about the effects of stimuli on evaluations and behavior. *Social Psychology, 41*, 118–131.

DeWall, C. N., Pond, R. S. Jr, Campbell, W. K., & Twenge, J. M. (2011). Tuning in to psychological change: Linguistic markers of psychological traits and emotions over time in popular US song lyrics. *Psychology of Aesthetics, Creativity, and the Arts, 5*(3), 200.

Eibach, R. P., Libby, L. K., & Gilovich, T. D. (2003). When change in the self is mistaken for change in the world. *Journal of Personality and Social Psychology, 84*(5), 917.

Exline, J. J., & Lobel, M. (1999). The perils of outperformance: Sensitivity about being the target of a threatening upward comparison. *Psychological Bulletin, 125*(3), 307.

Fiedler, E. R., Oltmanns, T. F., & Turkheimer, E. (2004). Traits associated with personality disorders and adjustment to military life: Predictive validity of self and peer reports. *Military Medicine, 169*(3), 207–211.

Forrester, R. L., Slater, H., Jomar, K., Mitzman, S., & Taylor, P. J. (2017). Self-esteem and non-suicidal self-injury in adulthood: A systematic review. *Journal of Affective Disorders, 221*, 172–183.

Forsyth, D. R., Berger, R. E., & Mitchell, T. (1981). The effects of self-serving vs. other-serving claims of responsibility on attraction and attribution in groups. *Social Psychology Quarterly, 44*, 59–64.

Forsyth, D. R., Lawrence, N. K., Burnette, J. L., & Baumeister, R. F. (2007). Attempting to improve the academic performance of struggling college students by bolstering their self–esteem: An intervention that backfired. *Journal of Social and Clinical Psychology, 26*(4), 447–459.

Gilovich, T., Medvec, V. H., & Savitsky, K. (2000). The spotlight effect in social judgment: An egocentric bias in estimates of the salience of one's own actions and appearance. *Journal of Personality and Social Psychology, 78*(2), 211.

Gilovich, T., Savitsky, K., & Medvec, V. H. (1998). The illusion of transparency: Biased assessments of others' ability to read one's emotional states. *Journal of Personality and Social Psychology, 75*(2), 332.

Gudykunst, W. B., & Lee, C. M. (2003). Assessing the validity of self construal scales: A response to Levine et al. *Human Communication Research, 29*(2), 253–274.

Heatherton, T. F., & Vohs, K. D. (2000). Interpersonal evaluations following threats to self: Role of self-esteem. *Journal of Personality and Social Psychology, 78*(4), 725.

Huang, C. M., & Park, D. (2013). Cultural influences on Facebook photographs. *International Journal of Psychology, 48*(3), 334–343.

James, W. (1890/1981). *The principles of psychology*. Harvard University Press.

Jones, E. E., & Berglas, S. (1978). Control of attributions about the self through self-handicapping strategies: The appeal of alcohol and the role of underachievement. *Personality and Social Psychology Bulletin, 4*(2), 200–206.

Kahan, T. L., & Johnson, M. K. (1992). Self effects in memory for person information. *Social Cognition, 10*(1), 30–50.

Kahneman, D., & Tversky, A. (1977). *Intuitive prediction: Biases and corrective procedures* (p. 0044). Decision Research, Perceptronics.

Kim, H., & Markus, H. R. (1999). Deviance or uniqueness, harmony or conformity? A cultural analysis. *Journal of Personality and Social Psychology, 77*(4), 785.

Koestner, R., Losier, G. F., Worren, N. M., Baker, L., & Vallerand, R. J. (1995). False consensus effects for the 1992 Canadian referendum. *Canadian Journal of Behavioural Science/Revue canadienne des sciences du comportement, 27*(2), 214.

Kruger, J., & Evans, M. (2004). If you don't want to be late, enumerate: Unpacking reduces the planning fallacy. *Journal of Experimental Social Psychology, 40*(5), 586–598.

Kuhn, M. H., & McPartland, T. S. (1954). Twenty statements test. *American Sociological Review.18*, 68–76.

Kuiper, N. A. (1981). Convergent evidence for the self as a prototype: The "inverted-U RT effect" for self and other judgments. *Personality and Social Psychology Bulletin, 7*(3), 438–443.

Ma, V., & Schoeneman, T. J. (1997). Individualism versus collectivism: A comparison of Kenyan and American self-concepts. *Basic and Applied Social Psychology, 19*(2), 261–273.

MacDonald, T. K., & Ross, M. (1999). Assessing the accuracy of predictions about dating relationships: How and why do lovers' predictions differ from those made by observers? *Personality and Social Psychology Bulletin, 25*(11), 1417–1429.

Miller, R. S., & Schlenker, B. R. (1985). Egotism in group members: Public and private attributions of responsibility for group performance. *Social Psychology Quarterly, 48*, 85–89.

Monin, B., & Norton, M. I. (2003). Perceptions of a fluid consensus: Uniqueness bias, false consensus, false polarization, and pluralistic ignorance in a water conservation crisis. *Personality and Social Psychology Bulletin, 29*(5), 559–567.

Mor, N., Doane, L. D., Adam, E. K., Mineka, S., Zinbarg, R. E., Griffith, J. W., Craske, M., Waters, A., & Nazarian, M. (2010). Within-person variations in self-focused attention and negative affect in depression and anxiety: A diary study. *Cognition and Emotion, 24*(1), 48–62.

Murray, S. L., Rose, P., Bellavia, G. M., Holmes, J. G., & Kusche, A. G. (2002). When rejection stings: How self-esteem constrains relationship-enhancement processes. *Journal of Personality and Social Psychology, 83*(3), 556.

Myers, D., Abell, J., & Sani, F. (2014). *Social psychology*. McGraw-Hill.

Nisbett, R. (2004). *The geography of thought: How Asians and Westerners think differently ... and why*. Simon and Schuster.

Nisbett, R. E., & Schachter, S. (1966). Cognitive manipulation of pain. *Journal of Experimental Social Psychology, 2*(3), 227–236.

Oyserman, D., Coon, H. M., & Kemmelmeier, M. (2002). Rethinking individualism and collectivism: Evaluation of theoretical assumptions and meta-analyses. *Psychological Bulletin, 128*(1), 3.

Renzetti, C. M. (1992). *Violent betrayal: Partner abuse in lesbian relationships*. Sage Publications.

Rhodewalt, F., Saltzman, A. T., & Wittmer, J. (1984). Self-handicapping among competitive athletes: The role of practice in self-esteem protection. *Basic and Applied Social Psychology, 5*(3), 197–209.

Rogers, T. B., Kuiper, N. A., & Kirker, W. S. (1977). Self-reference and the encoding of personal information. *Journal of Personality and Social Psychology, 35*(9), 677.

Ross, L., Greene, D., & House, P. (1977). The "false consensus effect": An egocentric bias in social perception and attribution processes. *Journal of Experimental Social Psychology, 13*(3), 279–301.

Salmela-Aro, K., & Nurmi, J. E. (2007). Self-esteem during university studies predicts career characteristics 10 years later. *Journal of Vocational Behavior, 70*(3), 463–477.

Savitsky, K., & Gilovich, T. (2003). The illusion of transparency and the alleviation of speech anxiety. *Journal of Experimental Social Psychology, 39*(6), 618–625.

Schoeneman, T. J. (1994). Individualism. In V. S. Ramachandran (Ed.), *Encyclopedia of human behaviour*. Academic Press.

Sedikides, C., Meek, R., Alicke, M. D., & Taylor, S. (2014). Behind bars but above the bar: Prisoners consider themselves more prosocial than non-prisoners. *British Journal of Social Psychology*, *53*(2), 396–403.

Sieff, E. M., Dawes, R. M., & Loewenstein, G. (1999). Anticipated versus actual reaction to HIV test results. *The American Journal of Psychology*, *112*(2), 297.

Smith, T. W., Uchino, B. N., Berg, C. A., Florsheim, P., Pearce, G., Hawkins, M., Henry, N. J. M., Beveridge, R. M., Skinner, M. A., & Yoon, H. C. (2008). Associations of self-reports versus spouse ratings of negative affectivity, dominance, and affiliation with coronary artery disease: Where should we look and who should we ask when studying personality and health? *Health Psychology*, *27*(6), 676.

Smithies, D. (2012). A simple theory of introspection. In D. Smithies & D. Stoljar (Eds.), *Introspection and consciousness*. Oxford: Oxford University Press.

Stewart, A. E. (2005). Attributions of responsibility for motor vehicle crashes. *Accident Analysis & Prevention*, *37*(4), 681–688.

Svenson, O. (1981). Are we all less risky and more skillful than our fellow drivers? *Acta Psychologica*, *47*(2), 143–148.

Thunström, L., Nordström, J., Shogren, J. F., Ehmke, M., & van't Veld, K. (2016). Strategic self-ignorance. *Journal of Risk and Uncertainty*, *52*, 117–136.

Tordesillas, R. S., & Chaiken, S. (1999). Thinking too much or too little? The effects of introspection on the decision-making process. *Personality and Social Psychology Bulletin*, *25*(5), 625–631.

Twenge, J. M., & Campbell, W. K. (2009). *The narcissism epidemic: Living in the age of entitlement*. Simon and Schuster.

Twenge, J. M., Konrath, S., Foster, J. D., Keith Campbell, W., & Bushman, B. J. (2008). Egos inflating over time: A cross-temporal meta-analysis of the narcissistic personality inventory. *Journal of Personality*, *76*(4), 875–902.

Urdan, T., & Midgley, C. (2001). Academic self-handicapping: What we know, what more there is to learn. *Educational Psychology Review*, *13*, 115–138.

Vaillancourt, T. (2013). Students aggress against professors in reaction to receiving poor grades: An effect moderated by student narcissism and self-esteem. *Aggressive Behavior*, *39*(1), 71–84.

Van Dijk, W. W., Ouwerkerk, J. W., van Koningsbruggen, G. M., & Wesseling, Y. M. (2012). "So you wanna be a pop star?": Schadenfreude following another's misfortune on TV. *Basic and Applied Social Psychology*, *34*(2), 168–174.

Vazire, S. (2010). Who knows what about a person? The self–other knowledge asymmetry (SOKA) model. *Journal of Personality and Social Psychology*, *98*(2), 281.

Weiner, B. (2005). Motivation from an attribution perspective and the social psychology of perceived competence. *Handbook of Competence and Motivation*, *2005*, 2–3.

Wilson, T. D. (2002). 5 knowing why. In *Strangers to ourselves* (pp. 93–116). Harvard University Press.

Wilson, T. D., & Schooler, J. W. (1991). Thinking too much: Introspection can reduce the quality of preferences and decisions. *Journal of Personality and Social Psychology*, *60*(2), 181.

Wolfson, S. (2000). Students' estimates of the prevalence of drug use: Evidence for a false consensus effect. *Psychology of Addictive Behaviors*, *14*(3), 295.

Woodzicka, J. A., & LaFrance, M. (2001). Real versus imagined gender harassment. *Journal of Social Issues*, *57*(1), 15–30.

Youyou, W., Kosinski, M., & Stillwell, D. (2015). Computer-based personality judgments are more accurate than those made by humans. *Proceedings of the National Academy of Sciences*, *112*(4), 1036–1040.

Zell, E., Strickhouser, J. E., Sedikides, C., & Alicke, M. D. (2020). The better-than-average effect in comparative self-evaluation: A comprehensive review and meta-analysis. *Psychological Bulletin*, *146*(2), 118.

Chapter 2

The psychology of physical attraction

In the previous chapter, we learnt that as much as we like to think we have better knowledge about ourselves than anyone else, the evidence doesn't always align with that and we are constantly looking to other people to find out more about ourselves. You may be familiar with the story of Cupid, a young boy who would fire golden arrows which could induce love in the recipients. You may not be so aware that Cupid also carried leaden arrows which could create aversion in the recipients! In an ancient Latin poem written by Ovid (one of fifteen poems in the book "Metamorphoses") Cupid fired a golden arrow at Apollo, the god of archery (amongst other things) who had been taunting him about his archery skills. As a result, Apollo instantly fell in love with a nymph, Daphne. Cupid was looking for a little payback though and unfortunately for Apollo, had fired a leaden arrow at Daphne causing her to run off. Poor Apollo.

Even though Cupid may not have been the innocent child-like god of love that we typically see portrayed in Valentine's Day cards, the idea of love being like an arrow through the heart has certainly got its place firmly secured in the scientific literature. Fisher et al. (2010) recruited ten women and five men to have an MRI scan conducted. Whilst in the scanner, they were shown photos either of a person who had recently rejected them in love whom they wished would return to the relationship or a familiar but neutral person such as a co-resident of their dormitory or a fellow classmate. In those that had been rejected, the insular cortex and anterior cingulate were both highly active. Both of these areas have been implicated in experience of physical pain and distress or pain regulation. The connection between physical and emotional pain has also been demonstrated by Eisenberger et al. (2003). They asked participants to play a virtual "Cyberball" game with two other players. In the first instance, they were asked to watch the other players, due to a technical difficulty. In the second phase, they were able to participate and were included. In the final phase, after seven ball throws, the two players stopped throwing the ball to the participant. In this third phase, participants reported feeling ignored and excluded and during this phase, an area of the brain known as the dorsal anterior cingulate cortex was highly active, more so than during the other phases of the study. The same area has been associated with experience of physical pain (Sawamoto et al., 2000).

So, Dan McCafferty of the pop group Nazareth was really on to something when he sang "love hurts". If it has the potential to hurt, then why are we so keen to find a partner? Well, believe it or not, being attached to a significant other is good for us. Coan et al. (2006) asked married couples to take part in a study of hand-holding. The wife of each couple was placed in an MRI scanner and had two electrodes placed on one of her ankles. Whilst in the scanner, she was able to see a series of cues

■ **Figure 2.1** Was Cupid the cheeky, fun-loving chappie we like to imagine?

presented in a random order, which would either be "safety" cues (a blue O against a black background) or "threat" cues (a red X on a black background). Whenever the threat cue was seen, this signalled a 20% chance that an electric shock would be delivered through the electrodes. During one block of the experiment, the woman was able to hold her husband's hand, in a second block, she held the hand of an anonymous male experimenter and in the third block, no hand-holding occurred at all. Holding anyone's hand did reduce the activation of neural pathways involved in a threat response but this was particularly the case if it was the husband's hand that the wife was holding.

Not only can a strong relationship attachment reduce our stress but it can also serve other protective functions too. Coyne et al. (2001) reported that marital quality predicted 4-year survival rates for individuals with congestive heart failure equally as well as the severity of their illness. Johnson et al. (2000) suggest that unmarried individuals have a higher rate of mortality across all causes of death than married individuals. Although this appears to be true for men and women, it is important to note that the protection offered from marriage in terms of mortality is five times higher for men (Robles & Kiecolt-Glaser, 2003). Holt-Lunstad et al. (2010) conducted a large meta-analysis of 148 studies in which they report a 50% increased likelihood of survival for those with strong social relationships.

It is probably no surprise then that psychologists are particularly interested in what attracts us to a significant other. In fact, the field of research on physical attraction is vast. To try and rein in the huge literature on this subject, I have compiled a series of ten "top tips" which, I hope, will stand you in good stead for finding your future partner, if you are single. If you are already in a relationship, you may be able to look at these top tips with your critical thinking glasses on to see if your experience matches the predictions that we get from the literature.

TOP TIP NUMBER 1: GET FAMILIAR

I have a question for you to ponder. Is the Mona Lisa liked because it is such an exceptional work of art or because we have seen it so many times? The reason I ask is because we do have an extraordinary ability to develop liking for things that are familiar. Monahan et al. (2000) demonstrated a significantly higher positive rating for Chinese ideographs that had been repeatedly presented compared to those that had been presented just once and Sluckin et al. (1973) reported a preference for familiar letters in children. When presented with either letters from the Roman-alphabet or the Cyrillic-alphabet, children strongly preferred the Roman-alphabet letters, even though the letters presented had been matched for aspects such as the number of straight- or curved-line components.

It works in other species too. Sometime back now, Cross et al. (1967) exposed rats to music by Schonberg or Mozart. Poor things had the music playing for 12 hours each day for 52 days! Anyway, would you believe it? After a 15-day break, the rats developed a preference for the music they had listened to in the earlier part of the study. Rajecki (1974) even demonstrated this

■ **Figure 2.2** Do we like the Mona Lisa simply because we have seen her a lot?

effect when music was played to fertile chicken eggs. When the chicks hatched, they consistently showed a preference for the tone that they had heard whilst in the egg!

So, what has this got to do with physical attraction? Well, we like things that we are familiar with and that includes people! Harmon-Jones and Allen (2001) demonstrated this neatly with a study in which facial muscle activity was measured whilst participants were shown photographs of women. Some of the faces shown had been viewed repeatedly but others were novel and had only been presented in the test phase of the study. Not only were the familiar faces rated as more likeable but also, they induced more activity in facial muscles in the cheek. It is known that activity in this area is associated with positive emotions so the interpretation was that the more familiar faces led to more positive affect. Take note of who you sit next to in your lectures. Back et al. (2008) asked undergraduates attending their psychology lecture to sit in a randomly assigned seat. They were asked to introduce themselves by stepping forward in front of the class. One year later, when shown photos of their classmates and asked to rate the intensity of their friendship, what do you think happened? That's right! The closer they sat in the rows of seats, the greater their friendship. Those who had sat next to each other or on the same row were much more likely to be good friends than those who sat in different rows.

A similar study was conducted by Moreland and Beach (1992). They asked four women to attend undergraduate classes, pretending to be fellow students. One woman attended five classes, another attended ten and another fifteen. The final woman did not attend any (please note: this is NOT a good strategy for learning!). Once the end of term arrived, all students were asked to comment on each woman's familiarity, attractiveness, and similarity. The woman who attended the most classes was rated as being the most attractive even though the four women were very similar in appearance. They were also considered to be someone that the students would enjoy spending time with and believed they could be good friends with. The woman who attended the most was rated as being the most similar to the students themselves. Monin (2003) refers to this positive feeling of liking that arises from familiarity as the "warm glow heuristic".

It is no accident that living in close proximity to someone increases the chances of a relationship forming. A long time before I suspect many of us were born, Bossard (1932) studied over 5000 marriage licences in Philadelphia during the first five months of 1931. Only 17% of marriages occurred between individuals from different cities but over a third occurred between individuals who lived within five blocks of each other. Perry (1969) reported something similar in the United Kingdom where over 80% of marriages in West Dorset, took place between individuals who lived in the same parish, no more than a few miles apart. It certainly isn't a pattern that has diminished as our ability to travel has expanded. In 2004, in a study that involved over 144,000 couples, Haandrikman et al. (2008) reported that over half of cohabiters had met within a six-kilometre radius. The most common distance between cohabiting couples before they met was only 1 km! Haandrikman et al. suggest:

Cupid may have wings but apparently, they are not adapted for long flights.

(2008, p. 387)

It works also in student accommodation. Marmaros and Sacerdote (2006) studied students at Dartmouth College in the United States. Those living on the same floor were more likely to exchange emails than those living on different floors and Priest and Sawyer (1967) reported that roommates were more likely to be named as friends than those living on the same floor but in a different room and they in turn were more likely to be friends that those living on a different floor entirely. And don't think that it is just students that this applies to. Segal (1974) demonstrated a similar effect in Maryland Police trainees. The closer two trainees sat, the more likely they were to be friends.

Shin et al. (2019) asked male students to read excerpts from Shakespeare's Romeo and Juliette with a female confederate who either sat at a distance or close to them. For men not involved in a relationship already, liking for the female confederate was significantly higher when she sat close by.

There is just one word of caution here however. Berlyne (1970) suggests that repeated exposure can lead to satiation, Bornstein et al. (1990) suggest boredom can set in and Montoya et al. (2017) point to how familiarity starts to lose its novelty. Perhaps this is a top tip only for finding a partner at the start of a relationship!

TOP TIP NUMBER 2: TRUST YOUR SENSE OF SMELL

Top tip number 2 may not be the first thing you think of when you think of physical attraction but, research suggests that your nose is hard at work detecting potential partners' odour even if you are not consciously aware of this. Time for a bit of biology ... Just above our hard palate, either side of the nasal septum which divides our nose into a left and right side, we have something called the vomeronasal organ (VNO). This VNO is lined with receptor cells that extend right through to the olfactory bulb, a mass of tissue that is involved in our sense of smell. From there, they extend to the hypothalamus, a part of the brain which is involved in secreting hormones involved in sexual reproduction. Are you still following this? Well, assuming so, the key part of this story is that the receptor cells detect human pheromones, chemical molecules produced by the apocrine glands. And guess where they are? Mainly in the armpits (Grammer et al., 2005). Because of the connections from these receptors, it is believed that these pheromones therefore influence sexual behaviour.

Word has it that we can detect family members by body odour (Ferdenzi et al., 2010), a phenomenon that helps bonding but also prevents inbreeding and it is commonly known that "comfort smelling" often helps to maintain relationships when partners are apart. This is where we seek security and comfort from

■ **Figure 2.3** Our noses play a bigger role in physical attraction than we like to think.

smelling items belonging to our partners. If those around us are in a happy mood, then exposure to their body odour will likely induce a happy state in us too (de Groot et al., 2015). Women report olfactory information as being the single most important sensory input in mate selection (Herz & Cahill, 1997). The main pheromone produced by males is androstenol. It is this that is meant to be involved in attraction. When it is exposed to oxygen, however, it forms androstenone which is not so pleasant! It is important to note that when sexuality is factored into the equation, this does make a difference also. White and Cunningham (2017) report that homosexual males value the sound of a partner's voice more than their smell in contrast to heterosexual males who show the reverse.

So how do we know this is involved in attraction to a significant other? In what can only be described as a truly delightful study, female participants had secretions from males' apocrine glands (in their armpits) spread on their upper lips. Whilst the secretions were being collected, the men were not permitted to use deodorant or perfume. The effect was that the women had more regular menstrual cycles. Cowley and Brooksbank (1991) impregnated a necklace with pheromones and asked participants to wear it overnight. The effect on women was noticeable. They were likely to interact with more males the next day! When pheromones were added to aftershave, a noticeable increase in sexual behaviours was reported, particularly in sexual intercourse and sleeping next to a romantic partner (58% of those who added the pheromones reported an increase in two or more sexual behaviours compared to 19% of the control group).

Kirk-Smith and Booth (1980) sprayed androstenone onto a chair in a dentist waiting room. They used different intensities and recorded where visitors to the waiting room sat. Women were significantly more likely to choose the sprayed chair to sit on.

So male pheromones can have a powerful effect on heterosexual women. How about the other way round? Tan and Goldman (2015) exposed heterosexual males to female pheromones by asking them to smell a t-shirt that had been worn by a fertile female. They not only drank more alcohol but also engaged in more "approach" behaviours compared to if the t-shirt had been worn by a non-fertile female. Approach behaviours here were measured by noting which chair out of a choice of 4, the men chose to sit in. They were arranged at different distances from a chair which had a woman's jumper on the back and a purse and clipboard on it.

Why is smell so important? One theory is that we use smell to detect something called MHC. If you want to impress your friends, this stands for "Major Histocompatibility Complex". MHC is important in the maintenance of our immune system. When finding a partner to potentially mate with, evidence suggests that we look for someone who has a different MHC to us. We want our offspring to have the best possible chance of survival so having different MHC strengthens their immune system further. Wedekind et al. (1995) demonstrated this by asking women to smell the t-shirts of men after they had been worn for two days. They rated the smell of the t-shirts worn by men with similar MHC as less pleasant than those with dissimilar MHC. It is important to note that women who were taking the contraceptive pill showed the opposite preference and Wedekind et al. suggested that the pill may therefore interfere with natural mate choice and may have a role to play in predicting the stability of relationships longer-term.

Next time you go shopping for perfume or aftershave, however, do think of this top tip. As Wedekind (2007) reminds us:

> ... the finest and most expensive perfumes contain notes of a urinary nature ...
>
> (p. 315)

And, if the ladies amongst us choose a musky perfume, be aware that we are 1000 times more sensitive to this smell than the men we may be trying to influence (Fox, 2006). If you are buying scents for another person, you might also do well to remember that Milinski and Wedekind (2001) demonstrated that we unconsciously choose perfumes that enhance our *own* body odours even when buying for other people. The closer the pheromones resemble our own MHC, the more we like it. (If the person you are buying for doesn't like the scent you bought for them, crying won't help – Gelstein et al. (2011) report that tears resulting from negative emotions induce reductions in sexual appeal in men who sniff them!)

Hopefully, I have convinced you now that we are very sensitive to pheromones and your nose may be working hard to help you make the right choice of future partner even if you are not fully aware of this. Just be grateful, however, that we do not respond in the same way to pheromones as the female boar. Exposure to boar odour causes the female boar to adopt a mating posture immediately. There is always something to be grateful for.

TOP TIP NUMBER 3: BE NICE

Imagine you have just read a description of Mr X. In that description, you are told that Mr X is intelligent, independent, and very honest. Sounds like a nice guy, yes? Ok, now imagine that you are shown a picture of Mr X, just a head and shoulders picture but you are asked to make judgements about things such as his health, how kind he looks, and how attractive he is. Chances are that you will report Mr X to be in good health, to look kind, and to be pretty attractive. Paunonen (2006) ran just such a study with 256 undergraduate students and found exactly this pattern occurring. Being described as honest, in particular, seemed to lead participants to attribute a whole host of other positive attributes to the target person.

It also works if you see a picture first and then get information about the personality of that individual after. Lewandowski et al. (2007) presented participants with 36 pictures and asked them to rate the attractiveness of the person in each picture. They were then asked to complete a distraction task to try and disrupt their memories of how they had rated the pictures. In the next part of the study, they saw the pictures again but this time with a description of that individual's personality. Some of the descriptions were positive, making mention of personality traits such as humorous, mature, or intelligent. Some of the descriptions were less positive, mentioning traits such as offensive, abusive, and unstable. Participants were then asked to say how attractive they thought the person in the photo was, how much they would like to be friends with that person and how much they would like to date them. Lewandowski et al. found a remarkable effect of the personality information on feelings towards the person in the photo. Where positive traits were mentioned, participants were more likely to see the person in the photo as a potential friend and dating partner and were more likely to evaluate them as being physically attractive.

It is not just positive personality traits that lead to greater attractiveness. Being seen as a morally just character counts too. He et al. (2022) reported that a morally prosocial act (e.g. Giving a homeless person money) led to greater ratings of attractiveness compared to a morally anti-social act (taking money from your father as self-compensation for low pay) and to a non-moral act (eating a banana after not eating breakfast before an exam).

And it also helps if you pull your weight in a group task. One of the studies reported by Kniffin and Wilson (2004) asked members of a university rowing team to complete a survey at the end of the season, rating all team members on a scale from 0 to 99 for a number of attributes such as talent, effort, liking, and physical attractiveness. Attractiveness ratings were strongly correlated with performance on the group task (rowing in this case). One individual who Kniffin and Sloan Wilson described as "a slacker", was uniformly rated as physically unattractive by his team-mates.

It even works in criminal contexts too. Veenvliet and Paunonen (2005) reported that if participants had a negative view of a witness (for example, knowing that the witness did not help), they tended to perceive their physical appearance in less appealing ways too (more pale, thinner lips, narrow, square faces)! So, to remember this top tip, think about the quote from Gross and Crofton (1977) who wrote "What is good is beautiful".

TOP TIP NUMBER 4: FIND SOMEONE WHO IS REALLY LIKE YOU

If you have read Chapter 1, you will know that we are obsessed with the self. You might not find it so surprising then to find that when it comes to relationships, we like people who are like us. Birds of a feather do indeed flock together as the saying goes and that saying even featured in the title of a research paper by Mackinnon et al. (2011). In a naturalistic observation, they observed where people chose to sit in a computer lab at a Canadian university. They noted who was sitting where and whether that person was wearing glasses or not. In accordance with the saying, people chose to sit next to people who were like them. Males sat next to males more often than next to females. People wearing glasses sat next to people wearing glasses more often than to those who didn't wear glasses. In a second study, they showed a similar effect occurred when looking at hair length! DeBruine (2004) actually morphed participant's faces with that of children and found a strong preference was reported for these images that contained elements of the participants' own faces.

The similarity effect even extends to names. Jones et al. (2004) provide evidence to suggest that we are more likely to marry others whose first or last names resemble our own. Similarly, we show a preference for tea samples that have a name containing the same letters as in our own name (Brendl et al., 2005). Jones et al. (2004) refer to this phenomenon as "Implicit Egotism". The positive view that we like to hold of ourselves "spills over" into the way we evaluate others associated with us.

It isn't just physical appearance that counts here though. Similarity in attitudes is also important. Byrne (1961) asked participants to complete a questionnaire which focused on their attitudes to a range of issues varying in importance to the individual. They were asked to determine which were the most and least important issues to them. Two weeks later, they returned to evaluate a person based on the answers they had given two weeks earlier. The answers they were presented with were actually fake and had been manipulated to create four conditions: one group received answers that mirrored their own, another received answers that were exactly opposite to what they themselves had put, another group received answers that were similar on the important issues but dissimilar on the unimportant issues and the last group had the reverse. As you might well be predicting by now, the group that saw answers that mirrored their own, reported significantly greater positivity towards the stranger than those who saw answers that deviated from their own. Notably, they also went on to rate the similar stranger as being more intelligent, knowledgeable, and moral than for those evaluating dissimilar strangers.

The attractiveness of similarity has been referred to as the Homophily Principle (Lazarsfeld & Merton, 1954). Similarity breeds liking. Our social groups therefore are usually made up of homogeneous individuals. Fiore and Donath (2005) demonstrated this principle works even in online dating. Similarity, they report, is sought after much more often than expected by chance alone. Wanting children and marital status were particularly important but even pet ownership and preferences were considered important. Imagine you happen to find out that the person sitting next to you shares your birthday. According to research reported by Burger et al. (2004), you would be significantly more likely to agree to a request to read their essay and provide feedback.

It doesn't even have to be *actual* similarity that is important. It can be *perceived* similarity. Montoya et al. (2008) conducted a meta-analysis of over 313 investigations, reporting an equally high association between attraction and both actual and perceived similarity. Selfhout et al. (2009) demonstrated the link between perceived similarity and attraction in a study of peer friendships at a university in the Netherlands. During the second week of their freshman year, students were asked to complete a questionnaire online which assessed their personality. Every month, ratings of friendship intensity in peers in their tutor group were collected as well as a measure of how much they had spoken to each of the group members during the previous week. The greater the perceived similarity in personality, the greater the friendship intensity claimed. This was the case even very early on in the study. Having the illusion of similarity is sufficient to predict liking it would appear.

However, there are limits to this principle it would seem. Similarity only seems to matter, Cheney (1975) argues, if the aspect we are similar on, is important to us. Cheney studied prison inmates at a county penitentiary who had been sentenced for public intoxication. After completing a questionnaire which contained items designed to measure attitudes to alcoholism, inmates were asked to listen to a 15-minute tape recording of a psychotherapy session. Finally, the inmates completed a questionnaire to measure attraction towards the therapist and were asked if they would be willing to meet with the therapist. Their ratings were higher when she shared similar views about alcohol but only for those inmates for whom this was an important issue.

Rosenbaum (1986) suggested that it is not similarity that is the driving force behind attraction as much as dissimilarity. If we perceive another person to be dissimilar, it causes repulsion, hence his concept of the Repulsion Hypothesis. Rosenbaum suggests that experiencing or encountering inconsistent attitudes to one's own, creates stress and tension so we seek to eliminate this just as we would with any other source of conflict. This is not to

■ **Figure 2.4** We are attracted to people who are like us.

say that similarity isn't important, but dissimilarity is a powerful force too!

So, before we move to top tip number 5, it is worth noting, even if you are not looking for a relationship currently, that the similarity effect can work wonders for increasing your tips if you are working in hospitality. Van Baaren et al. (2003) demonstrated how repeating back a customer's order to them would increase the size of the tip left. Mimicry of the order given leads to a positive feeling of greater liking!

TOP TIP NUMBER 5: LOOK INTO EACH OTHERS' EYES

If you are currently sitting next to someone, stop for 2 minutes and gaze into each other's eyes. Chances are this will increase your liking for each other. Kellerman et al. (1989) asked their participants to do just this and reported a significant increase in feelings of passionate love, dispositional love, and liking for the person whose eyes they were gazing into and who was gazing back at them. The study was presented to the participants as a study of ESP or extrasensory perception. The effect didn't work if participants were asked to stare at each other's hands or count the number of eye blinks made by their partner. It also didn't work if the participant was just gazed at.

Croes et al. (2020) suggest that eye contact leads to more self-disclosure – that is, revealing more about ourselves to the other person, compared to meeting someone in a situation with no eye contact possible. Cross-culturally, the importance of the eyes has been demonstrated. Karandashev et al. (2016) studied four different cultures reporting the importance of the eyes in romantic attraction in at least three of them and points to studies that have suggested that they are the most important of all facial features in evaluating attractiveness. Indeed, some have argued that large eyes in females are evaluated as attractive by males (Bereczkei & Mesko, 2006) irrespective of whether they are looking at them or not. And it is looks to which we now turn for top tip number 6.

TOP TIP NUMBER 6: IT'S GOOD TO BE AVERAGE … MOST OF THE TIME

The beauty industry is booming. But research suggests that average is good when it comes to attractiveness. Imagine taking 40 photos and morphing them all together to create a blended image. This is what psychologists refer to as a composite image. Langlois and Roggman (1990) presented participants with composite images made up of either 2, 4, 8, 16, or 32 faces morphed together. They also showed them some individual (not morphed) faces too. The task for the participants was to rate these in terms of attractiveness. What came out on top? You've guessed it. The composite images. Langlois and Roggman argue that this is largely due to the evolutionary pressure to find a good, healthy mate. Average looks are the norm because they must carry the best chance of survival. Therefore, we are drawn towards them.

Rhodes and Tremewan (1996) argued similarly that average is good when it comes to attraction. They constructed what they called caricatures and anti-caricatures and presented these to their participants along with the undistorted original photos. A caricature deviates from average – it emphasises the most distinctive features. An anti-caricature does the opposite. It makes a photo closer to the average so reduces any distinctive features. Similar to the findings of Langlois and Roggman 6 years earlier, the nearer to the average the images were, the more attractive they were rated as being. Caricatures were rated as the least attractive, followed by the undistorted images and then the anti-caricatures as the most attractive.

The idea that distinctiveness is not linked to attractiveness is also supported by studies that have looked at ratings of attractiveness of tattooed individuals. Swami -and Furnham. (2007) reported ratings of low attractiveness for women with tattoos. They were also assumed to be heavier drinkers and more sexually promiscuous. This is somewhat ironic given Forbes's (2001) finding that a common reason for getting a tattoo is to make ourselves look more attractive. It is even more strange when you consider that women who have a tattoo appear to rate themselves as less attractive as a result according to Molloy and Wagstaff (2021).

So averageness is good. However, it isn't just average *looks* that we are attracted to. Halberstadt and Rhodes (2000) demonstrated a preference for averages with other stimuli too such as dogs, wristwatches, and birds. When asked to judge how unusual each example was, the average was always preferred. Halberstadt and Rhodes (2003) also showed the same phenomenon with fish, cars, and passerines (birds). It seems hard to imagine then that our preference for average looks is adaptive in quite the way suggested by Langlois and Roggman. Instead, Halberstadt and

Rhodes argue that we are drawn to prototypical exemplars. It isn't just being average that is important, but being familiar. Now where have we heard that before …

There is one exception to the rule though, that we do need to mention. Deviations from the average, of features that signal good health or sexual maturity, do seem to be attractive (Perrett et al., 1994). Alley and Cunningham (1991) for example point to the attractiveness of large eyes and cheekbones. Kret and De Dreu (2019) even suggest that large pupils may be advantageous if we are asking someone to lend us money!

TOP TIP NUMBER 7: PICK A POSITIVE PERSON

The most powerful determinant of interpersonal attraction is an indication that one is liked.

(Sharma & Kaur, 1996, p. 635)

Let's be honest here. We all like to be liked. And that is no less true when it comes to physical attraction. Aronson and Worchel (1966) suggested that if someone claims they like us that is sufficient for us to find them attractive irrespective of whether they share the same attitudes as us. Being positive breeds liking it would seem. Folkes and Sears (1977) answered their own question "Does everybody like a liker?" with an emphatic yes! They asked participants to rate their liking for people who gave evaluations of a range of objects such as political figures, movies, and cities. Consistently, across stimuli, those who gave more positive evaluations were liked best.

Is consistency important? It depends. Berscheid and Hatfield (1969) claim that we like people better if they are consistently positive about us compared to if they say nine positive and one negative thing about us. Not so surprising when we consider that we remember negative information better than positive information (Skowronski & Carlston, 1987). But that only deals with information gained at one-time point. Normally, in a relationship, we build up a picture over time. Does consistency play a role then too? Aronson and Linder (1965) claim not. They created a laboratory experiment in which female students were asked to conduct seven short conversations with another student seated in another room as part of a study on verbal conditioning. After each conversation, they would be able to hear the other student evaluate them. In one condition, the evaluations changed from being rather negative to more positive. In a second condition, the evaluations changed from being more positive to rather negative

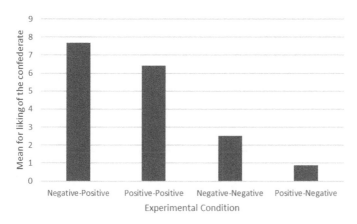

■ **Figure 2.5** Mean rating of liking for a confederate in each of Aronson and Linder's conditions. Data taken from Aronson and Linder (1965).

and in the last two conditions, evaluations remained either all positive or all negative. At the end of the study, the participants were interviewed and asked about their feelings towards the other student. What did they find? They identified a very strong liking for the other student in the condition where evaluations had started off a little negative but then gradually become more and more positive. The liking for the other student in this condition even outstripped that obtained in the condition where the other student had been positive throughout!

This has since been replicated by Sharma and Kaur (1996) who refer to this as the loss-gain hypothesis. We like others best when they grow to like us and certainly like them better than people who initially like us but then become more negative about us.

Perhaps what is at work here is detection of flattery. It is nice to be liked but only if that feeling is genuine. Coleman et al. (1987) claim that criticism can often be considered to be more sincere (they actually studied students' views of feedback from teachers in this study!). Vonk (1998) demonstrated the effect of insincerity in a series of studies designed to illustrate what he refers to as the "slime effect". If someone is always positive to superiors but not so towards subordinates, then they tend to be liked significantly less. This "licking upward – kicking downward" effect is not a great way to attract those around you! As Aronson (1980) reported:

> *As a relationship ripens toward greater intimacy, what becomes increasingly important is authenticity ...*
>
> (p. 323)

TOP TIP NUMBER 8: MEET YOUR DATE IN A NICE PLACE

For love to blossom, the smell of blossom (or something equally flowery) might be an asset. And I am not just talking about perfumes. The smell of the room you meet your amore in can have a big influence on attraction. Rotton (aptly named!) (1983) sprayed a room with ethyl mercaptan. This is a chemical that smells a bit like rotting cabbage. Urgh. Participants were asked to enter the room and complete ratings of attractiveness for four photographic negatives, four paintings, and four people described by adjectives. The smell was put down to an accident. Those at least were the unlucky participants. The others got shown to a room that was odourless where they were asked to complete the same rating exercises. The people in the photographs were rated as significantly less attractive when viewed in the smelly room as were the paintings and the people described by adjectives, at least as long as the descriptions were not too extreme.

The effect of odours in the environment seems to be largely down to the negative effect of unpleasant odours rather than to any beneficial effect of pleasant ones (Cook et al., 2018). Bensafi et al. (2003) sprayed a pleasant floral scent into a room where female volunteers were asked to rate female faces for attractiveness. The odour had no effect.

It isn't just the smell that is influential though. The décor has a big effect on us too. Maslow and Mintz (1956) demonstrated this with photographs being rated as less attractive if they were viewed in an "ugly" room. The "beautiful" room had two large windows, beige coloured walls (would you call that beautiful? Hmmm), an overhead indirect light, and nice furnishings. The "ugly" room had two half-windows, battleship-grey walls, an overhead bulb with a dirty and poorly fitting lampshade and furnishings that looked like they had come from a "janitor's storeroom". Kitchens et al. (1977) reported a similar effect but used real interactions with others as the basis for judgements rather than photographs. Participants were asked to get to know each other for a few minutes (which turned out to be 20!) before being escorted to a quiet, adjacent room to be interviewed about the partners they had conversed with. In the getting to know you stage of the study, participants were in either an unattractive room, an attractive room or the control room. The unattractive room had old paint splattered on wooden chairs, a green couch which had torn cushions on it and a broken leg. The walls were painted a dull green and lightbulbs were un-shaded. The attractive room by

■ **Figure 2.6** There are many reasons why a walk in the woods might help to promote attraction.

contrast was freshly painted with modern paintings on the wall, wicker furniture with decorative cushions and attractive shaded lamps. The control room was a standard university classroom, judged to be of average attractiveness compared to the other two rooms. No prizes for guessing who thought their conversational partner was the most attractive? Yes, that's right. Those who met them in the attractive room.

Miwa and Hanyu (2006) suggest dim lighting helps too. Eighty undergraduates were asked to evaluate a counsellor that had interviewed them either in a room with bright lighting or one with dim lighting. The dim lighting was regarded as creating a more relaxed and pleasant atmosphere and the counsellor was consequently perceived as being more attractive.

Ambience is important then but how about temperature? Someone might want to tell Snoop Dogg who sang "I wanna make you sweat" as the research suggests this is probably not a good strategy for love to thrive. Griffit and Veitch (1971) exposed participants to a room with either a high temperature (a stifling 93 degrees!) or a more modest 73 degrees and reported significantly more negative evaluations given by those in the hot room when asked to rate their liking of an anonymous stranger based on their responses to an attitude questionnaire.

As a final message for this top tip, just make sure the TV or radio isn't relaying bad news items when you meet your potential suitor. Veitch and Griffitt (1976) demonstrated how listening to bad news items reduced liking of a stranger immediately after.

TOP TIP NUMBER 9: TRY SOMETHING SCARY FOR YOUR FIRST DATE

For the next top tip, I am going to take you (in your mind's eye at least) to Canada. Specifically, to North Vancouver and to the Capilano River. There you will see the Capilano Canyon Suspension Bridge. This bridge is not small – it spans a 450 ft long gap and there is a 230-foot drop from it to rocks and rapids below. This bridge is made of wooden boards attached to wire cables which means that it has a remarkable ability to sway and tilt. If you happen to be upriver, you will see a very different sort of bridge. This one is made of a heavy cedar wood, is solid and has just a 10-foot drop to a rivulet below. The handrails are high on this one and because it is solid, it doesn't tilt or sway at all. The reason I am bringing you to this location is because this is where a famous study by Dutton and Aron (1974) was conducted.

Participants in this study were all male and were visiting one or other of these bridges. Whilst crossing the bridge, they were approached by an interviewer who claimed to be conducting a study looking at the effect of scenic attractions on creative expression. Participants were asked to complete a short questionnaire followed by a request to write a brief and dramatic story based on a picture of a young woman covering her face with one hand whilst reaching out with the other. Once participants had agreed and completed these tasks, the interviewer tore off a corner of paper and wrote her name and phone number on it to give to the participant so that she could explain more about the study if they wanted to talk further.

Of course, not everyone agreed to participate and not everyone who did, accepted the interviewers' number. However, of those that did, they were more likely to call the interviewer if they had met her on the wobbly bridge. They were also significantly more likely to include sexual imagery in their dramatic story. In a further experiment, they invited participants to take part in a study of electric shock and its effect on learning. Male participants were introduced to a female confederate whom they believed was also doing the experiment. Through the use of a manipulated coin flip, the male participants were told that they would be allocated to the strong shock condition whilst the confederate would be allocated to the mild shock condition. Prior to the main part of the study, they were asked to complete a questionnaire to assess feelings and reactions which could, they were told, influence learning. How much shock the female confederate would receive made little difference to the answers given but the amount of shock that was anticipated for themselves did. Those anticipating a strong shock reported significantly greater attraction to the female confederate! What is happening in these situations? According to Dutton and Aron, participants misattribute their arousal to being attracted to the other person rather than to the scary (or potentially scary) experience.

Remember this effect next time you go to a theme park. Meston and Frohlich (2003) compared the attractiveness ratings given to a photograph of an averagely attractive, opposite-sex individual, before and after taking a ride on a rollercoaster. For those exiting the ride, ratings of attractiveness given to the person in the photo were significantly higher than from those just getting on the ride. The arousal experienced as a result of the ride intensified the later feelings of attraction.

Even if theme parks are not your thing, physical exercise can serve the same purpose as far as arousal and attraction are concerned. Lewandowski and Aron (2004) asked mixed sex stranger pairs to participate in one of four physical activities presented as games. For example, one game required participants to stand on opposite corners of a rectangle, marked on the floor, and to bounce a ball in a circle near the centre so that the other person could catch it without coming off of their corner. Once a catch had occurred, they had to move to the next corner along the long side of the rectangle and repeat the task. The aim was to get as many catches as possible in 2 minutes and to do so whilst wearing ankle weights. This was the high arousal/high challenge condition. A low arousal condition might involve slowly walking from one corner to the next without any ankle weights. Regardless of the level of challenge, those who had participated in a high arousal condition showed a significantly higher level of attraction to their partner.

One final word on this is if you are going to go on a scary date, do make sure you look forward to it. Darley and Berscheid (1967) suggest that the anticipation of meeting up with someone can increase our liking for that person in itself.

TOP TIP NUMBER 10: SELF-DISCLOSE

How much of yourself do you disclose to a potential future partner? Your answer may contribute to how attracted you are to that person and how attracted they are to you. Altman and Taylor

(1973) proposed the Social Penetration Theory which proposes that deeper levels of self-disclosure lead to greater intimacy in a relationship. However, this takes time and is dependent on reciprocity. The process usually starts with relatively low-level disclosure moving to more intimate disclosure as the relationship develops.

What happens when we speed up that process? Aron et al. (1997) tried to explore this by increasing the intimacy of self-disclosure over three 15-minute intervals. Aron -et al. paired students who were strangers together and asked them to engage in conversation for 45 minutes by asking each other a set list of questions. In one condition, pairs worked through three sets of questions that reflected "small talk" such as "When was the last time you walked for over an hour?" After each 15-minute block, the next set of questions was moved to. In the other condition, pairs worked through three sets of questions that were designed to generate closeness such as "If you could change anything about the way you were raised, what would it be?". With each set, the questions delved a little deeper into personal topics. For example, one of the questions in the third set was, "Complete this sentence: I wish I had someone with whom I could share …". After the 45 minutes was up, a post-experiment questionnaire was completed. The questionnaire asked participants to compare the relationship with their conversation partner with other relationships. Those who had increasingly self-disclosed by responding to the closeness-generating questions, rated their relationship with their partner in this task to be as close as the average relationship in their lives and over 50% had had a subsequent conversation in the 7 weeks following the study and 35% had done something together.

The reciprocity of disclosure, however, does seem to be important. Sprecher et al. (2013) compared what happened when participants either just disclosed or just listened to an initial interaction and then switched roles in a second interaction or when they took turns asking in answering questions. Greater liking and closeness were reported only when reciprocal disclosure had occurred.

The effect appears to be robust. Collins and Miller (1994) conducted a meta-analysis exploring the effects of disclosure on attraction. They concluded that we like those who disclose to us, we disclose to those we like and after disclosing to them, we like them even more. It is an interesting observation that the process of self-disclosure happens more quickly online (Whitty, 2008).

ADDICTION TO LOVE

Well that's ten top tips covered. Hopefully, these will prove useful to those of you looking for love. Once we fall in love, evidence suggests that it is akin to an addiction (Fisher et al., 2016). Using brain scanning methodology, Fisher et al. point to a number of studies that demonstrate the activation of the same dopamine pathways when feeling intense romantic love as when taking drugs such as ecstasy. These pathways form part of the reward systems of the brain, driving pleasure. The same symptoms of addiction can be seen when we experience intense love too such as cravings, emotional dependence, and withdrawal.

Bartels and Zeki (2000) asked participants to look at a photograph of someone they were deeply in love with and then a photograph of someone they were friends with whilst in an fMRI scanner. When looking at a loved one, there was noticeably more dopamine activity in the Ventral Tegmental Area of the brain. This just happens to be part of the reward pathway and an area associated with euphoria-inducing drugs.

THE ROLE OF CULTURE

As we come to the end of our journey through the psychology of physical attraction, it is important to note that we have focused very much on Western culture in the studies covered. For this topic, more than most, there are important cultural differences that need to be considered. Gupta and Singh (1982) for example, point to the way that love often follows rather than precedes marriage in arranged marriage. They asked 50 couples to complete a questionnaire and reported a diminishing of love after 5 years for those who married for love. For those in arranged marriages, however, more love was reported after 5 years. It is important to note that only a minority of cultures strictly enforce monogamy (Eastwick, 2013).

Given these findings, it may come as no surprise to learn that the attraction to people who are similar to us is not culturally universal. Heine et al. (2009) suggest that the similarity-attraction effect is only pronounced for those from a Western culture. Canadian participants showed a strong attraction to those similar to them but in Japanese samples, the effect was only noticeable when the most powerful statistical methods were used.

Swami and Furnham (2008) point to differences in what individuals look for in the ideal partner dependent on culture. For example, in Japan, ink-dying of teeth (ohaguro) used to be popular, facial scarring is still practised in some African communities and even in our own culture, historically Renaissance Europe showed an obsession with men's thighs! Cunningham et al. (1995) pointed to the greater attractiveness of heavier women in cultures where food is often scarce, perhaps due to the greater chance they would have of successfully reproducing. Perrett (2017) points to the different ways that readiness to marry or adulthood is signalled in different cultures. Karen-Padaung women in Thailand lengthen their necks using neck rings, the Mursi women of Ethiopia wear pottery plates in their bottom lips and Kikuyu men in Kenya enlarge their earlobes using weights.

You may also have noticed that the majority of studies in this area focus on heterosexual relationships but we need to be careful to acknowledge the heterogeneity in approaches to physical attraction. Cohen and Tannenbaum (2001) for example suggested that lesbians and bisexual women prefer heavier figures in a partner than heterosexual women and Swami (2021) points to the different ways that an "ideal" relationship is conceptualised amongst gay men in the United States. Tylka and Andorka (2012) for example identified the need for muscularity as a strong force in physical attractiveness amongst gay men.

COMPANIONATE LOVE

Most of what we have covered does refer to physical attraction in its earliest stages. But, and I hate to disappoint, that initial feeling of passionate love cannot be sustained for long. As Hatfield et al. (2008) put it:

> *Passionate love is a fragile flower.*
>
> (p. 38)

Hatfield et al. argue that passionate love declines fairly quickly. They interviewed 53 couples who had recently been married and followed them up one year later. Time did indeed have what Hatfield et al. described as a "corrosive" effect on love although one year later, feelings of love were still, thankfully, high. Huston and Chorost (1994) suggest that after just two years of marriage, affection is expressed about half as often and marital satisfaction declines.

So what happens to a relationship over time? According to Hatfield, "companionate" love endures. Companionate love is defined as:

> *The affection and tenderness we feel for those with whom our lives are deeply entwined.*
>
> (Hatfield & Rapson, 1993, p. 9)

Underwood (2008) argues that this is not just about fulfilling our own needs and desires but is about acting in the significant other's best interests. It doesn't have the same elements of yearning, passion, or sexual desire as passionate love. Berscheid (2010) does point out that compassionate love can develop early on in a relationship but it is the enduring nature over time that is the true test of love.

Perhaps Mark Twain was really onto something when he suggested "No man or woman really knows what love is until they have been married a quarter of a century"!

REFERENCES

Alley, T. R., & Cunningham, M. R. (1991). Article commentary: Averaged faces are attractive, but very attractive faces are not average. *Psychological Science*, *2*(2), 123–125.

Altman, I., & Taylor, D. A. (1973). *Social penetration: The development of interpersonal relationships*. Holt, Rinehart & Winston.

Aron, A., Melinat, E., Aron, E. N., Vallone, R. D., & Bator, R. J. (1997). The experimental generation of interpersonal closeness: A procedure and some preliminary findings. *Personality and Social Psychology Bulletin*, *23*(4), 363–377.

Aronson, E. (1980) *The social animal* (5th ed). Freeman.

Aronson, E., & Linder, D. (1965). Gain and loss of esteem as determinants of interpersonal attractiveness. *Journal of Experimental Social Psychology*, *1*(2), 156–171.

Aronson, E., & Worchel, P. (1966). Similarity versus liking as determinants of interpersonal attractiveness. *Psychonomic Science*, *5*(4), 157–158.

Back, M. D., Schmukle, S. C., & Egloff, B. (2008). Becoming friends by chance. *Psychological Science*, *19*(5), 439.

Bartels, A., & Zeki, S. (2000). The neural basis of romantic love. *NeuroReport*, *11*(17), 3829–3834.

M. Bensafi, W.M. Brown, T. Tsutsui, J.D. Mainland, B.N. Johnson, E.A. Bremner, N. Young, I. Maus, B. Ray, J. Gross, J. Richards, I. Stappen, R.W. Levenson, & N. Sobel (2003). Sex-steroid derived compounds induce sex-specific effects on autonomic nervous system function in humans. *Behavioral Neuroscience*, *117*(6), 1125.

Bereczkei, T., & Mesko, N. (2006). Hair length, facial attractiveness, personality attribution: A multiple fitness model of hairdressing. *Review of Psychology*, *13*(1), 35–42.

Berlyne, D. E. (1970). Novelty, complexity, and hedonic value. *Perception & Psychophysics*, *8*(5), 279–286.

Berscheid, E. (2010). Love in the fourth dimension. *Annual Review of Psychology*, *61*, 1–25.

Berscheid, E., & Hatfield, E. (1969). *Interpersonal attraction* (Vol. 69, pp. 113–114). Addison-Wesley.

Bornstein, R. F., Kale, A. R., & Cornell, K. R. (1990). Boredom as a limiting condition on the mere exposure effect. *Journal of Personality and Social Psychology*, *58*(5), 791.

Bossard, J. H. (1932). Residential propinquity as a factor in marriage selection. *American Journal of Sociology*, *38*(2), 219–224.

Brendl, C. M., Chattopadhyay, A., Pelham, B. W., & Carvallo, M. (2005). Name letter branding: Valence transfers when product specific needs are active. *Journal of Consumer Research*, *32*(3), 405–415.

Burger, J. M., Messian, N., Patel, S., Del Prado, A., & Anderson, C. (2004). What a coincidence! The effects of incidental similarity on compliance. *Personality and Social Psychology Bulletin*, *30*(1), 35–43.

Byrne, D. (1961). Interpersonal attraction and attitude similarity. *The Journal of Abnormal and Social Psychology*, *62*(3), 713.

Cheney, T. (1975). Attitude similarity, topic importance, and psychotherapeutic attraction. *Journal of Counseling Psychology*, *22*(1), 2.

Coan, J. A., Schaefer, H. S., & Davidson, R. J. (2006). Lending a hand: Social regulation of the neural response to threat. *Psychological Science*, *17*(12), 1032–1039.

Cohen, A. B., & Tannenbaum, I. J. (2001). Lesbian and bisexual women's judgments of the attractiveness of different body types. *Journal of Sex Research*, *38*(3), 226–232.

Coleman, L. M., Jussim, L., & Abraham, J. (1987). Students' reactions to Teachers' evaluations: The unique impact of negative feedback 1. *Journal of Applied Social Psychology*, *17*(12), 1051–1070.

Collins, N. L., & Miller, L. C. (1994). Self-disclosure and liking: A meta-analytic review. *Psychological Bulletin*, *116*(3), 457.

Cook, S., Fallon, N., Wright, H., Thomas, A., Giesbrecht, T., Field, M., & Stancak, A. (2018). Simultaneous odour-face presentation strengthens hedonic evaluations and event-related potential responses influenced by unpleasant odour. *Neuroscience Letters*, *672*, 22–27.

Cowley, J. J., & Brooksbank, B. W. (1991). Human exposure to putative pheromones and changes in aspects of social behaviour. *The Journal of Steroid Biochemistry and Molecular Biology*, *39*(4), 647–659.

Coyne, J. C., Rohrbaugh, M. J., Shoham, V., Sonnega, J. S., Nicklas, J. M., & Cranford, J. A. (2001). Prognostic importance of marital quality for survival of congestive heart failure. *The American Journal of Cardiology*, *88*(5), 526–529.

Croes, E. A., Antheunis, M. L., Schouten, A. P., & Krahmer, E. J. (2020). The role of eye-contact in the development of romantic attraction: Studying interactive uncertainty reduction strategies during speed-dating. *Computers in Human Behavior*, *105*, 106218.

Cross, H. A., Halcomb, C. G., & Matter, W. W. (1967). Imprinting or exposure learning in rats given early auditory stimulation. *Psychonomic Science*, *7*(7), 233–234.

Cunningham, M. R., Roberts, A. R., Barbee, A. P., Druen, P. B., & Wu, C. H. (1995). "Their ideas of beauty are, on the whole, the same as ours": Consistency and variability in the cross-cultural perception of female physical attractiveness. *Journal of personality and social psychology*, *68*(2), 261.

Darley, J. M., & Berscheid, E. (1967). Increased liking as a result of the anticipation of personal contact. *Human Relations*, *20*(1), 29–40.

de Groot, J. H., Smeets, M. A., Rowson, M. J., Bulsing, P. J., Blonk, C. G., Wilkinson, J. E., & Semin, G. R. (2015). A sniff of happiness. *Psychological Science*, *26*(6), 684–700.

DeBruine, L. M. (2004). Facial resemblance increases the attractiveness of same–sex faces more than other–sex faces. *Proceedings of the Royal Society of London. Series B: Biological Sciences*, *271*(1552), 2085–2090.

Dutton, D. G., & Aron, A. P. (1974). Some evidence for heightened sexual attraction under conditions of high anxiety. *Journal of Personality and Social Psychology*, *30*(4), 510.

Eastwick, P. W. (2013). Cultural influences on attraction. In J.A. Simpson, L. Campbell (Eds.), *The Oxford Handbook of Close Relationships*, Oxford University Press, pp. 161–181.

Eisenberger, N. I., Lieberman, M. D., & Williams, K. D. (2003). Does rejection hurt? An fMRI study of social exclusion. *Science*, *302*(5643), 290–292.

Ferdenzi, C., Schaal, B., & Roberts, S. C. (2010). Family scents: Developmental changes in the perception of kin body odor? *Journal of Chemical Ecology*, *36*, 847–854.

Fiore, A. T., & Donath, J. S. (2005). Homophily in online dating: when do you like someone like yourself? In Conference on Human Factors in Computing Systems - Proceedings, pp. 1371–1374.

Fisher, H. E., Brown, L. L., Aron, A., Strong, G., & Mashek, D. (2010). Reward, addiction, and emotion regulation systems associated with rejection in love. *Journal of Neurophysiology*, *104*(1), 51–60.

Fisher, H. E., Xu, X., Aron, A., & Brown, L. L. (2016). Intense, passionate, romantic love: A natural addiction? How the fields that investigate romance and substance abuse can inform each other. *Frontiers in Psychology*, *7*, 687.

Folkes, V. S., & Sears, D. O. (1977). Does everybody like a liker? *Journal of Experimental Social Psychology*, *13*(6), 505–519.

Forbes, G. B. (2001). College students with tattoos and piercings: Motives, family experiences, personality factors, and perception by others. *Psychological Reports*, *89*(3), 774–786.

Fox, K. (2006). The smell report. *Social Issues Research Centre*, *334*, 385–400.

Gelstein, S., Yeshurun, Y., Rozenkrantz, L., Shushan, S., Frumin, I., Roth, Y., & Sobel, N. (2011). Human tears contain a chemosignal. *Science*, *331*(6014), 226–230.

Grammer, K., Fink, B., & Neave, N. (2005). Human pheromones and sexual attraction. *European Journal of Obstetrics & Gynecology and Reproductive Biology*, *118*(2), 135–142.

Griffit, W., & Veitch, R. (1971). Hot and crowded: Influence of population density and temperature on interpersonal affective behavior. *Journal of Personality and Social Psychology*, *17*(1), 92.

Gross, A. E., & Crofton, C. (1977). What is good is beautiful. *Sociometry*, *40*, 85–90.

Gupta, U., & Singh, P. (1982). An exploratory study of love and liking and type of marriages. *Indian Journal of Applied Psychology*, *19*, 92–97.

Haandrikman, K., Harmsen, C., Van Wissen, L. J., & Hutter, I. (2008). Geography matters: Patterns of spatial homogamy in the Netherlands. *Population, Space and Place*, *14*(5), 387–405.

Halberstadt, J., & Rhodes, G. (2000). The attractiveness of nonface averages: Implications for an evolutionary explanation of the attractiveness of average faces. *Psychological Science*, *11*(4), 285–289.

Halberstadt, J., & Rhodes, G. (2003). It's not just average faces that are attractive: Computer-manipulated averageness makes birds, fish, and automobiles attractive. *Psychonomic Bulletin & Review*, *10*(1), 149–156.

Harmon-Jones, E., & Allen, J. J. (2001). The role of affect in the mere exposure effect: Evidence from psychophysiological and individual differences approaches. *Personality and Social Psychology Bulletin*, *27*(7), 889–898.

Hatfield, E. C., Pillemer, J. T., O'Brien, M. U., & Le, Y. C. L. (2008). The endurance of love: Passionate and companionate love in newlywed and long-term marriages. *Interpersonal: An International Journal on Personal Relationships*, *2*(1), 35–64.

Hatfield, E., & Rapson, R. L. (1993). *Love, sex, and intimacy: Their psychology, biology, and history*. HarperCollins.

Heine, S. J., Foster, J. A. B., & Spina, R. (2009). Do birds of a feather universally flock together? Cultural variation in the similarity-attraction effect. *Asian Journal of Social Psychology*, *12*(4), 247–258.

Herz, R. S., & Cahill, E. D. (1997). Differential use of sensory information in sexual behavior as a function of gender. *Human Nature*, *8*, 275–286.

He, D., Workman, C. I., He, X., & Chatterjee, A. (2022). What is good is beautiful (and what isn't, isn't): How moral character affects perceived facial attractiveness. *Psychology of Aesthetics, Creativity, and the Arts*, 1–9. https://doi.org/10.1037/aca0000454

Holt-Lunstad, J., Smith, T. B., & Layton, J. B. (2010). Social relationships and mortality risk: A meta-analytic review. *PLoS Medicine*, *7*(7), e1000316.

Huston, T. L., & Chorost, A. F. (1994). Behavioral buffers on the effect of negativity on marital satisfaction: A longitudinal study. *Personal Relationships*, *1*(3), 223–239.

Johnson, N. J., Backlund, E., Sorlie, P. D., & Loveless, C. A. (2000). Marital status and mortality: The national longitudinal mortality study. *Annals of Epidemiology*, *10*(4), 224–238.

Jones, J. T., Pelham, B. W., Carvallo, M., & Mirenberg, M. C. (2004). How do I love thee? Let me count the Js: Implicit egotism and interpersonal attraction. *Journal of Personality and Social Psychology*, *87*(5), 665.

Karandashev, V., Zarubko, E., Artemeva, V., Neto, F., Surmanidze, L., & Feybesse, C. (2016). Sensory values in romantic attraction in four Europeans countries: Gender and cross-cultural comparison. *Cross-Cultural Research*, *50*(5), 478–504.

Kellerman, J., Lewis, J., & Laird, J. D. (1989). Looking and loving: The effects of mutual gaze on feelings of romantic love. *Journal of Research in Personality*, *23*(2), 145–161.

Kirk-Smith, M. D., & Booth, D. A. (1980). Effects of androstenone on choice of location in other's presence. *Olfaction and taste VII*. IRL Press, 397–400.

Kirk-Smith, M., Booth, D. A., Carroll, D., & Davies, P. (1978). Human social attitudes affected by androstenol. *Research Communications in Psychology, Psychiatry, and Behavior*, *3*, 379–384.

Kitchens, J. T., Herron, T. P., Behnke, R. R., & Beatty, M. J. (1977). Environmental esthetics and interpersonal attraction. *Western Journal of Communication (Includes Communication Reports)*, *41*(2), 126–130.

Kniffin, K. M., & Wilson, D. S. (2004). The effect of nonphysical traits on the perception of physical attractiveness: Three naturalistic studies. *Evolution and Human Behavior*, *25*(2), 88–101.

Kret, M. E., & De Dreu, C. K. (2019). The power of pupil size in establishing trust and reciprocity. *Journal of Experimental Psychology: General*, *148*(8), 1299.

Langlois, J. H., & Roggman, L. A. (1990). Attractive faces are only average. *Psychological Science*, *1*(2), 115–121.

Lazarsfeld, P. F., & Merton, R. K. (1954). Friendship as a social process: A substantive and methodological analysis. *Freedom and Control in Modern Society*, *18*(1), 18–66.

Lewandowski, G. W., & Aron, A. P. (2004). Distinguishing arousal from novelty and challenge in initial romantic attraction between strangers. *Social Behavior and Personality: An International Journal*, *32*(4), 361–372.

Lewandowski, G. W. Jr, Aron, A., & Gee, J. (2007). Personality goes a long way: The malleability of opposite-sex physical attractiveness. *Personal Relationships*, *14*(4), 571–585.

Mackinnon, S. P., Jordan, C. H., & Wilson, A. E. (2011). Birds of a feather sit together: Physical similarity predicts seating choice. *Personality and Social Psychology Bulletin*, *37*(7), 879–892.

Marmaros, D., & Sacerdote, B. (2006). How do friendships form. *The Quarterly Journal of Economics*, *121*(1), 79–119.

Maslow, A. H., & Mintz, N. L. (1956). Effects of esthetic surroundings: I. Initial effects of three esthetic conditions upon perceiving "energy" and "well-being" in faces. *The Journal of Psychology*, *41*(2), 247–254.

Meston, C. M., & Frohlich, P. F. (2003). Love at first fright: Partner salience moderates roller-coaster-induced excitation transfer. *Archives of Sexual Behavior*, *32*, 537–544.

Milinski, M., & Wedekind, C. (2001). Evidence for MHC-correlated perfume preferences in humans. *Behavioral Ecology*, *12*(2), 140–149.

Miwa, Y., & Hanyu, K. (2006). The effects of interior design on communication and impressions of a counselor in a counseling room. *Environment and Behavior*, *38*(4), 484–502.

Molloy, K., & Wagstaff, D. (2021). Effects of gender, self-rated attractiveness, and mate value on perceptions tattoos. *Personality and Individual Differences*, *168*, 110382.

Monahan, J. L., Murphy, S. T., & Zajonc, R. B. (2000). Subliminal mere exposure: Specific, general, and diffuse effects. *Psychological Science*, *11*(6), 462–466.

Monin, B. (2003). The warm glow heuristic: when liking leads to familiarity. *Journal of personality and social psychology*, *85*(6), 1035.

Montoya, R. M., Horton, R. S., Vevea, J. L., Citkowicz, M., & Lauber, E. A. (2017). A re-examination of the mere exposure effect: The influence of repeated exposure on recognition, familiarity, and liking. *Psychological bulletin*, *143*(5), 459.

Montoya, R. M., Horton, R. S., & Kirchner, J. (2008). Is actual similarity necessary for attraction? A meta-analysis of actual and perceived similarity. *Journal of Social and Personal Relationships*, *25*(6), 889–922.

Moreland, R. L., & Beach, S. R. (1992). Exposure effects in the classroom: The development of affinity among students. *Journal of Experimental Social Psychology*, *28*(3), 255–276.

Paunonen, S. V. (2006). You are honest, therefore I like you and find you attractive. *Journal of Research in Personality*, *40*(3), 237–249.

Perrett, D. (2017). *In your face: The new science of human attraction.* Bloomsbury Publishing.

Perrett, D. I., May, K. A., & Yoshikawa, S. (1994). Facial shape and judgements of female attractiveness. *Nature, 368*(6468), 239–242.

Perry, P. J. (1969). Working-class isolation and mobility in rural Dorset, 1837–1936: A study of marriage distances. *Transactions of the Institute of British Geographers, 46,* 121–141.

Priest, R. F., & Sawyer, J. (1967). Proximity and peership: Bases of balance in interpersonal attraction. *American Journal of Sociology, 72*(6), 633–649.

Rajecki, D. W. (1974). Effects of prenatal exposure to auditory or visual stimulation on postnatal distress vocalizations in chicks. *Behavioral Biology, 11*(4), 525–536.

Rhodes, G., & Tremewan, T. (1996). Averageness, exaggeration, and facial attractiveness. *Psychological Science, 7*(2), 105–110.

Robles, T. F., & Kiecolt-Glaser, J. K. (2003). The physiology of marriage: Pathways to health. *Physiology & Behavior, 79*(3), 409–416.

Rosenbaum, M. E. (1986). The repulsion hypothesis: On the nondevelopment of relationships. *Journal of Personality and Social Psychology, 51*(6), 1156.

Rotton, J. (1983). Affective and cognitive consequences of malodorous pollution. *Basic and Applied Social Psychology, 4*(2), 171–191.

Sawamoto, N., Honda, M., Okada, T., Hanakawa, T., Kanda, M., Fukuyama, H., Konishi, J., & Shibasaki, H. (2000). Expectation of pain enhances responses to nonpainful somatosensory stimulation in the anterior cingulate cortex and parietal operculum/posterior insula: An event-related functional magnetic resonance imaging study. *Journal of Neuroscience, 20*(19), 7438–7445.

Segal, M. W. (1974). Alphabet and attraction: An unobtrusive measure of the effect of propinquity in a field setting. *Journal of Personality and Social Psychology, 30*(5), 654.

Selfhout, M., Denissen, J., Branje, S., & Meeus, W. (2009). In the eye of the beholder: Perceived, actual, and peer-rated similarity in personality, communication, and friendship intensity during the acquaintanceship process. *Journal of Personality and Social Psychology, 96*(6), 1152.

Sharma, V., & Kaur, I. (1996). Interpersonal attraction in relation to the loss—Gain hypothesis. *The Journal of Social Psychology, 136*(5), 635–638.

Shin, J. E., Suh, E. M., Li, N. P., Eo, K., Chong, S. C., & Tsai, M. H. (2019). Darling, get closer to me: Spatial proximity amplifies interpersonal liking. *Personality and Social Psychology Bulletin, 45*(2), 300–309.

Skowronski, J. J., & Carlston, D. E. (1987). Social judgment and social memory: The role of cue diagnosticity in negativity, positivity, and extremity biases. *Journal of Personality and Social Psychology, 52*(4), 689.

Sluckin, W., Miller, L. B., & Franklin, H. (1973). The influence of stimulus familiarity/novelty on children's expressed preferences. *British Journal of Psychology, 64*(4), 563–567.

Sprecher, S., Treger, S., Wondra, J. D., Hilaire, N., & Wallpe, K. (2013). Taking turns: Reciprocal self-disclosure promotes liking in initial interactions. *Journal of Experimental Social Psychology, 49*(5), 860–866.

Swami, V. (2021). *Attraction explained: The science of how we form relationships*. Routledge.

Swami, V., & Furnham, A. (2008). *The psychology of physical attraction*. Routledge.

Swami, V., & Furnham, A. (2007). Unattractive, promiscuous and heavy drinkers: Perceptions of women with tattoos. *Body Image, 4*(4), 343–352.

Swami, V., Furnham, A., Georgiades, C., & Pang, L. (2007). Evaluating self and partner physical attractiveness. *Body Image, 4*(1), 97–101.

Tan, R., & Goldman, M. S. (2015). Exposure to female fertility pheromones influences men's drinking. *Experimental and Clinical Psychopharmacology, 23*(3), 139.

Tylka, T. L., & Andorka, M. J. (2012). Support for an expanded tripartite influence model with gay men. *Body Image, 9*(1), 57–67.

Underwood, L. G. (2008). Compassionate love: A framework for research. In: Fehr B, Sprecher S, Underwood LG, editors. *The science of compassionate love: Theory, research, and applications*. West Sussex, United Kingdom: Wiley-Blackwell; pp. 3–25.

Van Baaren, R. B., Holland, R. W., Steenaert, B., & Van Knippenberg, A. (2003). Mimicry for money: Behavioral consequences of imitation. *Journal of Experimental Social Psychology, 39*(4), 393–398.

Veenvliet, S. G., & Paunonen, S. V. (2005). Person perception based on rape-victim testimony. *Deviant Behavior, 26*(3), 209–227.

Veitch, R., & Griffitt, W. (1976). Good news-bad news: Affective and interpersonal effects 1. *Journal of Applied Social Psychology, 6*(1), 69–75.

Vonk, R. (1998). The slime effect: Suspicion and dislike of likeable behavior toward superiors. *Journal of Personality and Social Psychology, 74*(4), 849.

Wedekind, C. (2007). Body odours and body odour preferences. In R.I.M. Dunbar & L.Barrett (Eds.) *The Oxford Handbook of Evolutionary Psychology* (pp.315–320). Oxford University Press.

Wedekind, C., Seebeck, T., Bettens, F., & Paepke, A. J. (1995). MHC-dependent mate preferences in humans. *Proceedings of the Royal Society of London. Series B: Biological Sciences, 260*(1359), 245–249.

White, T. L., & Cunningham, C. (2017). Sexual preference and the self-reported role of olfaction in mate selection. *Chemosensory Perception, 10*, 31–41.

Whitty, M. T. (2008). Revealing the 'real' me, searching for the 'actual' you: Presentations of self on an internet dating site. *Computers in Human Behavior, 24*(4), 1707–1723.

Chapter 3

Do we only help others to benefit ourselves?

Is there such a thing as true altruism? Do we really help others out of a genuine desire to ease another's suffering or is it more to do with preserving our reputation or alleviating guilt on our part? In this chapter, we will explore the psychology of what is often referred to as prosocial behaviour to see if it can offer us any answers. In our journey through this topic, we will uncover nine rules that seem to promote prosociality, three theories that have been proposed to explain why we engage in prosocial behaviour and two myths about what might make us more prosocial.

RULE 1: MAKE SURE IT'S A NICE DAY

The sun is shining. It's a beautiful day. On days like these, there is more good news. If you are in need of help, chances are you are more likely to receive it. Guéguen and Lamy (2013) looked to see how many individuals would alert a confederate to the fact they had "accidentally" dropped a glove from their handbag. They conducted this observation on both sunny and cloudy days in two different towns in France. When the sun was shining, over 65% of individuals who happened to be walking past, alerted the confederate. However, such help was reduced on cloudier days with only 53% doing so.

The idea of sunny weather promoting helpful behaviour is not a new one. Cunningham (1979) compared the number of individuals offering help in two off-campus locations in Minneapolis, USA and two locations at the University of Minnesota. A confederate asked passers-by if they would be prepared to answer at least some of the questions on their survey of social opinions. They were told that they didn't have to answer all 80 and were asked how many they would be willing to answer. Sunshine was found to be the strongest predictor of helping behaviour. The more sunshine there was in the hour before they were asked, the more helpful they were likely to be. Cunningham also found a link to other weather factors. In the summer months, if the temperature was warm and there was a slight breeze, then people really were prosocial. In the winter months, warmer temperatures and no wind chill led to more help offered.

It isn't just completing questionnaires that people are willing to help with. According to Schneider et al. (1980), a strong association exists between good weather and people's willingness to help an individual look for their missing contact lens and Rind and Strohmetz (2001) suggest that favourable weather leads to increased tipping for waiting staff. When a server wrote a positive message about the weather (i.e. "The weather is supposed to be really good tomorrow. I hope you enjoy the day!") on the back of customers' bills, the percentage of tip left rose significantly compared to when they wrote a negative message about the weather (i.e. The weather is supposed to be not so good tomorrow. I hope you enjoy the day anyway".) or didn't write a message at all.

This tipping effect has been demonstrated by Cunningham (1979) also in his second study where he reported increased tipping when outdoor sunshine levels were high. The interesting aspect of the tipping effect here is that it doesn't even have to be sunny in reality. Rind (1996) made use of a hotel setting where the windows had a dark, limo-tint effect which meant that it always looked cloudy outside. The room service waiter informed guests, when he delivered their orders, that it was either warm and sunny, cold and sunny, warm and rainy, or cold and rainy outside. Just being led to believe that it was sunny outside was sufficient for guests to give greater amounts of tips to the waiter.

So, why might sunshine make us more helpful? One idea proposed by Cunningham (1979) is that it puts us in a good mood and that is where rule number 2 comes into play.

RULE 2: MAKE SURE PEOPLE AROUND YOU ARE IN A GOOD MOOD

In an aptly named article "Effect of feeling good on helping: Cookies and kindness", Isen and Levin (1972) drew our attention to the effect of positive mood on prosocial behaviour. Some participants were given cookies to try and induce good moods. Others were offered none. In the main part of the study, half of each group were asked if they would be willing to volunteer to help in another psychology experiment. The other half were asked if they would be willing to volunteer to distract another student who was trying to study. As you can probably guess, those who had unexpectedly received cookies were more prepared to help in another experiment but were less willing to distract another student. This evidence, the authors suggest, supports the notion of a "warm glow" effect (Isen, 1970), in which feeling good about ourselves leads us to want to help others more.

In a second study, Isen and Levin (1972) demonstrated a similar outcome when participants unexpectedly found a dime in the coin return slot of a payphone. This does of course date this study given the advent of mobile phone technology but keep with me… On leaving the phone booth, they would have seen a confederate walking slightly ahead of them, carrying a folder full of papers. As luck would have it, the confederate dropped the folder and its contents. Who helped them to retrieve the papers? Yes, you've guessed it. The people who unexpectedly had found a dime. Fourteen people helped after having found one compared to only one person in a control condition where no dime was left for them to find.

These studies explore the effect of feeling positive on our willingness to help others but showing others that we are in a positive mood can also be a good way to get others to help us. Guéguen and Fischer-Lokou (2004) reported that hitch-hiking women who smiled, received more offers of help from motorists than those who didn't. (Unfortunately for the men amongst us, smiling didn't make much difference.) Solomon et al. (1981) suggested smiling confederates standing near to an elevator in a department store received more offers of help in finding an item than those who didn't smile and Otta et al. (1993) suggest that smiling leads to positive attributions which leads to greater willingness to help with directions or to find a contact lens.

The power of a smile extends beyond just receiving help ourselves or offering to help the smiler. Guéguen and De Gail (2003) observed the reaction of passers-by to a confederate who had dropped computer discs on the ground (yes, I know, I am showing the age of this study too!). In some cases, the passer-by had just seen a different confederate smile at them as they came down the stairs. In some cases, they hadn't seen this. You won't be surprised to know that being smiled at by a stranger enhances our willingness to help another person (not the smiler) after. It is of interest to note that members of the opposite sex were helped more, that is males helped females more than other males and vice versa.

The effect is so powerful that it doesn't even have to be another person that induces positivity. It can be a situation where we feel relieved about something. Dolinski and Nawrat (1998) illustrated this with the "fear-then-relief" technique. How many of you have parked illegally? How many of you have received a parking ticket for doing so? Dolinski and Nawrat wanted to use this scenario in their study of helping behaviour. Individuals who had parked in an area of Opole, Poland, notorious for illegal parking had a piece of paper placed under their windscreen wiper or stuck to their car door. The paper was made to look like a parking ticket, being the same size and colour. Rather than a parking ticket, the paper actually contained either an advertisement for a fake hair-growth medication or an appeal for people to give blood. The latter clearly has a prosocial connection. Once the driver returned to their car and saw the paper, they were approached by a confederate and asked if they would complete a survey that would take up to 15 minutes as part of a master project.

Those who found the paper under the windscreen wiper were much more likely to complete the survey than any of the other participants. Seeing that the paper was not in fact a parking ticket, as it had appeared at first, was a relief and that was sufficient to induce positivity.

Positive mood or relief from guilt?

In all of these studies, the emphasis is on the role that positive affect plays in our willingness to help others. We feel good, so we do good. However, is that the full story? The evidence suggests that sometimes, it is the avoidance of guilt that is the driving force behind our prosocial behaviour.

In Dolinski and Nawrat's study, it is possible that the increase in helping behaviour was caused not by good mood as such but by guilt or shame as the authors themselves consider. The individuals in their study were parking illegally and managed to "get away with it". The guilt they felt may well have impacted on their decision to help. Although the authors decide in favour of an alternative theory, there is abundant evidence that guilt can lead to increased prosocial behaviour.

Carlsmith and Gross (1969) asked male participants at Stanford University to act as a teacher in an experiment which required them to flick a switch whenever a learner (a confederate) made a mistake. Half of the participants were led to believe that flicking the switch caused an electric shock to be delivered to the learner. After this part of the study had finished, the learner asked the participant if they would be willing to help phone potential signers of a petition to save redwood trees in Northern California. Seventy-five percent of those who thought they had administered electric shocks to the learner agreed, compared to only 25% in the control condition. Not only were those who administered the shocks more likely to agree, but also, they were prepared to make more calls (mean number of calls agreed to was 32 in the shock condition compared to just 16 in the control condition).

In both Dolinski and Nawrat's study and in Carlsmith and Gross's study, a direct request was made to the participant. However, helping behaviour as a response to guilt seems to happen even in situations where a direct request is not made. Imagine you are in a shopping centre and someone asks you if you will use their camera to take a picture of them for a project they are doing. When you go to take the picture, the shutter just won't work. If you were a participant in Regan et al.'s (1972) study, you might then face a difficult situation where the owner of the camera suggests you did something to jam the camera and tells you he will have to get it fixed. You may, however, be lucky and find that the owner acknowledges that his camera "acts up a lot" and reassures you that you did not do anything wrong. Which one you experience will impact your willingness to help a confederate a little way ahead of where you are walking. As the confederate walks, candy falls from a torn corner of a shopping bag. Would you tell them? The answer is… it depends. If you faced the difficult situation and were made to feel guilty by the camera owner, then chances are you would. Fifty-five percent in this situation did so in Regan et al.'s study. Those who heard the owner say that the camera often played up and reassured them it was not their fault were less prosocial. Only 15% in this situation helped the confederate by letting them know about the candy.

Before we move onto our next rule, it is worth noting that guilt can also arise from unethical actions in our past. Zhong and Liljenquist (2006) reported that thinking of something we did in the past that was unethical led to greater willingness to volunteer to complete a different research study. However, this was only true for those individuals who had not had a chance to clean their hands with an antiseptic wipe! Cleaning hands was seen as akin to cleansing of their misdeeds. Seventy-four percent offered help if they had not cleaned their hands compared to 41% who had. A similar finding was obtained by

Xu et al. (2014). Having written about a past misdeed, those who were then given a chance to wash their hands were significantly less likely to offer help to a PhD student with their dissertation. Washing our hands, the authors claim:

> ...can wash away one's guilt and lead to less helpful behaviour.
>
> (p. 97)

The authors refer to this as the Macbeth effect. When people feel they have done wrong, they want to cleanse themselves, just as Lady Macbeth compulsively washes her hands in an attempt to rid herself of the guilt of plotting Duncan's murder.

■ **Figure 3.1** The Macbeth effect can guilt lead to more prosocial behaviour?

RULE 3: IF ITS AN EMERGENCY, GENDER MATTERS

On 7 July 2005, a terrorist attack on the London Underground led to 52 individuals losing their lives. In a report on this event (https://www.london.gov.uk/sites/default/files/gla_migrate_files_destination/archives/assembly-reports-7july-report.pdf), the help offered to victims was mentioned. Volunteers from Great Ormond Street Hospital set up a field hospital in a nearby hotel to receive the walking wounded. In Edgeware Road, a passer-by, Paul, set up a reception centre for those injured so that their condition could be assessed. Acts such as these, in emergency situations, have been the subject of much interest in social psychology and research suggests that in emergency situations, men are more likely to offer help than females (Eagly & Crowley, 1986).

This is reflected in the honouring of individuals for acts of heroism. The Carnegie Hero Fund Commission awards medals to those who have voluntarily risked their lives in order to save or attempt to save another person. Of the 7,000 people who have received this medal, 91% have been male (this was up until 2008). Eagly (2009) also highlights the gender skew in awarding of the Canadian government's Medal of Bravery. Eighty-seven percent of these medals honour males. This is not to say that women are not considered on an equal level but more that heroic actions that involve risk and require what Eagly refers to as "agentic" action are more likely to be delivered by males.

Females, on the other hand, are associated with providing emotional support more frequently. Kunkel and Burleson (1999) asked male and female students who they would be most likely to seek emotional support from, a friend of the same or the opposite sex. Seventy-one percent of males and 76% of females responded by saying they would seek emotional support from a female. Eagly and Koenig (2009) report that women are more likely to become volunteers in situations that involve helping others. This association of females with more empathic forms of helping does of course overflow into the family division of labour where, as Eagly (2009) points out, women have the lion's share of caring responsibilities, not just in terms of helping family members but also in caring for elderly members of the family unit.

Before we move to rule number 4, it is worth pointing out that male prosocial helping in emergencies is more likely to occur under certain conditions. As Eagly and Crowley (1986) report, in their meta-analysis, men are more likely to help women if they are not asked to but rather have to take the initiative, that is, if the need for help presents itself but the person doesn't make a request for it. They are also more likely to provide help when there are on-lookers present as opposed to when they are the sole bystander. And as Mims et al. (1975) found, they are more likely to offer help to an attractive female than a less attractive one. The age of romance may be dead but the age of chivalry is certainly alive and well!

RULE 4: MAKE SURE YOU ARE SOMEWHERE NICE (PREF SPAIN)

What a strange rule you may think. Make sure you are in Spain? Far from being a tourist advertisement, this is actually linked to a difference in the way that prosocial behaviour is encapsulated in language. Simpatia is a linguistic term that describes a culture oriented towards the social well-being of others. It suggests a recognition of the need to be prosocial towards strangers. Levine et al. (2001) conducted field studies in large cities in 23 different countries. They wanted to assess the level of help offered in three different situations. In one, an experimenter walked towards a pedestrian heading in the opposite direction, reached into his pocket and dropped a pen without appearing to notice. Would the pedestrian alert them or pick it up and return it to them? In a second situation, an experimenter appeared to walk with a heavy limp whilst wearing a leg brace. As they approached an oncoming pedestrian, they dropped and struggled to retrieve a pile of magazines. Would the pedestrian help? Finally, in a third situation, an experimenter enacted the role of a blind person. They wore dark glasses and carried a white cane. They approached a junction, held out their white cane and waited to see if anyone offered help.

Individuals in Latin American countries and in Spain, countries that have the concept of Simpatia culture, were significantly more likely to help than those in non-Simpatia cultures. The percentage of overall helping was 82.87% in Simpatia cultures compared to just 65.87% in non-Simpatia cultures. Those dropping a pen in Rio were four times more likely to be helped than those doing so in New York City for example. It is interesting to note that there is no English translation of this word. As Levine et al. point out:

Simpatia and simpatico emphasize prioritising amiable social behaviours as compared with, for example, emphasizing achievement and productivity.

(p. 555)

RULE 5: ASK ONE PERSON NOT MANY

For rule number 5, numbers matter. When it comes to obtaining help, in most cases, having one bystander is more likely to lead to you getting it, then when there are many. Markey (2000), for example, reported a longer time lapse before help was offered when the number of people present in a computer-mediated chat group increased. Markey observed individuals interacting in 400 different chat groups on Yahoo! Chat over a 30-day period. The confederate in the chatroom was named as either Jake Harmen or Suzy Harmen and they sought help by asking the following question:

Can anyone tell me how to look at someone's profile?

A linear relationship was identified between the number of people in the chat room and the time it took for anyone to provide help by answering this question. As the number of people present increased, so did the time taken to answer the question. Latané and Darley (1970) argue that when other people are present, an individual might be concerned that if they help, their behaviour will be evaluated negatively by others, something they termed "audience inhibition". They may also be subject to "diffusion of responsibility" where others may assume the responsibility does not lie solely on their shoulders to intervene.

In line with these ideas, when Markey (2000) asked the experimenter to direct the question to a specific named individual in the group, help was received significantly more quickly. It is important to note that this was not an emergency situation. Jones and Foshay (1984) demonstrated this effect even with a simple greeting. When a confederate said hello to a stranger they encountered, 77% returned the greeting. When they said hello to a stranger who was part of a group of 4–6 people, however, only 48% returned the greeting.

It doesn't even have to be an actual situation to promote prosocial behaviour. Even imagining yourself as part of a group will be sufficient to reduce your feeling of responsibility to help others. Garcia et al. (2002) asked undergraduate students from Princeton University to complete a questionnaire. For one group, they were asked to imagine they had won a dinner for themselves and 30 friends at their favourite restaurant. For a second group, they were asked to imagine a similar situation but for ten friends rather than thirty. The third group were asked to imagine they had won a dinner for just themselves and one friend. On the second page, participants were asked to imagine that they had graduated some

■ **Figure 3.2** Would you be more likely to get help when there are lots of people around? "Large Group Travel – Conference People, London to Brighton, return" by Luxury Train Club.

time back and were asked what percentage of their annual earnings they would be willing to donate to charity. Consistent with the effects described so far, those who were asked to imagine dinner with 30 friends pledged less of their income than individuals in either of the other groups. Those imagining dinner with ten friends pledged less than individuals who imagined dinner with just themselves and one other.

In a second study, Garcia et al. asked participants to imagine being in a movie theatre that was either crowded or that only they and a friend were present in. Imagining being in a crowded movie theatre was sufficient to reduce subsequent helping behaviour. They pledged fewer dollars towards a university yearly appeal fund after.

What about if someone is hurt though? Darley and Latané (1968) led participants to believe that an individual in a nearby cubicle was experiencing a seizure. Those who believed they were the only person who could hear were much more likely to seek help than if they thought others could hear what was going on too. Latané and Rodin (1969) asked participants to participate in a survey of game and puzzle preferences. On arrival, they were shown past an office where they could see a desk, filing cabinets and bookcases piled high with papers. In an adjacent room, they were given a questionnaire and a variety of games to look at. The experimenter then went into the office next door. After 4 minutes, a tape was played to make it sound as though the experimenter had climbed on a chair to retrieve some papers from the bookcase, and then fallen, hurting their foot. Seventy percent of those individuals who had been on their own in the adjacent room offered help compared to only 7% when a confederate was present in the room with them. On almost 40 occasions, the victim received no help at all. As Latané and Rodin report:

> *The idea of "safety in numbers" receives no support from the results of this experiment.*
>
> (p. 198)

THEORY 1: SOCIAL EXCHANGE THEORY

These studies might well suggest to you that when we make a decision to help another person, we are looking to maximise our rewards and minimise our costs (Cook & Rice, 2006). Helping behaviour is therefore like an economic exchange. In other words, we are "selfish helpers".

Zhang and Epley (2009) demonstrated how this might work in a series of six studies comparing the opinions of favour-givers and favour-receivers to reciprocation. Zhang and Epley compared outcomes in scenarios such as waiting in a queue to buy tickets, recalling a recent favour, and even working on a boring task. In all cases, those helping another person expected their good turn to be reciprocated on the basis of the cost they had incurred. The bigger the cost to them, the more they expected the receiver of help to "pay back". For those receiving help, however, their idea of how to reciprocate was very much based on the benefit they themselves had received for the favour. According to these findings, we might well expect people to only help another person if the cost to themselves is low.

Cialdini et al. (1987) argue that helping is sometimes a way of relieving our own distress rather than a true expression of altruism. If we believe that our own sad mood cannot be improved through helping, we are less likely to do so. According to this theory then, true altruism does not exist.

Piliavin and Piliavin (1972) suggest there might be some truth to this. They conducted an observational study on subway trains in New York. A confederate acted as the victim, falling over and remaining on the floor of the train carriage. Help was significantly slower to be offered when the victim appeared to be bleeding than when he wasn't. Piliavin et al. (1969) demonstrated how help is also less likely to be offered to an individual who appears to be drunk as opposed to ill. In both of these cases, the costs to the person offering help are likely to be high and the benefits low, reducing the likelihood of them stepping in to provide assistance.

RULE 6: CHOOSE SOMEONE SIMILAR TO YOURSELF

Time for another rule and hopefully one that will put a smile on your face after a somewhat uncomfortable theory! Talking of faces, would you be surprised to know that you are more likely to help someone who looks like you? Maybe not if you have read Chapter 1. DeBruine (2002) asked participants to participate in a computer game involving trust. The game required two players and participants would be shown a computer-generated picture of the other player. Unbeknown to the participants in the experimental group, some of the pictures had been morphed to include elements of their own faces. The result of this was that greater trust was shown in the gaming decisions made, when the face shown had elements of their own faces morphed into it.

It isn't just faces that influence our willingness to act in prosocial ways however. Emswiller et al. (1971) demonstrated how people were more willing to lend money to someone who resembled them. The confederate in this study dressed either as a clean-cut, typically collegiately dressed individual or as a jean-wearing, long-haired "hippie". The confederate approached each participant to ask if they would lend them a dime for a long-distance phone call. They were much more likely to receive the help they asked for if they had approached someone who looked similar to them.

Levine et al. (2005) suggest that similarity might be important in signalling shared identity in these situations. They chose to use Manchester United fans studying at Lancaster University as the participants for their first study. On arrival at the psychology department, each participant was asked to complete a questionnaire which quizzed them on their allegiance to a football club. A second questionnaire tested their identification with other supporters of their team. The experimenter then explained that for the next part of the study, they would need to move to move to an adjacent building so that a video about football teams could be shown. Halfway across the car park, the experimenter explained where the participant should head to meet the person showing the video and headed back to the psychology department. Just as the participant approached the corner of the building, a confederate came jogging along a grass bank but slipped and fell over. He gripped his ankle and was clearly in some pain. Importantly, this individual was wearing either a Manchester United football shirt, a Liverpool football shirt, or an unbranded sports top. No request for help was made. Would the participant offer help?

Well, the answer, according to Levine et al., is "it depends". If the confederate was wearing a Manchester United football top, and hence, shared group membership with the participant, the participant was significantly more likely to offer help. In a second study, when the saliency of being a football fan more generally was emphasised, participants were more likely to help the confederate when he was wearing a football shirt, of any team, compared to when he wore a plain shirt. Social group membership plays a big role.

It isn't just similarity in physical appearance that seems to influence us. Burger et al. (2004) demonstrated how incidental similarity can be important also. Believing that someone who is requesting help (asking for feedback on an essay) shares the same birthday as us, the same first name or even similarities in fingerprints, is enough for us to comply with the request for help much more readily than if they don't. When participants believed the requester shared the same birthday as them, for example, 62% agreed to read and feedback on the essay compared to only 34% when birthdays were dissimilar.

There is an interesting exception to this rule however. van Leeuwen and Täuber (2011) argue that low-status group members may often offer help to high-status group members. This seems to contradict the role of similarity. However, van Leeuwen and Tauber suggest that this may be a way of increasing the reputation of the group, demonstrating their knowledge, and perhaps initiating a process of reciprocation. This may also go some way to explaining the effects identified by Piff et al. (2010). Across four studies, they reported significantly more willingness to act prosocially amongst lower-class individuals. This included being more generous, more charitable, more trusting, and more helpful. Being prosocial, the authors suggest, can be a powerful adaptation to a more threatening environment. It can open up prosocial connections and help individuals to build relationships. Piff et al., however, argue that this is unlikely to lead to a difference in social class standing so maybe more to do with the dependence on others to achieve particular outcomes.

THEORY 2: EMPATHY-ALTRUISM HYPOTHESIS

Is the motivation to help ever, in any degree, truly altruistic?

This question was asked by Toi and Batson (1982). Certainly, the picture we have painted so far doesn't suggest a positive answer. However, the Empathy-Altruism Hypothesis suggests something more promising. Helping can be altruistic as long as it is evoked by an "empathic emotional response" to distress. What does this mean exactly? Empathy is demonstrated when we can put ourselves in the other person's shoes and imagine how it feels to experience what they are going through.

Toi and Batson (1982) asked participants to listen to an audiotape of an interview with a student Carol Marcy. Participants believed they were selecting a tape at random from five possible audiotapes but in reality, all of these contained the same interview. In the interview, Carol reveals to listeners that due to a car accident, she has broken both legs and has had to spend the last month in hospital. Due to the amount of work missed, she is in danger of having to re-do the year. Whilst listening to the tape, some participants were instructed to listen carefully to the information whilst others were asked to imagine how Carol must have felt about the situation.

Having listened to the audiotape, the participants were asked to complete two questionnaires, the first assessed their emotional response and the second their evaluation of the broadcast. The experimenter explained that they had misplaced the evaluation form but whilst they went to get a copy, they handed an envelope to the participant. Stating that they did not know anything about the contents of the envelope, they explained that they had been asked by the research lead to give this to the student listening to the Carol Macy tape. Inside was a letter from the professor stating that he realised Carol needed help to catch up and had thought the participant might be able to help. He had asked Carol to write a letter asking for help. If the participant was willing to help, they should fill out the card enclosed in the envelope and return it to the experimenter to give to the professor.

In Carol's letter, some participants read that she was in the same discussion section of the class as they were and hoped to return to class the following week. Others read that she was studying at home due to her legs still being in casts.

So, who helped? Those who were asked to imagine how Carol felt of course. Regardless of whether Carol intended to return or not, they were significantly more likely to offer help. Those who were asked to focus on the information instead, only offered help if they thought Carol was going to be returning. For these individuals, it appeared they were focusing on their own distress rather than Carol's in making the decision to help. According to Toi and Batson, empathy is the key to true altruism.

Consistent with this idea is the finding that people tend to feel good after helping only if the act of helping has reduced the distress of the other person (Batson et al., 1988). Batson (2017) suggests that over four decades, at least 35 experiments have supported the empathy-altruism idea so there is hope after all!

RULE 7: MAKE SURE THEY HAVE JUST SEEN SOMEONE ELSE HELPING

A female stands by a 1965 Oldsmobile car which is raised on a jack whilst a male changes the tyre.

About ¼ of a mile further down the road, you notice a different girl standing by a 1964 Ford Mustang that has a flat tyre. A fully inflated tyre leans against the side of the car. Would you help? According to Bryan and Test (1967), you are more likely to if you have just witnessed someone else helping in a similar situation. It also works with donations. Bryan and Test got a confederate to walk past a Salvation Army kettle placed on the pavement that was being used to collect coins, and to drop some coins into it. Would you believe it? Those individuals who happened to be passing nearby and saw this action, were more likely to donate themselves. Generosity breeds generosity the authors claim.

Rushton and Campbell (1977) demonstrated this effect with blood donations. Trainee occupational health therapists took part in a videoed interaction with another individual described as a Visiting Lecturer to Oxford. The visiting lecturer was in fact a confederate of the experiment. On visiting the office in the Psychology Department to collect their payment, they passed a "blood collector", standing next to a table with lots of information about blood donation on it. The collector asked the confederate if they would be willing to donate blood and if so how much. The confederate agreed and was asked to complete a donation form.

Whilst the blood collector went to an adjacent table to collect the form, an accomplice either praised the confederate for volunteering, or suggested she would regret it. A third condition involved the accomplice merely greeting the confederate and asking after her. When the blood collector returned, she asked the participant if they too would be willing to donate blood and if so, how much. Significantly more participants volunteered to give at least one pint of blood if they had seen the confederate agree compared to a control condition where the confederate was not present. Moreover, they were significantly more likely to actually give blood compared to the condition where the confederate was not present.

Jung et al. (2020) suggest that this effect of modelling prosocial behaviour is robust. In a meta-analysis of over 80 different studies with more than 25,000 participants, they reported that the modelling of prosocial behaviour has a noticeable and moderate

■ **Figure 3.3** Watching someone else act prosocially can influence us too. "Charity donations" by Howard Lake.

effect on our own willingness to help. As Greitemeyer (2022) reported:

> *As prosocial behaviour seems to be contagious, exposure to prosocial models is an effective way to encourage positive social encounters.*
>
> (p. 135)

This brings us nicely on to rule number 8 because increasingly, prosocial behaviour is modelled not by other people directly but through the media and it is to this that we now turn our attention.

RULE 8: PLAY NICE GAMES OR LISTEN TO NICE MUSIC

What was the last TV programme you watched? Did it have any prosocial behaviour examples in it? How about the last song you listened to? Were the lyrics advocating prosocial behaviour? And how about video games – have you played any prosocial video games recently? These questions all relate to rule number 8.

Let's take our story to the movies. de Leeuw and van der Laan (2018) were keen to look at the effects of helping behaviour in Disney animated movies on children who view them. Padilla-Walker et al. (2013) had already pointed to the overwhelmingly prosocial content in Disney animated movies in an earlier content analysis. de Leeuw and van der Laan asked children between 7 and 11 years of age to watch one of two Disney clips from the film "Cars". In the prosocial clip, they saw one of the cars let another competitor win before reversing to help a friend who had broken down. In the control clip, they saw the same characters but at the beginning of the race where nothing special happened. After the film clip, each child was given 20 spot the difference puzzles to try and complete. They were led to believe that they all had different puzzles and were encouraged to ask their friends for help where needed.

Children who watched the prosocial Disney clip were significantly more likely to provide help, to provide it spontaneously, without waiting to be asked and to spend more time helping a peer than those who watched the control clip.

There is also evidence that if you are primed to think about superheroes, this can have a similar effect on prosocial behaviour. Rosenberg et al. (2013) asked participants to engage with virtual reality games where they were asked to deliver insulin to a child who needed this to survive or to tour around a virtual city.

Participants were either in a condition where they had the power to fly like Superman or to fly as a passenger in a helicopter. When the experimenter knocked over a cup of pens, presumably by accident, those who had been given the superhuman VR powers were significantly more likely to help by picking up the pens than those who had flown as a co-pilot.

Peña and Chen (2017) reported a similar finding using a simulated flight game on a Nintendo Wii. They first asked participants to think about and describe the characteristics of a superhero or supervillain for 3 minutes. They then played on the flight training part of an Ironman game. After the game had been played,

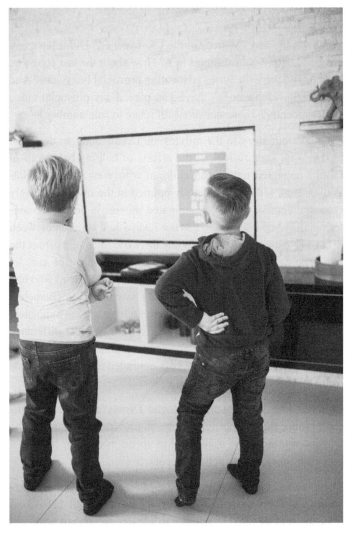

■ **Figure 3.4** The media we engage with can have a big effect on our behaviour. "Kids playing video games at home" by shixart1985.

the experimenter appeared to knock over a pot of pens from the table. Those who had been primed to think about superheroes were much faster to respond in helping to pick them up.

Yoon and Vargas (2014) found a similar prosocial effect when assigning participants to play as either a heroic, villainous, or neutral avatar. They were then asked to do a taste test and to pour an unspecified amount of either chocolate or chilli sauce into a dish for the next participant to try. The next participant would be asked to consume whatever was in the dish. Those who played as the heroic superhero avatar were significantly more generous with the distribution of chocolate to a future participant compared to those playing as the villainous or neutral avatar. (Those who played as villainous avatars poured more chilli sauce!)

These studies of course used virtual reality or avatars but even games that don't have these features can have similar prosocial effects. Greitemeyer and Osswald (2010) distributed participants across two conditions. In the prosocial condition, participants played Lemmings. The idea here is that small creatures have to be saved by being led away from danger and towards an exit point. In the neutral condition, participants played Tetris. Different geometrical shapes that fall from the top of the screen have to be placed in such a way that they form a solid row. Participants then witnessed a male confederate harassing a female experimenter. Not only did he shout at the woman but also, he kicked the bin and pulled her arm to try and get her to leave the room with him. Would participants intervene to help? Why yes. Those who had played Lemmings, the prosocial game, were significantly more likely to do so. More than half did so in this group compared to only a fifth of those who had played Tetris. Doing nice things to game characters in the game, Greitemeyer (2011) suggests, can generalise to real world positive social interaction after.

These studies focus on video games and movies but how about music? Well, if Greitemeyer's (2009) study is anything to go by, do spend time listening to songs such as Love Generation by Bob Sinclair. Exposure to this music led to greater willingness to donate money to a non-profit making organisation. Greitemeyer found a similar prosocial influence from songs such as "Heal the world" by Michael Jackson, "We are the world" by Live Aid and "Help" by the Beatles. Listening to these songs led to more willingness to pick up pencils that had been dropped. Prosocial music has also been found to increase the tipping behaviour of visitors to a restaurant (Jacob et al., 2010) and to purchase more fair-trade as opposed to regular coffee (Ruth, 2017). It has even been claimed to reduce risky driving behaviour (Greitemeyer, 2013) and to promote volunteering amongst gym members to distribute leaflets (North et al., 2004)!

It remains to be seen how, with increasing technology, this rule evolves. Peter et al. (2021) suggest that observing prosocial behaviour in a robot works effectively. They presented children with Nao, a 57 cm tall humanoid robot. If the robot won a game, it gave away ten of the twelve stickers it received. In a separate condition, the robot would only give away two. Witnessing strongly prosocial behaviour in the robot was sufficient to increase prosocial behaviour in the child by a factor of just over 6! When asked how many stickers their friends would give to the robot if they played the game, those who had played a strongly prosocial robot were more likely to give a higher estimate.

RULE 9: MAKE SURE YOU HAVE A RELATIVE NEAR

Our final rule in our journey through prosocial behaviour has everything to do with family. Essock-Vitale and McGuire (1985) suggest that when help is needed, closer family members are more likely to be a source of help and are more likely to help to a greater degree. It is no coincidence that women are more likely to help with childcare for their close relatives than for individuals who are not related. For example, Bereczkei (1998) demonstrated this in Gypsy populations and Ivey (2000) demonstrated this in Efe hunter-gatherer tribes suggesting this is a cross-cultural phenomenon. Knijn and Liefbroer (2006) reported that 56% of their participants said their parents have helped them with caring for their children. Sear (2018, 2020) suggests that such help can have a significant effect on fertility with those who can rely on help from close family members, more likely to have more children.

Hamilton (1964) refers to this as kin selection. This is where an individual will engage in a behaviour, potentially that involves a cost to the self, to promote the continuation of genes of genetically related individuals. Burnstein et al. (1994) provided evidence of this. Japanese and American undergraduates were asked to complete two questionnaires. In one, three individuals are described as being in need of help. The situation is a life and death situation for all of them but only one of the individuals can be helped. Which one would they help? In the other questionnaire, they were asked to imagine that three individuals asked them to do a small favour whilst they were on their way to an appointment. As with the first situation, only one person could be helped. Who would they help? The three individuals varied in terms of how closely related they were to the individual, e.g. a cousin, a grandparent, or an acquaintance. What did they find? The closer the person in relatedness, the more often they were selected as the person they would offer help to.

Sime (1983) studied the reports of survivors of a fire at a seaside leisure complex. In their accounts of the events, survivors reported that before they left the building, they were more likely to search for family members than for friends.

Madsen et al. (2007) asked participants to complete a ski-training exercise in return for a reward. The exercise involved maintaining a sitting posture as though they were sitting on a chair but with their back against the wall and their calves and thighs at right angles to each other. After a short while, this can become physically painful. When participants were told that the recipient of the reward was a close relative, they invested significantly more effort in the task and endured more pain.

This does, of course, give us food for thought. As Wilson (1978) highlighted:

> *Altruism based on kin selection is the enemy of civilization. If human beings are to a large extent guided…to favour their own relatives and tribe, only a limited amount of global harmony is possible.*
>
> (p. 157)

MYTH 1: IT HELPS TO BE RELIGIOUS

One of the famous stories of the Bible, is the parable of the Good Samaritan. A man is set upon by robbers and left for dead at the side of the road. A Priest and a Levite (who provided assistance to priests) walked past and did nothing but the Good Samaritan stopped to provide aid and assist the man in getting to an inn. One might imagine the Priest and the Levite, as religious men, to be more inclined to help but they didn't. Darley and Batson (1973) used this parable as the basis for establishing their own study of helping behaviour. They even called their study "From Jerusalem to Jericho" in recognition of the biblical connection.

Darley and Batson enlisted the help of seminary students as participants. Seminary students study theology, the study of religious belief. They believed they were participating in a study of religious education and vocations. They were asked to give a 3–5-minute talk based on either the story of the Good Samaritan or the jobs that seminary students might be most effective at. The experiment began in one building but required the students to move to a second building to deliver the talk. For one-third of the students, they were told that they were late and should quickly make their way to the other building, for another third, they were told to go right over as the assistant was ready for them and the last third were told that they might as well head over although it would be a few minutes before the assistant would be ready.

As the students moved to the second building, they encountered a person slumped in the alleyway. The person coughed as the students passed and kept his head down. Who would stop? Would anyone stop?

After giving their talk, they were asked to complete a helping behaviour questionnaire which quizzed them on when they last saw a person in need of help and when they last stopped to help someone in need amongst others.

Even though these were seminary students, 60% of them did not offer any help at all. Whether they were expecting to give a talk on the Good Samaritan or on the jobs seminary students would be effective at, had no effect on helping behaviour at all. As the authors point out, on several occasions, several of those students going to give a talk on the Good Samaritan, literally stepped over the slumped man on their way to do so. Being in a hurry reduced the chances of offering help substantially with only 10% of students in that condition offering any assistance.

Mencken and Fitz (2013), using data from the 2005 Baylor Religion survey, observed that the more important religion is, for a politically conservative individual, the less likely they will be to volunteer (13% less), the less likely they are to donate money for non-religious purposes (12% less) and the smaller the donation they make if they do (almost $230 less on average).

How do we reconcile these findings with research that suggests that religious individuals are more likely to volunteer (Johnston, 2013)? Batson, in a series of articles (e.g. Batson & Flory, 1990; Batson & Gray, 1981; Darley & Batson, 1973) suggests that religious individuals have a need to be seen to be helpful. Batson et al. (1989) presented participants with a chance to help another. They were told that even if they volunteered to help, they would only be chosen if they passed a qualification task. When they were told the task would be difficult, those who scored highly on religious measures were highly likely to volunteer. When they were told the task would be easy, fewer did so. Batson interpreted this as evidence that volunteering was the result of the desire to obtain rewards for themselves. A sobering thought....

MYTH 2: IT HELPS IF YOU LIVE IN A CITY

It might be assumed that with more people present in a city, there is more opportunity to obtain help when needed. Hansson and Slade (1977) used the lost letter technique to assess helpfulness in towns and a city, Tulsa in Oklahoma. Two hundred and sixteen letters were "lost" on the pavement, in a phone booth or at a business. Each letter was addressed to a fictitious individual. In some cases, the individual was identified as being a member of the communist party. How many would be picked up and posted?

Those dropped in the city were returned regardless of who it was addressed to. However, in towns, those addressed to the communist were significantly less likely to be picked up and posted. Only 2.8% of these letters were returned compared to 52% of the control letters (addressed to a random name and address but with no political connection apparent).

However, Milgram (1970) suggested that urban environments lead to sensory overload. The amount of social and environmental stimulation is so great that residents deal with this by avoiding involvement with strangers. Amato (1983) reviewed 18 different studies of helping behaviour, 50% of which found people in urban settings to be less helpful than those in small towns. Amato decided to undertake a study of his own. He wanted to explore the rates of helpfulness in 55 cities and towns in Australia that differed in population size and geographical position. The helping scenarios used were varied: (a) Passers-by were asked to participate in a survey by writing their favourite colour on a piece of paper. (b) A confederate with a limp and a clearly bandaged leg (part of which had had theatrical blood put on it) fell to the floor and remained kneeling. (c) A confederate would drop 20 envelopes on the pavement, bend down and start to pick them up. (d) Passers-by were asked if they would buy a packet of greeting cards to raise funds for a charity. (e) A confederate would give the experimenter inaccurate directions in response to a request whilst in a shop.

In all of these scenarios, helping behaviour decreased as population size increased. In the colour-request scenario, for example, 82% of individuals helped in one of the towns compared to just 55% in the cities. This was mirrored in the other scenarios with 44% buying greetings cards in the smallest communities to only 9% in the cities.

Levine et al. (2001) suggest that economic productivity could be influencing these trends. They reported a tendency for countries with stronger economies to be those that had lower rates of helping behaviour occurring within them. Inkeles (1997) similarly suggests that economic productivity and attitudes to prosocial behaviour are negatively related. More recently, it appears that this is rather oversimplified. Whillans et al. (2017) demonstrated how wealth can lead to greater prosocial behaviour, as measured by both intentions to donate and actual donations to charity. However, there was a condition attached! This was only the case when the appeal emphasised agency, that is the pursuit of personal goals. When the pursuit of shared goals was emphasised, it was the less wealthy individuals who were more willing to engage in prosocial behaviour. Wealthy people will also donate more when this is done publicly (Kraus & Callaghan, 2016). Which brings us back to the question we started with – are we selfish helpers?

REFERENCES

Amato, P. R. (1983). Helping behavior in urban and rural environments: Field studies based on a taxonomic organization of helping episodes. *Journal of Personality and Social Psychology, 45*(3), 571.

Batson, C. D. (2017). The empathy-altruism hypothesis: What and so what. E.M. Seppälä, S. Simon-Thomas, S.L. Brown, M.C. Worline, C.D. Cameron, J.R. Doty (Eds.), *The Oxford Handbook of Compassion Science*, Oxford University Press, pp. 27–40.

Batson, C. D., Dyck, J. L., Brandt, J. R., Batson, J. G., Powell, A. L., McMaster, M. R., & Griffitt, C. (1988). Five studies testing two new egoistic alternatives to the empathy-altruism hypothesis. *Journal of Personality and Social Psychology, 55*(1), 52.

Batson, C. D., & Flory, J. D. (1990). Goal-relevant cognitions associated with helping by individuals high on intrinsic, end religion. *Journal for the Scientific Study of Religion, 29*, 346–360.

Batson, C. D., & Gray, R. A. (1981). Religious orientation and helping behavior: Responding to one's own or the victim's needs? *Journal of Personality and Social Psychology, 40*(3), 511.

Batson, C. D., Oleson, K. C., Weeks, J. L., Healy, S. P., Reeves, P. J., Jennings, P., & Brown, T. (1989). Religious prosocial motivation: Is it altruistic or egoistic? *Journal of Personality and Social Psychology, 57*(5), 873.

Bereczkei, T. (1998). Kinship network, direct childcare, and fertility among Hungarians and Gypsies. *Evolution and Human Behavior, 19*(5), 283–298.

Bryan, J. H., & Test, M. A. (1967). Models and helping: Naturalistic studies in aiding behavior. *Journal of Personality and Social Psychology, 6*(4p1), 400.

Burger, J. M., Messian, N., Patel, S., Del Prado, A., & Anderson, C. (2004). What a coincidence! The effects of incidental similarity on compliance. *Personality and Social Psychology Bulletin, 30*(1), 35–43.

Burnstein, E., Crandall, C., & Kitayama, S. (1994). Some neo-Darwinian decision rules for altruism: Weighing cues for inclusive fitness as a function of the biological importance of the decision. *Journal of Personality and Social Psychology*, *67*(5), 773.

Carlsmith, J. M., & Gross, A. E. (1969). Some effects of guilt on compliance. *Journal of Personality and Social Psychology*, *11*(3), 232.

Cialdini, R. B., Schaller, M., Houlihan, D., Arps, K., Fultz, J., & Beaman, A. L. (1987). Empathy-based helping: Is it selflessly or selfishly motivated? *Journal of Personality and Social Psychology*, *52*(4), 749.

Cook, K., & Rice, E. (2006). Social exchange theory. In J. Delamater (Ed.), *Handbook of social psychology* (pp. 53–76). Kluwer Academic/Plenum.

Cunningham, M. R. (1979). Weather, mood, and helping behavior: Quasi experiments with the sunshine Samaritan. *Journal of Personality and Social Psychology*, *37*(11), 1947.

Darley, J. M., & Batson, C. D. (1973). "From Jerusalem to Jericho": A study of situational and dispositional variables in helping behavior. *Journal of Personality and Social Psychology*, *27*(1), 100.

Darley, J. M., & Latané, B. (1968). Bystander intervention in emergencies: Diffusion of responsibility. *Journal of Personality and Social Psychology*, *8*(4p1), 377.

de Leeuw, R. N., & van der Laan, C. A. (2018). Helping behavior in Disney animated movies and children's helping behavior in the Netherlands. *Journal of Children and Media*, *12*(2), 159–174.

DeBruine, L. M. (2002). Facial resemblance enhances trust. *Proceedings of the Royal Society of London. Series B: Biological Sciences*, *269*(1498), 1307–1312.

Dolinski, D., & Nawrat, R. (1998). "Fear-then-relief" procedure for producing compliance: Beware when the danger is over. *Journal of Experimental Social Psychology*, *34*(1), 27–50.

Eagly, A. H. (2009). The his and hers of prosocial behavior: An examination of the social psychology of gender. *American Psychologist*, *64*(8), 644.

Eagly, A. H., & Crowley, M. (1986). Gender and helping behavior: A meta-analytic review of the social psychological literature. *Psychological Bulletin*, *100*(3), 283.

Eagly, A. H., & Koenig, A. M. (2009). Social role theory of sex differences and similarities: Implication for prosocial behavior. In K. Dindia & D. J. Canary (Eds.), *Sex differences and similarities in communication (2nd ed.)*: 161–177. Erlbaum

Emswiller, T., Deaux, K., & Willits, J. E. (1971). Similarity, sex, and requests for small favors 1. *Journal of Applied Social Psychology*, *1*(3), 284–291.

Essock-Vitale, S. M., & McGuire, M. T. (1985). Women's lives viewed from an evolutionary perspective. II. Patterns of helping. *Ethology and Sociobiology*, *6*(3), 155–173.

Garcia, S. M., Weaver, K. D., Moskowitz, G. B., & Darley, J. M. (2002). Crowded minds: The implicit bystander effect. *Journal of Personality and Social Psychology*, *83*, 843–853.

Greitemeyer, T. (2009). Effects of songs with prosocial lyrics on prosocial thoughts, affect, and behavior. *Journal of Experimental Social Psychology*, *45*(1), 186–190.

Greitemeyer, T. (2011). Effects of prosocial media on social behavior: When and why does media exposure affect helping and aggression? *Current Directions in Psychological Science*, *20*(4), 251–255.

Greitemeyer, T. (2013). Exposure to media with prosocial content reduces the propensity for reckless and risky driving. *Journal of Risk Research*, *16*(5), 583–594.

Greitemeyer, T. (2022). Prosocial modeling: Person role models and the media. *Current Opinion in Psychology*, *44*, 135–139.

Greitemeyer, T., & Osswald, S. (2010). Effects of prosocial video games on prosocial behavior. *Journal of Personality and Social Psychology*, *98*(2), 211.

Guéguen, N., & De Gail, M. A. (2003). The effect of smiling on helping behavior: Smiling and Good Samaritan behavior. *Communication Reports*, *16*(2), 133–140.

Guéguen, N., & Fischer-Lokou, J. (2004). Hitchhikers' smiles and receipt of help. *Psychological Reports*, *94*(3), 756–760.

Guéguen, N., & Lamy, L. (2013). Weather and helping: Additional evidence of the effect of the sunshine Samaritan. *The Journal of Social Psychology*, *153*(2), 123–126.

Hamilton, W. D. (1964). The genetical evolution of social behaviour. II. *Journal of Theoretical Biology*, *7*(1), 17–52.

Hansson, R. O., & Slade, K. M. (1977). Altruism toward a deviant in city and small town. *Journal of Applied Social Psychology*, *7*(3), 272–279.

Inkeles, A. (1997). *Continuity and change in popular values on the Pacific Rim (No. 19)*. Hoover Press.

Isen, A. M. (1970). Success, failure, attention, and reaction to others: The warm glow of success. *Journal of Personality and Social Psychology*, *15*(4), 294.

Isen, A. M., & Levin, P. F. (1972). Effect of feeling good on helping: Cookies and kindness. *Journal of Personality and Social Psychology*, *21*(3), 384.

Ivey, P. K. (2000). Cooperative reproduction in Ituri forest hunter-gatherers: Who cares for Efe infants? *Current Anthropology*, *41*(5), 856–866.

Jacob, C., Guéguen, N., & Boulbry, G. (2010). Effects of songs with prosocial lyrics on tipping behavior in a restaurant. *International Journal of Hospitality Management*, *29*(4), 761–763.

Johnston, J. B. (2013). Religion and volunteering over the adult life course. *Journal for the Scientific Study of Religion*, *52*(4), 733–752.

Jones, L. M., & Foshay, N. N. (1984). Diffusion of responsibility in a nonemergency situation: Response to a greeting from a stranger. *Journal of Social Psychology*, *123*(2), 155.

Jung, H., Seo, E., Han, E., Henderson, M. D., & Patall, E. A. (2020). Prosocial modeling: A meta-analytic review and synthesis. *Psychological Bulletin*, *146*(8), 635.

Knijn, T. C., & Liefbroer, A. C. (2006). More kin than kind: Instrumental support in families. In P. A. Dykstra, M. Kalmijn, G. C. M. Knijn, A. E. Komter, A. C. Liefbroer, & C. H. Mulder (Eds.), *Family solidarity in the Netherlands* (pp. 89–105). Dutch University Press.

Kraus, M. W., & Callaghan, B. (2016). Social class and prosocial behavior: The moderating role of public versus private contexts. *Social Psychological and Personality Science*, *7*(8), 769–777.

Kunkel, A. W., & Burleson, B. R. (1999). Assessing explanations for sex differences in emotional support: A test of the different cultures and skill specialization accounts. *Human Communication Research*, *25*(3), 307–340.

Latané, B., & Darley, J. M. (1970). The unresponsive bystander: Why doesn't he help? *Journal of Personality and Social Psychology*, *10*, 215–221.

Latané, B., & Rodin, J. (1969). A lady in distress: Inhibiting effects of friends and strangers on bystander intervention. *Journal of Experimental Social Psychology*, *5*(2), 189–202.

Levine, R. V., Norenzayan, A., & Philbrick, K. (2001). Cross-cultural differences in helping strangers. *Journal of Cross-Cultural Psychology*, *32*(5), 543–560.

Levine, M., Prosser, A., Evans, D., & Reicher, S. (2005). Identity and emergency intervention: How social group membership and inclusiveness of group boundaries shape helping behavior. *Personality and Social Psychology Bulletin*, *31*(4), 443–453.

Madsen, E. A., Tunney, R. J., Fieldman, G., Plotkin, H. C., Dunbar, R. I., Richardson, J. M., & McFarland, D. (2007). Kinship and altruism: A cross-cultural experimental study. *British journal of psychology*, *98*(2), 339–359.

Markey, P. M. (2000). Bystander intervention in computer-mediated communication. *Computers in Human Behavior*, *16*(2), 183–188.

Mencken, F. C., & Fitz, B. (2013). Image of God and community volunteering among religious adherents in the United States. *Review of Religious Research*, *55*, 491–508.

Milgram, S. (1970). The experience of living in cities: A psychological analysis. In *Annual meeting of the American Psychological Association, September, 1969, Washington, DC, US; This paper is based on an Invited Address presented to the Division of General Psychology at the aforementioned meeting.* American Psychological Association.

Mims, P. R., Hartnett, J. J., & Nay, W. R. (1975). Interpersonal attraction and help volunteering as a function of physical attractiveness. *The Journal of Psychology*, *89*(1), 125–131.

North, A. C., Tarrant, M., & Hargreaves, D. J. (2004). The effects of music on helping behavior: A field study. *Environment and Behavior*, *36*(2), 266–275.

Otta, E., Pereira, B., Delavati, N., Pimentel, O., & Pires, C. (1993). The effects of smiling and of head tilting on person perception. *The Journal of Psychology*, *128*, 323–331.

Padilla-Walker, L. M., Coyne, S. M., Fraser, A. M., & Stockdale, L. A. (2013). Is Disney the nicest place on earth? A content analysis of prosocial behavior in animated Disney films. *Journal of Communication*, *63*(2), 393–412.

Peña, J., & Chen, M. (2017). With great power comes great responsibility: Superhero primes and expansive poses influence prosocial behavior after a motion-controlled game task. *Computers in Human Behavior*, *76*, 378–385.

Peter, J., Kühne, R., & Barco, A. (2021). Can social robots affect children's prosocial behavior? An experimental study on prosocial robot models. *Computers in Human Behavior*, *120*, 106712.

Piff, P. K., Kraus, M. W., Côté, S., Cheng, B. H., & Keltner, D. (2010). Having less, giving more: The influence of social class on prosocial behavior. *Journal of Personality and Social Psychology*, *99*(5), 771.

Piliavin, J. A., & Piliavin, I. M. (1972). Effect of blood on reactions to a victim. *Journal of Personality and Social Psychology*, *23*(3), 353–361.

Piliavin, I. M., Rodin, J., & Piliavin, J. A. (1969). Good Samaritanism: An underground phenomenon? *Journal of Personality and Social Psychology*, *13*(4), 289.

Regan, D. T., Williams, M., & Sparling, S. (1972). Voluntary expiation of guilt: A field experiment. *Journal of Personality and Social Psychology*, *24*(1), 42.

Rind, B. (1996). Effect of beliefs about weather conditions on tipping. *Journal of Applied Social Psychology*, *26*(2), 137–147.

Rind, B., & Strohmetz, D. (2001). Effect of beliefs about future weather conditions on restaurant tipping. *Journal of Applied Social Psychology*, *31*(10), 2160–2164.

Rosenberg, R. S., Baughman, S. L., & Bailenson, J. N. (2013). Virtual superheroes: Using superpowers in virtual reality to encourage prosocial behavior. *PLOS ONE*, *8*(1), e55003.

Rushton, J. P., & Campbell, A. C. (1977). Modeling, vicarious reinforcement and extraversion on blood donating in adults: Immediate and long-term effects. *European Journal of Social Psychology*, *7*(3), 297–306.

Ruth, N. (2017). "Heal the world": A field experiment on the effects of music with prosocial lyrics on prosocial behavior. *Psychology of Music*, *45*(2), 298–304.

Schneider, F. W., Lesko, W. A., & Garrett, W. A. (1980). Helping behavior in hot, comfortable, and cold temperatures: A field study. *Environment and Behavior*, *12*(2), 231–240.

Sear, R. (2020). Do human 'life history strategies' exist? *Evolution and Human Behavior*, *41*(6), 513–526.

Sear, R. (2018). Family and fertility: does kin help influence women's fertility, and how does this vary worldwide?. *Population Horizons*, *14*(1), 18–34.

Sime, J. D. (1983). Affiliative behaviour during escape to building exits. *Journal of Environmental Psychology*, *3*(1), 21–41.

Solomon, H., Solomon, L. Z., Arnone, M. M., Maur, B. J., Reda, R. M., & Roth, E. O. (1981). Anonymity and helping. *The Journal of Social Psychology*, *113*(1), 37–43.

Toi, M., & Batson, C. D. (1982). More evidence that empathy is a source of altruistic motivation. *Journal of Personality and Social Psychology*, *43*(2), 281.

van Leeuwen, E., & Täuber, S. (2011). Demonstrating knowledge: The effects of group status on outgroup helping. *Journal of Experimental Social Psychology*, *47*(1), 147–156.

Whillans, A. V., Caruso, E. M., & Dunn, E. W. (2017). Both selfishness and selflessness start with the self: How wealth shapes responses to charitable appeals. *Journal of Experimental Social Psychology*, *70*, 242–250.

Wilson, E. O. (1978). *On human nature*. Harvard University Press.

Xu, H., Bègue, L., & Bushman, B. J. (2014). Washing the guilt away: Effects of personal versus vicarious cleansing on guilty feelings and prosocial behavior. *Frontiers in Human Neuroscience*, *8*, 97.

Yoon, G., & Vargas, P. T. (2014). Know thy avatar: The unintended effect of virtual-self representation on behavior. *Psychological science*, *25*(4), 1043–1045.

Zhang, Y., & Epley, N. (2009). Self-centered social exchange: Differential use of costs versus benefits in prosocial reciprocity. *Journal of Personality and Social Psychology*, *97*(5), 796.

Zhong, C. B., & Liljenquist, K. (2006). Washing away your sins: Threatened morality and physical cleansing. *Science*, *313*(5792), 1451–1452.

Chapter 4

Why do we want to be the same as everyone else? Or do we?

Bob walks into a very dark room. On the wall ahead of him, there shines a tiny spot of bright light. As Bob watches, the light appears to move. Mustafer, an experimenter, asks Bob to estimate how far he thinks the light moved. Having done this once, Bob is then asked to repeat it, 100 times! Mustafer notices that by the end, Bob has established a median estimate for himself. The following week, Bob returns to the dark room but this time he is with two other individuals. When they are asked to discuss their estimates, Mustafer notices that something strange has started to happen. Bob is now altering his estimates to be more in line with those of the others in the group.

This scenario was exactly the one that a participant in Mustafer Sherif's (1935) study would have demonstrated. Sherif argued that each group was setting its own norm. That is, they were "conforming". Conformity was defined by Claidière and Whiten (2012) as:

> ... the fact that an individual displays a particular behaviour because it is the most frequent the individual witnessed in others.
>
> (p. 126)

Rohrer et al. (1954) demonstrated that the norms established by the groups are long-lasting, even after the experiment has been completed and Postmes et al. (2000) suggest that this process is accelerated in computer-mediated interactions due to the individual anonymity that is possible. Abrams and Levine (2017) point to how Sherif believed that our basic needs and activities often rest on establishing norms and "frames of reference" and claim that 75 years after the original study, Sherif's study continues to serve as a solid reference point in social psychology.

There is an important aspect of Sherif's studies, however, that needs to be acknowledged. In the autokinetic effect, it is an illusion. There is no clear right answer to the experimenter's question. We may therefore not be surprised to see group norms converge. Deutsch and Gerard (1955) refer to this type of social influence as informational influence. What might happen though in a situation where the answer is blatantly obvious? This was a question that Solomon Asch wanted to explore. In 1956, he conducted a study that aimed to illustrate "true conformity". A participant would be shown to a room to participate in a group study of visual perception. On entering the room, they would see between seven and nine other people already seated, waiting to start the study. The participant would take the only available seat which was always one from the end of a row. This ensured that in the study, the participant would hear most of the other group members' decisions before giving their judgement. The task itself was a line judgement task. Each member of the group was asked, in turn, to say which of three lines, A, B, or C matched a target line. In each case, the answer was unambiguous. There were 18 trials in total. In six of these, all members of the group answered correctly. However, in 12 of the trials, members of the group gave a unanimous incorrect response. Would the participant conform to the group and give an obviously incorrect answer? Or would they trust their judgement and give a correct answer?

Asch reported that over 36.8% of participants conformed and gave a blatantly wrong answer. In a control condition where no deliberately incorrect answers were given, the participants gave an incorrect answer only 1% of the time.

> *That we have found the tendency to conformity in our society so strong that reasonably intelligent and well-meaning young people are willing to call White Black is a matter of concern. It raises questions about our ways of education and about the values that guide our conduct.*
>
> (Asch, 1955, p. 34)

CULTURE MATTERS!

Before we wholeheartedly accept Asch's rather grim outlook, we need to remember that conformity rates do seem to differ according to culture, both geographical and historical. Asch conducted his studies in the United States, a country known for encouraging the pursuit of individual goals and for valuing independence. In a large-scale meta-analysis of 133 studies, Bond and Smith (1996) reviewed findings from Asch-like studies across a range of cultures. Conformity, they reported, is higher in collectivist countries, that value working for the good of the group over working for personal gain (Triandis, 1990).

At the time that Asch conducted his original study, there was a political context that may well have influenced the drive to conform. McCarthyism ... It is not crazy to assume this had an impact. Larsen (1990) for example reports that they found a lower level of conformity 20 years later, at a time when the Vietnam War had caused individuals to question their own behaviour and to become militants. In 1979, however, just five years later still, conformity appeared to increase again, a finding aligned with a decline in activism. Perrin and Spencer (1981) certainly believed that Asch's study was

a child of its time.

(p. 405)

They asked British male university students studying engineering, chemistry and physics to take part in a line judgement task, similar to that used by Asch and reported only one instance of conformity at all across 396 trials. Young offenders on probation and a group of "alienated" (Perrin & Spencer, 1981) West Indian participants were used as comparison groups. They performed similarly to Asch's original participants. Perrin and Spencer argued that for the latter two groups, the personal costs of not yielding to the majority view are high.

It is possible that knowledge played a big role in Perrin and Spencer's outcomes. The participants were all engineering students who were no doubt well-versed with making judgements of line length. We know from the work of Walker and Andrade (1996) that confidence in our own understanding increases with age and reduces conformity. Working with participants aged from 3 to 17 years, they suggest the high rates of conformity in younger participants to be due to children looking to others to help aid their understanding of the task. We also know from the work of Rhodes and Wood (1992) that individuals rated as low in intelligence tend to be more "influenceable" than those rated as high in intelligence.

Knowledge has been shown experimentally to influence conformity by Baron et al. (1996). They asked students to participate in two eyewitness identification tasks. In the lineup task, they were shown a picture of a perpetrator on a slide. They were then shown a different slide showing the perpetrator dressed differently plus

■ Figure 4.1 Why do we want to be the same as everyone else?

three additional men. The task was to identify the perpetrator from the lineup of four. In the description task, participants were shown seven slides, each of which had pictures of two male individuals on them and were asked to try and remember as many details as possible. The task was to answer, as accurately as possible, two questions about each slide such as "Which man was taller?". To make the task more difficult for participants in one condition, the time that the slide was shown for was reduced to just 0.5 seconds for the lineup task and 1 second for the description task.

When completing these tasks, participants were seated on the end of a row of three chairs. The other two were taken by confederates. After each slide, each person had to call out their answer in turn, with the participant answering last. In seven of the trials, the confederates gave the deliberately incorrect answer. For half of the participants in each condition, they were told that the study results would be useful at some point in the future and the main aim was to find out what the best conditions were for presenting the materials. For the other half of the participants, the importance of the task was emphasised. They were told that the test would be adopted by police departments soon and their responses would be used to establish accurate norms. The most accurate participant would be awarded a $20 prize at the end of the study.

When the difficulty of the lineup task was increased, *and* the task was given high importance, conformity increased. Participants looked to others more to ensure they were accurate in their own responses. When the task was made more easy, however, conformity declined.

CONFORMITY OUTSIDE THE LAB

Since the studies of Sherif and Asch, there have been numerous attempts to demonstrate the power of conformity in day-to-day life. Cialdini (2005) points to a demonstration of conformity that took place in a busy spot in a town where a street musician was playing. If a confederate had modelled making a donation into the musician's hat, passersby were much more likely to do the same. Cialdini (2003) demonstrated conformity in Arizona in the Petrified Forest National Park. The park had experienced a high degree of theft of wood (estimates were of more than one tonne a month). The authorities had tried to stem this by placing signs which informed visitors that their heritage was being vandalised as a result. It made reference to the amount of theft, 14 tonnes a year and to the fact that this was the accumulation of visitors taking a small bit of wood at a time. Cialdini soon realised that this sign was causing efforts to backfire because it was essentially setting the "norm" for visitors. Most visitors, it seemed to suggest, do take a small bit of wood from this forest. Cialdini therefore replaced these signs with new ones. These were alternated so that a comparison could be made of theft occurrences whilst each was in place. The first sign urged people not to take wood and showed a picture depicting three thieves. The second again urged people not to take wood but this time depicted a lone thief. The question was whether this would have any effect on conformity. When the first sign was displayed, about 7.92% of visitors were likely to steal. When the second sign was displayed, this dropped to 1.67%!

Conformity has powerful effects on health too. Koban and Wager (2016) have suggested that exposure to other fictitious people's pain ratings does have a strong influence on our own pain responses after. Akerlof et al. (1996) suggest that teenage girls are more likely to fall pregnant if they see other teenagers are having children and Harakeh and Vollebergh (2012) suggest that conformity has a role to play in teenage smoking. Peer smoking predicted smoking in participants during a music task. Knowing what other people have suggested is sufficient to create a frame of reference or norm that guides our own experience.

Martin and Randal (2011) explored the potential use of conformity in increasing donations to museums and art galleries. Many offers free admission but have a donation box in the entrance hall for visitors to make voluntary donations in. Martin and Randal wanted to see whether the contents of the box made any difference to the frequency and amount of donations made. They varied the contents that were visible as follows: in condition 1 the box was visibly empty. In condition 2, the box contained a lot of coins. In condition 3, there were several small denominations notes visible. In condition 4, there were just a few large denominations notes visible. The study took place in New Zealand, in an art gallery and ran for 52 days. As you may have guessed, seeing that other people had donated led to a much greater chance of visitors donating themselves. The strongest signal of all was condition 2 where a large number of coins had been deposited. Seeing that lots of donations had been made was sufficient for visitors to confirm and donate themselves.

As Martin and Randal (2011) point out this is in line with other illustrations of the power of conformity in donation decisions. Frey and Meier (2004) for example, suggest that giving individuals information about the frequency of donations that others have made in the past, has a big impact on willingness to donate to social funds for future students and Goldstein et al. (2008) report a greater willingness to reuse towels in a hotel room when guests are told that 75% of guests already do so. Goldstein et al.'s study is also useful in showing how similarity to the self is an important factor in our conformity actions. Being told that 75% of guests who stayed in the same room as a current guest re-used their towels led to the highest towel reuse rate of all.

WE CONFORM TO THOSE WHO ARE MOST LIKE US

It may seem to you like we just conform to social norms regardless but actually we are a lot more discerning than this suggests. You may not be surprised to know that we are much more likely to conform to those who are most like us. Platow et al. (2005) demonstrated this in a study that exploited the use of canned laughter. Canned laughter is pre-recorded laughter of an audience that is used to suggest to viewers what aspects of a performance or show should be funny. Platow asked participants to watch a stand-up comedy routine presented on video. For half of the clips, the participants heard canned laughter in the background at various points. In the other condition, there was no canned laughter at all. Within each condition, half of the participants were led to believe that the audience contained people like them, that is, fellow university students. For the other half, they were led to believe that the people in the audience were all members of a far-right political party that the students were less likely to identify with.

When no canned laughter was heard, the constitution of the audience had no effect at all on the amount of laughter produced by the participants. When canned laughter was heard, however, there was a marked effect. For those who believed the audience contained fellow university students, the amount of laughter produced was significantly higher than when they believed the audience were members of the far-right political party, or when they heard no laughter at all. We conform to those who are most like us.

Ušto et al. (2019) demonstrated this with Asch's original study. A conformity rate of 35.4% was obtained overall. However, this effect was stronger when the participant believed that others in the group were from their own in-group (Bosniaks, the same ethnic group as the participant) as opposed to when they believed others were from an out-group (Serbs). The mean number of errors made (hence a measure of conformity) was over 52% for the in-group condition but only 15% for the out-group condition.

WHY DO WE CONFORM SO MUCH?

So, why do we feel the need to conform so much? Stanley Schachter, in a seminal study in 1951 gave us a good idea of why. He constructed a scenario that was meant to look like the first meeting of a club. There were four in total, for example a movie club. The experimenter observed the 45-minute discussion that took place in each group and at the end of each meeting, members of the group would be chosen to be on different committees. Members of all clubs were asked to read a short version of a case study of a fictitious individual called Johnny Rocco. The participants believed this was a real person. Johnny was described as being a juvenile delinquent. The task was to decide what should be done with Johnny. A seven-point scale was used for members of the group to gauge their opinions.

Unbeknown to most in the group, of the five to seven members, three were paid to make specific judgements. One would always take the most commonly occurring view of the group (the mode), one would take an extreme position, of harsh punishment (the deviant) and one would start with an extreme position but be persuaded to change more towards the group norm (the slider). All opinions were expressed aloud.

At the end of the discussion, groups were asked to make a judgement about which group members should ideally stay together with them if there was a need to reduce the number of members in the club or to redistribute members to another group. The deviant was rejected significantly more often than the mode or slider. The more cohesive the group, the stronger the rejection. When asked to nominate individuals for committee roles, the deviant was significantly more likely to be nominated for the correspondence committee which had secretarial roles only as opposed to the Executive Committee which decided on the discussion topics and the Steering Committee which determined procedure.

Janes and Olson (2000) reported a similar effect more recently. Those who had watched an 8-minute video of someone ridiculing other people were much more likely to conform on a rating task than those who had seen a video where there was no target or where the ridicule was directed at the self. Participants who saw bogus ratings of a cartoon strip and had experienced someone else being ridiculed were more likely to agree with the ratings that had already been given. We want to avoid standing out because this could make us a target for ridicule. Janus and Olsen call this "jeer pressure".

CONFORMING WITHOUT KNOWING IT!

Of course, all of this so far suggests that we make a conscious and explicit decision to conform. But are we always fully aware? Pendry and Carrick (2001) primed participants with either an accountant category or a punk category. They were shown a photo of an individual dressed as either a business man or a punk and were asked to study the photo and then read out the text that accompanied each photo which introduced the person in the photo as either an accountant or a punk. This initial part of the study was done under the guise of being an additional extra to the main study, to check some materials for clarity.

Participants were then introduced into a group of four confederates and were invited to sit in the furthest seat. All were then asked to listen to an audiotape and keep a mental tally of how many beeps they heard. In a scenario reminiscent of Asch's, each individual was then asked to say aloud what their estimate was. The actual number of beeps heard was 100 but the confederates were told to give estimates ranging from 120 to 125. Did conformity occur? Why yes, of course, but more so for those who had been shown the photo of the accountant in the pre-task. Those who had been primed with the photo of the punk, conformed but

■ **Figure 4.2** Can conformity be used to improve conservation of energy?

to the same level as a group of participants that had not completed the initial task at all. Pendry and Carrick believe the photo of the punk had served to activate concepts of non-conformity whilst the accountant photo had done the opposite.

The idea that we often lack awareness of the power of others on our behaviour is also supported by Nolan et al. (2008) in their study of energy conservation. They believe that we often under-detect the role that such social influence plays in our decisions. They used random-digit-dialling to obtain interviewees in California. The interviews quizzed participants on their self-reported efforts to conserve energy, their beliefs about the benefits of energy conservation and their beliefs about energy conservation norms. In the latter case, participants were asked to decide how important it was to them that using less energy:

a. Saves money.
b. Protects the environment.
c. Benefits society.
d. Is something that a lot of other people are trying to do.

The reason rated as the most important was (b), followed by (c) and then (a). Reason (d), the idea that others are also trying to conserve energy was rated as the least important. However, beliefs about neighbours' conservation efforts were in fact strongly related to participants' own efforts to conserve energy. In a second study, door hangers were placed on the doors of residences in an area of California appealing to residents to conserve energy. Five different messages were used on the door hangers with each household receiving only one type of message:

- Information-only door hangers advocated a particular energy-conserving behaviour such as taking shorter showers.
- Self-interest door hangers also had an additional message that pointed to the monetary savings that could be had from conserving energy.
- Environmental protection door hangers pointed to the value for the environment such as cutting greenhouse gases.
- Social responsibility door hangers emphasised the possible reduction in demand for energy as a result of making socially responsible choices.
- Descriptive norm door hangers suggested that 77% of residents in the neighbourhood took action to conserve energy such as using fans instead of air conditioning.

Those receiving the descriptive norm door hangers used significantly less energy than participants in all other conditions combined. So, those messages that people view as being the most persuasive and important actually were not the ones that influenced behaviour the most. Nolan et al. suggest this is very much in line with findings of minority influence where people often deny the influence of others on their decision-making even though the evidence suggests otherwise. We don't like to think that others have such a powerful sway over our thinking. They do, however, advise against making individuals aware of such influence as it may result in efforts to correct this. The boomerang effect is just one example which brings us to our next consideration

BEWARE THE BOOMERANG

Sometimes conformity can be a helpful thing but sometimes the desire to get people to conform can backfire. Schultz et al. (2007) demonstrated this using the topic of energy conservation. Once a week, for four weeks, they put door hangers onto doorknobs of residents in a California community. These door hangers contained an appeal message about energy conservation. They contained a message about their energy consumption in the 2 weeks prior to the study, how they compared to others in the neighbourhood in terms of energy consumption and information about ways to conserve energy. For half of the participants, they also received what Schultz et al. refer to as an injunctive message, that is an indication of approval or disapproval. This was communicated via either a happy or a sad face alongside the message.

In the descriptive message condition (without the happy or sad faces), those who had been told they were using more than average compared to their neighbours, reduced their energy consumption. However, for those that were told they were using less than average compared to their neighbours, energy consumption increased! That is, the classic boomerang effect occurred. When the happy or sad faces accompanied the message, however, those households that were consuming less energy than average, continued to consume less than average. Even over a longer term, these patterns were sustained.

Borsari and Carey (2003) in discussing the effect of social norms and conformity on drinking behaviour in college students suggest that perceived norms can be less than helpful. If students think that their peers are drinking less than they are, they are likely to reduce their own drinking but if they perceive their peers to be drinking more than they are, this can serve to increase their own drinking behaviour. Neighbors et al. (2007) similarly suggest that overestimation of drinking behaviour in peers or even just the view that friends approve of heavy drinking can be sufficient to increase drinking behaviour ourselves.

■ **Figure 4.3** Richter, Thøgersen, and Klöckner used social norms to try and increase the purchase of sustainable seafood.

Richter et al. (2018) posted information about social norms in a supermarket where they wanted consumers to purchase more sustainably sourced seafood. A sign saying "More than 75% of the seafood customers in this store bought MSC-labelled seafood" (MSC stands for Marine Stewardship Council) had the opposite effect from what was intended. A decrease in the purchase of sustainably sourced seafood was found. The authors argue that customers were primed with the food group rather than the sustainability message!

THE THEORY OF UNIQUENESS

So far, our story suggests that we are particularly keen to be seen as fitting in with others, to be the same as everyone else, and to follow social norms, even if this means engaging in behaviour that is not so healthy. How do we reconcile this fact with the observation that we like to think of ourselves as unique and individual?

Pronin et al. (2007) give us one idea. Across a series of five studies, they demonstrated how individuals see other people as being more conforming than they are. Asked to assess their own susceptibility to 16 different examples of conformity, participants rated themselves as significantly less susceptible than their peers. They thought of themselves as more immune to social influence when purchasing a trendy electronic item than their peers and when making decisions about how to vote. Pronin, Berger, and Molouki refer to this asymmetry as the introspection illusion. We refer to information about our thoughts in trying to predict our behaviour rather than information about our actual behaviour.

The idea that we may lack awareness of how social norms are affecting our behaviour is something that Jaeger and Schultz (2017) similarly support. They conducted their study during a period of drought in California. Water use restrictions were in force. Receipt of a normative message informing residents that a majority of their neighbours were reducing their water consumption was just as effective as a strong warning threatening a substantial fine for breaking the drought restrictions but was more effective in reducing water consumption over a longer time period. This was the case even though there was no external reason such as the avoidance of a fine, for doing so.

These studies suggest we may not be aware of just how conformist we are. Instead, we have a positive striving to be seen as distinctive and unique. Snyder and Fromkin (1977, 1980) refer to this as the theory of uniqueness. Being seen to behave just like everyone else can be aversive if extreme. We like to think that in matters such as ability, beliefs, and even appearance, we have at least some uniqueness. Bellezza et al. (2014) give us reason to think this is because non-conformity is often associated with higher status. Individuals who were seen to be wearing non-conformist clothing such as a pair of red trainers, were seen to be of higher status than those who wore more conformist clothing. Bellezza et al. refer to this as the red sneakers effect.

As a demonstration of the uniqueness effect, Fromkin and Snyder (1980) asked students to list their ten most important attitudes. For half of the students, they were led to believe that their attitudes were quite unique compared to 10,000 other students that had been quizzed. For the other half, they were led to believe that their attitudes were pretty similar. When these same students were then asked to participate in a conformity experiment, guess who were the non-conformists? Yes, the students who had been led to believe their attitudes were the same as those of everyone else.

This idea of wanting to be seen as unique was exploited by cigarette advertisers in the 50s. The tobacco industry had advertised Camel cigarettes with the slogan "More doctors smoke Camels than any other cigarette". Somewhat ironic given what we now know about the health issues linked to smoking. However, this campaign emphasises the authority of medicine and a push to conform to expert opinion. In 1955, a new campaign was launched to promote the purchase of Marlboro cigarettes. The advertising featured a cowboy, the "Marlboro Man" who was depicted as independent and individualist. He made his own decisions and choices and rebuffed authority. Advertisers promoted uniqueness in an effort to make their product more desirable. (White et al., 2012).

A different way of marking uniqueness is tattooing. Tiggemann and Golder (2006) compared tattooed and non-tattooed individuals and found that those with tattoos scored higher on the need for uniqueness scale. Tattooing served as a means for differentiating themselves from others. This was confirmed more recently by Swami et al. (2012) who also reported a greater need to invest in creating a unique appearance in these individuals.

The uniqueness effect can work both ways however. Zweigenhaft (1981) suggests that individuals with unusual names score higher on the need for uniqueness. (Although be aware that individuals with unusual names are less likely to graduate with academic honours according to Joubert (1983)!)

So, it's good to be different. Indeed, Friend et al. (1990) remind us that Asch himself believed his results to demonstrate the power of independence. Most individuals did in fact, resist group pressure. However, we don't like to be too different. There is, however, just one exception (isn't there always). Men who are looking to attract a mate tend to be non-conformist in order to make themselves look unique, according to Griskevicius et al. (2006). (This is, of course, assuming they can't be proven wrong!)

REFERENCES

Abrams, D., & Levine, J. M. (2017). Norm formation. *Social Psychology: Revisiting the Classic Studies*, 58–76.

Akerlof, G. A., Yellen, J. L., & Katz, M. L. (1996). An analysis of out-of-wedlock childbearing in the United States. *The Quarterly Journal of Economics*, *111*(2), 277–317.

Asch, S. E. (1955). Opinions and social pressure. *Scientific American*, *193*(5), 31–35.

Asch, S. E. (1956). Studies of independence and conformity: I. A minority of one against a unanimous majority. *Psychological Monographs: General and Applied*, *70*(9), 1.

Baron, R. S., Vandello, J. A., & Brunsman, B. (1996). The forgotten variable in conformity research: Impact of task importance on social influence. *Journal of Personality and Social Psychology*, *71*(5), 915.

Bellezza, S., Gino, F., & Keinan, A. (2014). The red sneakers effect: Inferring status and competence from signals of nonconformity. *Journal of Consumer Research*, *41*(1), 35–54.

Bond, R., & Smith, P. B. (1996). Culture and conformity: A meta-analysis of studies using Asch's (1952b, 1956) line judgment task. *Psychological Bulletin*, *119*(1), 111.

Borsari, B., & Carey, K. B. (2003). Descriptive and injunctive norms in college drinking: A meta-analytic integration. *Journal of Studies on Alcohol*, *64*(3), 331–341.

Cialdini, R. B. (2003). Crafting normative messages to protect the environment. *Current Directions in Psychological Science*, *12*(4), 105–109.

Cialdini, R. B. (2005). Basic social influence is underestimated. *Psychological Inquiry*, *16*(4), 158–161.

Claidière, N., & Whiten, A. (2012). Integrating the study of conformity and culture in humans and nonhuman animals. *Psychological Bulletin*, *138*(1), 126.

Deutsch, M., & Gerard, H. B. (1955). A study of normative and informational social influences upon individual judgment. *The Journal of Abnormal and Social Psychology*, *51*(3), 629.

Frey, B. S., & Meier, S. (2004). Social comparisons and pro-social behavior: Testing "conditional cooperation" in a field experiment. *American Economic Review*, *94*(5), 1717–1722.

Friend, R., Rafferty, Y., & Bramel, D. (1990). A puzzling misinterpretation of the Asch 'conformity' study. *European Journal of Social Psychology*, *20*(1), 29–44.

Fromkin, H. L., & Snyder, C. R. (1980). The search for uniqueness and valuation of scarcity: Neglected dimensions of value in exchange theory. In *Social exchange: Advances in theory and research* (pp. 57–75). Boston, MA: Springer US.

Goldstein, N. J., Cialdini, R. B., & Griskevicius, V. (2008). A room with a viewpoint: Using social norms to motivate environmental conservation in hotels. *Journal of Consumer Research, 35*(3), 472–482.

Griskevicius, V., Goldstein, N. J., Mortensen, C. R., Cialdini, R. B., & Kenrick, D. T. (2006). Going along versus going alone: When fundamental motives facilitate strategic (non) conformity. *Journal of Personality and Social Psychology, 91*(2), 281.

Harakeh, Z., & Vollebergh, W. A. (2012). The impact of active and passive peer influence on young adult smoking: An experimental study. *Drug and Alcohol Dependence, 121*(3), 220–223.

Jaeger, C. M., & Schultz, P. W. (2017). Coupling social norms and commitments: Testing the underdetected nature of social influence. *Journal of Environmental Psychology, 51*, 199–208.

Janes, L. M., & Olson, J. M. (2000). Jeer pressure: The behavioral effects of observing ridicule of others. *Personality and Social Psychology Bulletin, 26*(4), 474–485.

Joubert, C. E. (1983). Unusual names and academic achievement. *Psychological Reports, 53*, 266.

Koban, L., & Wager, T. D. (2016). Beyond conformity: Social influences on pain reports and physiology. *Emotion, 16*(1), 24.

Larsen, K. S. (1990). The Asch conformity experiment: Replication and transhistorical comparison. *Journal of Social Behavior and Personality, 5*(4), 163.

Martin, R., & Randal, J. (2011). How social norms, price, and scrutiny influence donation behavior: Evidence from four natural field experiments. In D.M. Oppenheimer & C.Y. Olivola (Eds.), *The science of giving: Experimental approaches to the study of charity* (pp. 81–113). Taylor and Francis.

Neighbors, C., Lee, C. M., Lewis, M. A., Fossos, N., & Larimer, M. E. (2007). Are social norms the best predictor of outcomes among heavy-drinking college students? *Journal of Studies on Alcohol and Drugs, 68*(4), 556–565.

Nolan, J. M., Schultz, P. W., Cialdini, R. B., Goldstein, N. J., & Griskevicius, V. (2008). Normative social influence is underdetected. *Personality and Social Psychology Bulletin, 34*(7), 913–923.

Pendry, L., & Carrick, R. (2001). Doing what the mob do: Priming effects on conformity. *European Journal of Social Psychology, 31*(1), 83–92.

Perrin, S., & Spencer, C. (1981). Independence or conformity in the Asch experiment as a reflection of cultural and situational factors. *British Journal of Social Psychology, 20*(3), 205–209.

Platow, M. J., Haslam, S. A., Both, A., Chew, I., Cuddon, M., Goharpey, N., Maurer, J., Rosini, S., Tsekouras, A., & Grace, D. M. (2005). "It's not funny if they're laughing": Self-categorization, social influence, and responses to canned laughter. *Journal of Experimental Social Psychology, 41*(5), 542–550.

Postmes, T., Spears, R., & Lea, M. (2000). The formation of group norms in computer-mediated communication. *Human Communication Research, 26*(3), 341–371.

Pronin, E., Berger, J., & Molouki, S. (2007). Alone in a crowd of sheep: Asymmetric perceptions of conformity and their roots in an introspection illusion. *Journal of Personality and Social Psychology*, *92*(4), 585.

Rhodes, N., & Wood, W. (1992). Self-esteem and intelligence affect influenceability: The mediating role of message reception. *Psychological Bulletin*, *111*(1), 156.

Richter, I., Thøgersen, J., & Klöckner, C. A. (2018). A social norms intervention going wrong: Boomerang effects from descriptive norms information. *Sustainability*, *10*(8), 2848.

Rohrer, J. H., Baron, S. H., Hoffman, E. L., & Swander, D. V. (1954). The stability of autokinetic judgments. *The Journal of Abnormal and Social Psychology*, *49*(4p1), 595.

Schachter, S. (1951). Deviation, rejection, and communication. *The Journal of Abnormal and Social Psychology*, *46*(2), 190.

Schultz, P. W., Nolan, J. M., Cialdini, R. B., Goldstein, N. J., & Griskevicius, V. (2007). The constructive, destructive, and reconstructive power of social norms. *Psychological Science*, *18*(5), 429–434.

Sherif, M. (1935). A study of some social factors in perception. *Archives of Psychology (Columbia University)*, *187*, 60.

Snyder, C. R., & Fromkin, H. L. (1977). Abnormality as a positive characteristic: The development and validation of a scale measuring need for uniqueness. *Journal of Abnormal Psychology*, *86*(5), 518.

Snyder, C. R., & Fromkin, H. L. (1980). Theory of uniqueness. *Uniqueness: The Human Pursuit of Difference*, Plenum Press: New York 31–55.

Swami, V., Pietschnig, J., Bertl, B., Nader, I. W., Stieger, S., & Voracek, M. (2012). Personality differences between tattooed and non-tattooed individuals. *Psychological Reports*, *111*(1), 97–106.

Tiggemann, M., & Golder, F. (2006). Tattooing: An expression of uniqueness in the appearance domain. *Body Image*, *3*(4), 309–315.

Triandis, H. C. (1990). Theoretical concepts that are applicable to the analysis of ethnocentrism. *Applied Cross-Cultural Psychology*, *14*, 34–55.

Ušto, M., Drače, S., & Hadžiahmetović, N. (2019). Replication of the "Asch effect" in Bosnia and Herzegovina: Evidence for the moderating role of group similarity in conformity. *Psychological Topics*, *28*(3), 589–599.

Walker, M. B., & Andrade, M. G. (1996). Conformity in the Asch task as a function of age. *The Journal of Social Psychology*, *136*(3), 367–372.

White, C., Oliffe, J. L., & Bottorff, J. L. (2012). From the physician to the Marlboro Man: Masculinity, health, and cigarette advertising in America, 1946–1964. *Men and Masculinities*, *15*(5), 526–547.

Zweigenhaft, R. L. (1981). Unusual names and uniqueness. *The Journal of Social Psychology*, *114*(2), 297–298.

Chapter 5
The art of persuasion

What are your thoughts on electric cars? Would you be persuaded to buy one? Which political party do you find the most convincing? And what are your thoughts on the dangers of binge drinking? The reason I ask is because all of these relate to our topic of persuasion. We are constantly bombarded with attempts to convince us to adopt a particular view, to act in a certain way or to purchase a product. This is not a new phenomenon. In Germany from 1933 to 1945, Josef Goebbels published a weekly newspaper "Der Sturmer" which aimed to persuade people of the Nazi point of view on everything from radio to rallies to the arts. More recently, few of us can have escaped the persuasive techniques used by so-called "instagram influencers" and you may be familiar with the controversies over using gambling companies to sponsor sports teams because of the impact this has in terms of persuading others to gamble.

Some of these examples are what is referred to as propaganda. This term is used to describe negative instances of persuasion. These contrast with education-based persuasion which aims to improve quality of life or to seek resolutions and are more interactive.

THE PERSON TRYING TO PERSUADE US

So, let's paint a portrait of what the successful persuader is … credible, like us, talks fast and perhaps is even good-looking and trustworthy. Good-looking? Yes, indeed there is evidence to support this. So, let's embark on our journey through the world of persuasion psychology and see if we can add more details to our portrait.

The successful persuader is … credible

I want you to imagine you are listening to a podcast in which you hear a person warn of the dangers of frequent toothbrushing. The person is Dr James Rundle of the Canadian Dental Association. James has been leading research in the field of dentistry for some years. Do you think you would be persuaded

DOI: 10.4324/9781003396208-5

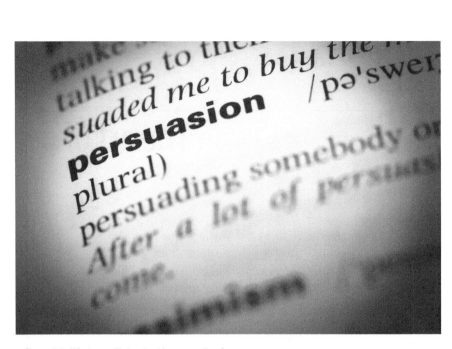

■ **Figure 5.1** Who is most likely to be able to persuade us?

of the argument? Imagine now, that instead of Dr James Rundle, you are told that the speaker is Jim Rundle, a high school student who has just completed a project with his classmates looking at the issue of dental hygiene. Would it make a difference to your behaviour?

This was exactly the scenario used by Olson and Cal (1984) (albeit it was not a podcast but an audio recording). In their study, those who believed the message came from Dr James Rundle were more likely to report brushing their teeth less often in the 4 weeks following the audio message. I pity their dentist now ... The critical factor seemed to be credibility. Dr James Rundle was seen as the high-credibility speaker and therefore was more persuasive.

So, it would seem that credibility matters but is this the whole story? Not according to Tormala et al. (2006). They asked undergraduates to sit at a computer terminal. On the screen, information suggested the study was designed to aid the development of a new aspirin product "Comfrin". Participants then saw a persuasive message promoting this drug but with a strong argument (it works faster, lasts longer, and has no harmful side effects compared to other aspirin products) or a weak argument (it lasts as long as other brands, has very few harmful side effects and contains only small amounts of caffeine and sodium). They were asked to document their thoughts one at a time on the screen. Once the participants had completed this task, they were told about the source of the message. For those in the high credibility condition, they were led to believe that this was information provided by a medical research federal agency. For those in the low credibility condition, they were led to believe it was taken from a class report written by a high school student. They were then asked to document their attitudes towards the product and to classify their earlier recorded thoughts in terms of how positive or negative they were to the product.

From Olsen and Cal's work, we might imagine that the high-credibility source led to greater positivity towards the product. This was indeed the case when the argument presented was strong. However, when the argument was weak, the high-credibility source weakened the persuasiveness of the participant. In other words, it backfired! The key message is that if we want to persuade another person, choose a high-credibility source with a strong argument.

But even this is not the full story. Tormala and Petty (2004) argue that it is important to consider what an individual's initial attitudes are before attempting to persuade them. High-credibility sources who attempt to persuade people of a counter-attitudinal point of view can actually make people more rather than less confident in their existing attitude. Where an issue is of low interest to an individual, high-credibility sources tend to be most persuasive (Petty & Cacioppo, 1979). We are less likely to want to invest lots of effort to process the arguments and so, are more influenced by the source. If it's an issue we are highly involved in or really care about, however, well, that is a different story. We scrutinise the messages more. This has important implications for how persuasive internet information can be (Wathen & Burkell, 2002), particularly when so many low-credibility sources can generate information. The idea that people need to be motivated and engaged with an issue to really engage with it fits with the Elaboration Likelihood Model developed by Petty et al. (1986). In these situations, people focus on the arguments given, the so-called central route to persuasion. Where arguments are strong, persuasion may occur. If people are not so engaged with an issue, then a peripheral route may be used instead. Here we may be more influenced by factors that are easily processed such as how attractively the message is delivered or how easy it is to understand.

So, how do we explain this contradiction in credibility? One possibility is that there is another factor at play here, the factor of similarity to the self and it is to that that we will turn next.

The successful persuader is .... similar to us

Back in 1965, Brock investigated similarity and its effect on persuasion in a field study conducted in a paint shop. An experimenter tried to persuade a customer to buy a different brand of paint. Customers were more likely to be persuaded if the experimenter had recently bought a similar amount of paint to them for a similar project than by someone who had bought twenty times as much paint or who had been working on a dissimilar project. For example, 73% changed their decision when the persuader was seen as similar to themselves but only 45% did so when the persuader was dissimilar. This was the case even when the dissimilar persuader was seen as being more credible in terms of knowledge.

More recently, Howard and Kerin (2011) wanted to explore the effect of similarity on persuasion in advertising. In one of their experiments, participants were asked to evaluate advertisements for a new brand of cranberry juice. In one condition, the name of the juice was manipulated to be similar to the participant's own name. The first letter of the participant's name was used and the complete last name was used. I don't know about you but I might be a bit suspicious if I saw a cranberry juice called W-Garnham! In a second condition, the name was completely unrelated to the participant's own. For some participants in each condition, they saw information about the juice that referred to "strong" attributes such as that the juice was "vitamin fortified". For some, they saw information that referred to "weak" attributes such as "contains 40% real fruit juice". As you may well have predicted by this point, more favourable thoughts were reported when strong arguments were seen but only when the brand had a similar name to themselves. In these conditions, the researchers argue, participants are more likely to thoughtfully examine the information and relate it to themselves.

Gamer (2005) suggests this is also important when it comes to getting students to complete and return questionnaires. Students (and college professors) are more likely to return these when the name on the cover letter is similar to their own! This is an example of what Pelham et al. (2005) refer to as implicit egotism, that is liking things that remind us of ourselves.

This phenomenon is also highly applicable to political voting situations. Wiegman (1985) asked Liberal and Socialist political leaders who were working in the Dutch parliament to present exactly the same arguments, even using the identical words, to either their own or an opposition party. Consistent with the similarity effect, they were more successful at persuading members of their own party than those of the opposition. Similarity can also be influential in the lead-up to an election. Edwards-Levy (2015) explored attitudes towards universal health care. When Republicans were told that Donald Trump has endorsed these ideas, they were significantly more likely to support them than when they were led to believe they came from Barack Obama. Give the same information to Democrats and you find the reverse picture – they are significantly less likely to support the ideas if they believe they came from Trump!

The successful persuader is ... a fast talker

Whilst similarity might be important, there are other factors that increase our persuasiveness. How fast do you talk? The reason I ask is because this might be influential if you are trying to persuade someone else of a point of view or to behave in a certain way. Miller et al. (1976) compared the persuasiveness of a message about the deleterious effects of caffeine on the body, when the speaker averaged 102 words a minute compared to when they averaged 195 words a minute. Speaking fast was significantly more effective in persuading another person of the message compared to speaking slowly. Rapid speech, Miller et al. claim, acts as a cue to credibility which in turn, as we have seen, is a variable that has a big influence over our persuasive tendencies.

Perhaps it is not so much speed but fluency that is important. Certainly, if we are seen to stumble over our words or stutter, we are more likely to be seen as low in credibility and our persuasiveness diminishes (Carpenter, 2012). This has implications for the law court where fluency of witnesses has been shown to influence how much they can persuade a jury (Kaminski and Sporer, 2018).

The successful persuader is ... trustworthy

Trustworthiness is a good quality to have as a persuader. Hemsley and Doob (1978) tested this using a courtroom simulation. When a witness averted rather than held their gaze when giving testimony, they were seen to be less trustworthy and the defendant that they acted as a witness for, was judged as guilty more often.

One of the key questions when trying to assess trustworthiness is the question of *why* someone is trying to persuade you. If you believe that someone has something to gain from trying to convince you, you are less likely to be persuaded. So, no wonder then that when we overhear someone without them realising, we are more likely to be influenced by them. The speaker is not intending to be heard so cannot possibly have any ulterior motive.

To explain, let's look at Walster and Festinger's (1962) "hidden camera" method. New undergraduates were required to sign up for a short tour of the psychology department's laboratory observation room. As they walked to this room, they were informed that graduate students sometimes used this as a lounge. In one condition, the participants saw the experimenter enter the room and ask the students to continue their conversation so that the new undergraduates could try a bit of "blind listening", that is noticing pauses, incomplete sentences, etc. In the other condition, the experimenter didn't enter the room so the participants were under the impression that the graduate students were unaware of their presence. In both conditions, participants listened into the conversation which happened to be about what they saw as a misconception of the link between smoking and lung cancer. One week later, the participants were asked to complete a questionnaire which claimed to be from the National Institute of Health. Amongst the questions on this questionnaire, were four questions relating to the relationship between smoking and cancer. Shortly after, students were asked to evaluate their tour of the laboratory.

■ **Figure 5.2** If we believe someone is not trying to influence us but we overhear their message, we may be more easily persuaded by it.

Those who overheard the conversation without the graduate students being aware of their presence, were much more influenced by what they heard than those who thought the graduate students were aware they were listening. Smokers were particularly influenced compared to non-smokers. This latter finding is important. Brock and Becker (1965) similarly reported that overheard conversations are powerful in persuading others but only when listeners are involved and when the content of the conversation is "acceptable". That is, when the information aligns with the person's existing position on the issue.

One of the clearest indicators that we use to assess trustworthiness is looking to see whether someone is persuading us in line with their self-interests. Environmental concerns are often at the forefront of attempts to persuade others and with climate change a growing political agenda, this is no less true now than it was at the time that Eagly et al. (1978) conducted their study. They asked undergraduates to participate in an "opinion formation" experiment. The task involved reading some background material on the issue of water pollution, specifically about the Farraday Aluminium Company's waste disposal methods and the impact of these on the local waterways. The company, it suggested, had been polluting an ecologically important river by dumping its waste into it. Two possible resolutions for the issue were proposed. One resolution was to allow the company to gradually change its waste disposal methods but to continue operating. The second was to stop production straight away and to make radical changes. At this point, participants were asked to state their opinion about the matter.

In the next stage of the study, participants read a transcript of a meeting that had been held to explore this issue. A mayoral candidate, described as a well-liked person, Jack Reynolds, had spoken in the meeting. Reynolds was always described as having favoured the resolution of stopping production immediately. However, for half of the participants, they were led to believe that Reynolds was a pro-environmentalist who had had success in stopping dumping of pollutants previously. For the other half, they were led to believe that Reynolds had previously acted successfully on behalf of the Farraday company. That is, he had a business background. In some cases, the background information described the audience as being citizens for the environment and in others, it described them as being citizens for industrial growth. All participants were asked to give their judgement after this second stage.

Who was most likely to be persuaded by Reynolds? Those who heard that he had a business background. Why? According to the researchers, he was considered to be expressing his true opinion. His message seemed to contradict what they had expected him to say. Why would he argue for something that conflicts with his interest in industry? Well, he must really genuinely believe in it. In contrast, when he confirmed expectation by arguing in a way consistent with a pro-environmentalist background, he was considered to be biased and hence less persuasive. Similarly, when he was speaking to a pro-environmentalist audience, he was less persuasive than when he was speaking to a pro-business audience. Being seen to argue against our personal self-interest is a strong characteristic to show when trying to persuade another. Edwards and Potter (2007) refer to this as the dilemma of stake and interest. If people are seen as having something to gain from persuading us, or have a personal grievance that underlies their persuasion attempts, we are less likely to be convinced by them as they appear to be less trustworthy.

The successful persuader is … good-looking

Can this be true? Are we so shallow? Well, the evidence suggests so. Mills and Aronson (1965) reported that an attractive persuader was more effective when announcing his intention to persuade than a less attractive persuader. Similarly, Chaiken (1979) suggested that attractive communicators were able to persuade others more than unattractive communicators on both verbal (agreement with a statement) and behavioural (signing a petition) tasks. Communicators wanted to convince people on a university campus that the university should stop serving meat at breakfast and lunch at all campus food outlets. Two arguments were presented after which participants were asked to complete a questionnaire asking for their opinion on the issue as well as their ratings of friendliness, attractiveness, and knowledgeability of the communicator. They were then asked if they would be willing to sign a petition on this issue. Attractive communicators were not only more successful at persuading others of their argument but also were rated as more friendly.

Ozanne et al. (2019) identified an attractiveness effect even for review-writing. They constructed a fake Facebook page for a hotel which had a review written underneath. Having read this, participants completed a survey. A positive review left by an attractive reviewer led to significantly enhanced brand evaluations covering trust, quality, desirability, and the likelihood of purchase. As Ozanne et al. point out, social media reports suggest an excess of 75 billion items of content are posted every day on Facebook alone and this platform can be influential in persuading others of the value (or otherwise) of products. It is important therefore to consider the role that profile pictures might play in the impact of such content.

It is no wonder then that attractive celebrities are commonly used to endorse products. Schimmelpfennig and Hunt (2020) suggest that attractive celebrities can influence not just attitudes to the advertisement but also evaluations of products. Have we made this sound too simple though? Well yes because as Sääksjärvi et al. (2016) found, this is not the case for individuals who have low self-esteem. For these consumers, attractive celebrities can have a negative effect on the intention to purchase an item. It is also increasingly the case that the effect of attractiveness is limited to attractiveness-related products and services (Trampe et al., 2010).

This factor is not an isolated factor, however, as we have seen. If an attractive communicator produces a weak argument in an essay, then this can backfire with them being less persuasive than an unattractive counterpart (Puckett et al., 1983). Similarly, Maddux and Rogers (1980) suggest that being attractive simply isn't sufficient to persuade another person. You also need to be seen as either possessing expertise or have strong arguments to be successful.

So, we now have an idea of what the successful persuader might look like. However, even the most trustworthy, credible, and good-looking communicator needs to think carefully about what it is they want to say to another individual to persuade them. So, what do we know about the effect of message content on persuasion?

THE CONTENT OF THE MESSAGE
Should we appeal to hearts or to minds?

You may be familiar with Comic Relief as a charity organisation. Every year they try to persuade the general public to donate money to the charity through appealing to us in short film clips or with comedy sketches. Many of the films they show depict individuals in very challenging circumstances and as such appeal to viewer's sense of compassion and empathy in trying to persuade us to part with money. Erlandsson et al. (2018) suggest that negatively framed appeals tend to lead to greater donations. They appeal to our hearts by highlighting negative consequences that may occur if we don't take a particular action. Some argue that such appeals lead us to want to alleviate our

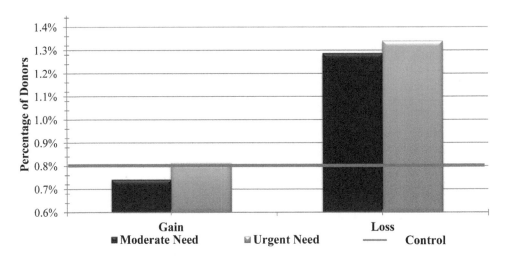

■ **Figure 5.3** Chou and Murnighan (2013) suggest that the framing of a message can make a big difference to our success in persuading others.

own distress (Choi & Park, 2021). Chou and Murnighan (2013) increased the number of students who agreed to donate blood by framing this as a way to prevent death than to save a life. Banks et al. (1995) reported a higher number of women getting a mammogram within 12 months of viewing a video that emphasises the risks of not getting one compared to those who saw a video emphasising the benefits. Avoiding loss works.

Uncomfortable emotions caused by threat or fear messages work in contexts outside of health concerns also. Aagerup et al. (2019) demonstrated how appealing to emotions can lead to greater persuasion in getting people to commit to green packaging. They contrasted claims that contained rational appeals (pointing to effects on soil erosion, carbon dioxide, and deforestation) with claims that contained emotional appeals (asking readers whether they want to drink coffee in their old age and how choosing a more sustainable option will help secure coffee's future). The propensity to purchase sustainable products was significantly enhanced with the emotional message.

One word of warning here though – don't include statistics in an emotional appeal. Small et al. (2013) reported a decrease in donations if the number of people in need was mentioned in an emotional appeal. Deliberative thinking, they argue, can serve to undermine emotional responses, blunting them. And it is also worth considering gender in appealing. Kemp et al. (2013) presented participants with a message designed to elicit either pride or sympathy. When sympathy was emphasised, women expressed greater intention to donate than men. When pride was emphasised, men expressed greater intention to donate than women. So, the type of emotional appeal might be important.

Should we scare people?

One of the dominant emotions we experience is fear. And believe me, there have been many attempts to explore the role of fear in persuasion. The key question is, does it work? Janis and Feshbach (1953) chose to explore this using dentistry as their focus. I'm not sure there are many of us who relish a trip to the dentist chair. Janis and Feshbach presented high school students with one of three illustrated lectures focused on the causes of tooth decay and ways to minimise this. In the strong fear condition, the students were told about the painful consequences of decay including diseased gums, the spread of infection to other bodily organs and the link to other consequences such as blindness or paralysis. Students themselves were told this could happen to them. In the moderate fear condition, dangers were described in a more factual and impersonal way and in the low fear condition, the consequences of tooth decay were barely mentioned. Instead, they had more information about the structure and function of teeth. A control group heard a lecture on the structure and function of the eye instead.

Questionnaires on general health were administered one week before, immediately after and one week later with the questions concerning dental hygiene being of interest to the researchers. In terms of feeling worried about what they had heard, 74% of those in the strong group reported this compared to only 60% in the moderate fear group and 48% in the low fear group. When it came to changing their dental hygiene practices, however, those in the strongest group showed virtually no change at all in their practices. Fifty-two percent of the individuals in this group had not changed their hygiene behaviours at all and 20% reported less conformity to the recommendations than previously! In the minimal fear group, however, only 36% reported no change but 50% had changed to align with the recommendations. Janis and Feshbach believe that defensive avoidance may have occurred for those who were in the strong fear group. These students reported experiencing uncomfortable feelings about the lecture even in the follow-up survey one week later, feelings that were not alleviated by the recommendations provided. When this happens, Janis and Feshbach claim, the audience become motivated to ignore or resist the communication as a way of alleviating the emotional tension.

Witte and Allen (2000) conducted a meta-analysis of studies that explored the use of fear in public health campaigns. They suggested that the stronger the fear caused by an appeal, the more persuasive it is. However, similar to Janis and Feshbach, they argue that if the message fails to make people believe the recommended response is effective, then people tend to show defensive responses instead of following the recommendation. Dillard and Anderson (2004) presented participants with a message that described the dangers of influenza followed by a recommendation to obtain a free vaccination. Fear did indeed predict persuasion in this context.

How about the case of improving driver safety? This is one area where fear has been used extensively to try and persuade drivers to take more care, for example by not speeding or by not drink-driving. Tay and Ozanne (2002) reported on a fear-based advertising campaign used in New Zealand for this very purpose. The campaign presented a number of high-fear scenarios where fatal consequences arose from drink-driving, speeding or not wearing a seatbelt. The campaign was successful in reducing the number of fatal crashes in a number of age groups but the target demographic of young male drivers was completely unaffected.

Why is this group immune to the effects of fear in persuading them to drive more carefully? One idea put forward by Lewis et al. (2007) is that such appeals may not be seen as relevant by this particular group. As McKenna et al. (1991) report, there is a tendency to see oneself as better than the average driver, a positive "self-bias" and this can lead to a third-person effect occurring (Lewis et al., 2007). This is where individuals think that a persuasive message will have more effect on other people than it will on them. As Lewis et al. suggest, it is the perception of vulnerability that is more important in terms of whether a person can be persuaded rather than simply making them fearful.

Should we always use emotional appeals then?

So is it worth appealing to the mind at all? Of course! Lindauer et al. (2020) compared emotional and rational appeals in their success at persuading participants to donate to an organisation working with children in developing countries. The emotional appeal focused on a single individual who was one of the children helped by charitable donations. The rational appeal focused on scientific views of moral behaviour. Both appeals were found to be successful in increasing donations. Zajonc (1984) believes emotions take precedence over rational considerations in cases where the issues are of low relevance.

One factor that is important to consider here is age. McKay-Nesbitt et al. (2011) argue that negative emotional appeals are recalled more easily by younger individuals and are considered more persuasive whereas older adults prefer and are more easily persuaded by rational, positive messages.

A second factor that influences this choice is the "need for cognition", that is the motivation to process information. Those high in need for cognition tend to be influenced by the rational arguments presented whereas those low in need for cognition are more easily swayed by emotional appeals (Petty & Cacioppo, 1982). Indeed, Cacioppo et al. (1983) suggest that rational appeals are more successful with well-educated individuals. Many advertising campaigns focus on knowledge of a product and according to Keshari and Jain (2016) this does mean that rational persuasive attempts may be more effective in this context.

Perhaps what we need to look at is whether initial attitudes are based on information or emotions. Horne et al. (2015) suggest this makes a difference to how successful our attempts to persuade might be. They used the issue of vaccination distrust in their study. Participants held strong emotion-based attitudes to this issue so when they were asked to read an emotional story about a child who was unvaccinated and then went on to contract measles, they responded more positively to the issue. However, focusing on information only had little effect.

Should we present two sides of the argument?

One additional consideration in terms of the content of the message is the nature of the argument in terms of whether it is one or two-sided. When we are trying to persuade someone, particularly if we think they may disagree, we are probably anticipating counterarguments. What if we pre-empt this by presenting both sides of the story ourselves? Does this make us more persuasive or does it weaken our attempts to persuade the other person?

In 1949, Hovland provided some initial answers. Hovland presented one of two radio broadcasts to groups of US soldiers. For context, the war with Japan was continuing at this time. For one group of soldiers, they heard a broadcast that claimed the war would last for two more years and they heard one-sided arguments about how the war would not be easy. For the other half, they also heard the war would last for two more years but they heard two-sided arguments. Which worked best at persuading the soldiers? The one-sided appeal worked best if soldiers already agreed with the message being delivered. However, the two-sided appeal worked best for those who initially disagreed.

Some years later, Chu (1967) conducted an experiment with participants from a boy's high school in Taiwan. They chose to examine the effect of a one or two-sided message about the creation of an international trade zone in Southern Taiwan. After completing a questionnaire asking them about a range of issues from the Vietnam War to the link between smoking and lung cancer, the participants were then asked to listen to an argument presented by a local university staff member. For half of the participants, the argument was one-sided, presenting evidence in favour of the trade zone. For the other half of the participants, the argument was two-sided. Arguments against the trade zone were noted but they were also argued against. A final questionnaire was then issued.

For those who were initially supportive of the idea, there was very little difference in one or two-sided arguments in terms of their persuasiveness. However, for those who were not supportive initially, the one-sided argument had the most effect. But this was only the case if those individuals were not already familiar with the issue. When they were familiar, the two-sided argument had more impact. This aligns with Hovland's original findings as he found that those soldiers who were more highly educated tended to be more persuaded by two-sided arguments.

More recently, Werner et al. (2002) demonstrated the power of two-sided arguments in persuading students to recycle aluminium cans. Many more cans were recycled when the inconvenience of doing so was acknowledged than when it wasn't. Signs read "No Aluminium Cans Please!!!! Use the Recycler Located on the First Floor, near the entrance. It may be inconvenient but it is important". The rate of recycling reached 80% where the sign was present, a level that was significantly higher than when no message was given.

The impact of two-sided messages, especially for educated audiences, has an impact on our view of a communicator's trustworthiness too. Hendriks et al. (2023) asked German residents to complete a survey which asked about their attitudes to mask-wearing. They were then given a statement to read which was written by either a scientist or a politician and asked to rate the trustworthiness of the source and the motivations behind the statement. Regardless of occupation, the source of the information was seen as being an expert more often and being more trustworthy when a two-sided message was given.

■ **Figure 5.4** Werner et al. (2002) demonstrated the power of two-sided arguments in persuading students to recycle aluminium cans.

THE WAY THE MESSAGE IS DELIVERED
Is face-to-face persuasion best?

In the run-up to a General Election, there are usually party-political broadcasts aired on TV. The aim of these is to try and persuade you to vote for a particular party based on the information contained therein. Is watching a pre-recorded message the best way to persuade your audience though?

Chaiken and Eagly (1976) compared the effectiveness of a persuasive message delivered by videotape, audiotape or as text. For half of the participants, the message was difficult to comprehend. For the other half of the participants, the message was considered easy to comprehend. When the message content was considered difficult, videotape certainly didn't prove successful. In fact, it fared almost as bad as the audiotape version. Chaiken and Eagly argue that the presentation of a message in these formats takes control of the timing of presentation away from the person trying to understand it. The written message was by far the most persuasive. However, when the message to be delivered was simple and straightforward, then video excelled.

How does this compare to face-to-face persuasion? The results of a study conducted by Crawford (1974) might well lead us to think that face-to-face persuasion is pretty ineffective. He interviewed parishioners of 12 different churches before and after they had heard sermons which argued against racial injustice. When asked if they had heard anything about racial injustice since the initial interview, only 10% mentioned the sermon. When specifically asked if the priest had mentioned this, 29% flatly denied it! Eldersveld et al. (1954) suggested a more positive outcome from face-to-face encounters. Residents of Ann Arbor in Michigan who intended not to vote for a revision of the city charter, were either sent mailings, visited personally or simply heard the arguments in the media. Those who visited personally were significantly more likely to cast their votes in support (75% compared to only 19% who heard the media reports only). Perhaps Crawford's participants were just not that motivated by the message they heard?

The role of repetition

One of the strategies that many politicians use when trying to convince us to vote for them is the use of repetition. For example, Theresa May used the slogan "Strong and Stable" repeatedly in the lead-up to the 2017 election, Tony Blair reminded us repeatedly of the role of "Education, Education, Education" and Donald Trump is known to repeat "Believe me" in his political speeches. Hasher et al. (1977) claim that repeated statements are perceived as being more truthful, something which they refer to as the illusion of truth.

Moons et al. (2009) report that repetition increases persuasiveness. However, those who are particularly motivated to pay attention to the arguments are influenced more when the arguments are strong. When the arguments are seen to be weak, repetition has little effect. For those not particularly motivated, repetition is likely to increase agreement regardless of the strength of the argument.

Timing is everything

Criminal trials involve trying to convince the jury of a particular point of view about a situation that took place. Who is most likely to persuade the jury? Those who present first or those who present last? Miller and Campbell (1959) used an actual transcript from a civil trial in their experiment. They asked students to read both the defence and prosecution arguments. One week later, students were asked to make a judgement about the case. The primacy effect won out – that is, the information they read first dominated their judgement one week later. However, most court cases don't get finalised in one day. If the prosecution and defence testimony are separated out by a week, a recency effect occurs, with whatever information was presented last, dominating judgements (Miller & Campbell, 1959). Memory fades ... and with it the recollection of the initial argument it would seem.

Let's try this for ourselves. Think about your opinion of "John" having read this sentence:

> *John is intelligent, industrious, impulsive, critical, stubborn and envious.*

To what extent did the initial information colour your judgement of this individual? Imagine that you had read the same information but in this order:

> *John is envious, stubborn, critical, impulsive, industrious and intelligent.*

Do you think this would make a difference? Asch (1946) asked college students to do just this sort of task and reported a strong primacy effect – what we hear first, colours our judgement of what we hear later. The strength of the primacy effect in persuasion is so strong that even being listed first on a ballot paper advantages candidates in an election (Moore, 2004)!

Coker (2012) demonstrated the power of primacy in a study of hotel reviews. If reviews of a hotel are ordered from positive to negative, evaluations are much more positive in response than if they are ordered from negative to positive. What we hear first sticks with us.

This also works in reverse too. Once we make a commitment to a certain action, we are loathe to change. Cialdini (2001) refers to this as the "consistency" principle. He gives the example of Sherman's volunteering study. He called residents of town and asked them to participate in a survey. One of the questions asked was what they would say if they were asked to spend 3 hours collecting money for the American Cancer Society. Many said they would indeed volunteer. A few days later, a member of the society came calling to ask for help with canvassing. A 700% increase in volunteers resulted! Having committed to the first question, people wanted to seem consistent.

Beware the sleeper!

One phenomenon worth mentioning here before we draw our story to a close, is the sleeper effect. Quite often, we may think that our attempts at persuading another are hitting a brick wall, that is, we are not having any effect on the other person. However, at a later date, we find that actually our message has indeed had some impact. This "sleeper effect" refers to the way in which a message can have increased influence after an initial delay (Gruder et al., 1978). One idea about what causes this is the idea of dissociated memories. Over time, we forget negative sources that may have delivered a message but we remember the message itself that is the source becomes dissociated from the message (Hovland et al., 1949a, 1949b).

The sleeper effect is a controversial idea however. As Lariscy and Tinkham (1999) explain, some attempts at demonstrating the sleeper effect have failed miserably. Kumkale and Albaraccin (2004) conducted a large meta-analysis of sleeper effect studies and concluded that it does exist but only when the initial message has a strong impact, when the recipients of the message are motivated to think about it and when information about the source of the message is received after. It is interesting to note that many advertisements contain information before mentioning the source for this reason. Even when we find out later that the source was, as Petrocelli et al. (2023) call it "bullshitting", a message may be influential even 2 weeks after it was originally heard. In fact, Appel and Richter (2007) argue that messages received through reading of fiction can be particularly persuasive after 2-week delays even if we report less certainty in these messages immediately after reading them.

REFERENCES

Aagerup, U., Frank, A. S., & Hultqvist, E. (2019). The persuasive effects of emotional green packaging claims. *British Food Journal*, *121*(12), 3233–3246.

Appel, M., & Richter, T. (2007). Persuasive effects of fictional narratives increase over time. *Media Psychology*, *10*(1), 113–134.

Asch, S. E. (1946). Forming impressions of personality. *The Journal of Abnormal and Social Psychology*, *41*(3), 258.

Banks, S. M., Salovey, P., Greener, S., Rothman, A. J., Moyer, A., Beauvais, J., & Epel, E. (1995). The effects of message framing on mammography utilization. *Health Psychology*, *14*(2), 178.

Brock, T. C., & Becker, L. A. (1965). Ineffectiveness of "overheard" counterpropaganda. *Journal of Personality and Social Psychology*, *2*(5), 654.

Cacioppo, J. T., Petty, R. E., & Morris, K. J. (1983). Effects of need for cognition on message evaluation, recall, and persuasion. *Journal of Personality and Social Psychology*, *45*(4), 805.

Carpenter, C. J. (2012). A meta-analysis and an experiment investigating the effects of speaker disfluency on persuasion. *Western Journal of Communication*, *76*(5), 552–569.

Chaiken, S. (1979). Communicator physical attractiveness and persuasion. *Journal of Personality and Social Psychology, 37*(8), 1387.

Chaiken, S., & Eagly, A. H. (1976). Communication modality as a determinant of message persuasiveness and message comprehensibility. *Journal of Personality and Social Psychology, 34*(4), 605.

Choi, J., & Park, H. Y. (2021). How donor's regulatory focus changes the effectiveness of a sadness-evoking charity appeal. *International Journal of Research in Marketing, 38*(3), 749–769.

Chou, E. Y., & Murnighan, J. K. (2013). Life or death decisions: Framing the call for help. *PLOS ONE, 8*(3), e57351.

Chu, G. C. (1967). Prior familiarity, perceived bias, and one-sided versus two-sided communications. *Journal of Experimental Social Psychology, 3*(3), 243–254.

Cialdini, R. B. (2001). The science of persuasion. *Scientific American, 284*(2), 76–81.

Coker, B. L. (2012). Seeking the opinions of others online: Evidence of evaluation overshoot. *Journal of Economic Psychology, 33*(6), 1033–1042.

Crawford, T. J. (1974). Theories of attitude change and the "beyond family planning" debate: The case for the persuasion approach in population policy. *Journal of Social Issues, 30*(4), 211–233.

Dillard, J. P., & Anderson, J. W. (2004). The role of fear in persuasion. *Psychology & Marketing, 21*(11), 909–926.

Eagly, A. H., Wood, W., & Chaiken, S. (1978). Causal inferences about communicators and their effect on opinion change. *Journal of Personality and Social Psychology, 36*(4), 424.

Edwards, D., & Potter, J. (2007). Language and causation. *Psychological Review, 100*.

Edwards-Levy, A. (2015). Republicans like Obama's ideas better when they think they're Donald Trump's. In D. G. Myers, & J. M. Twenge (Eds.), *Social psychology*. McGraw Hill.

Erlandsson, A., Nilsson, A., & Västfjäll, D. (2018). Attitudes and donation behavior when reading positive and negative charity appeals. *Journal of Nonprofit & Public Sector Marketing, 30*(4), 444–474.

Eldersveld, S. J., Dodge, R. W., Katz, D., Cartwright, D., Eldersveld, S., & Lee, A. M. (1954). Personal contact or mail propaganda? An experiment in voting and attitude change. In D. Katz, D. Cartwright, S. Eldersveld, & A. M. Lee (Eds.), *Public opinion and propaganda*. Dryden Press, pp. 532–542.

Gamer, R. (2005). What's in a name? Persuasion perhaps. *Journal of Consumer Psychology, 15*(2), 108–116.

Gruder, C. L., Cook, T. D., Hennigan, K. M., Flay, B. R., Alessis, C., & Halamaj, J. (1978). Empirical tests of the absolute sleeper effect predicted from the discounting cue hypothesis. *Journal of Personality and Social Psychology, 36*(10), 1061.

Hasher, L., Goldstein, D., & Toppino, T. (1977). Frequency and the conference of referential validity. *Journal of Verbal Learning and Verbal Behavior, 16*(1), 107–112.

Hemsley, G. D., & Doob, A. N. (1978). The effect of looking behavior on perceptions of a Communicator's credibility 1. *Journal of Applied Social Psychology, 8*(2), 136–142.

Hendriks, F., Janssen, I., & Jucks, R. (2023). Balance as credibility? How presenting one-vs. two-sided messages affects ratings of scientists' and politicians' trustworthiness. *Health Communication*, *38*(12), 2757–2764.

Horne, Z., Powell, D., Hummel, J. E., & Holyoak, K. J. (2015). Countering antivaccination attitudes. *Proceedings of the National Academy of Sciences*, *112*(33), 10321–10324.

Hovland, C. I., Lumsdaine, A. A., & Sheffield, F. D. (1949a). Experiments on mass communication. In *Studies in social psychology in World War II* (Vol. 3).

Hovland, C. I., Lumsdaine, A. A., & Sheffield, F. D. (1949b). The effects of presenting "one side" versus "both sides" in changing opinions on a controversial subject. In *Experiments on mass communication: studies in social psychology in World War II*, Princeton University Press, Princeton.

Howard, D. J., & Kerin, R. A. (2011). The effects of name similarity on message processing and persuasion. *Journal of Experimental Social Psychology*, *47*(1), 63–71.

Janis, I. L., & Feshbach, S. (1953). Effects of fear-arousing communications. *The Journal of Abnormal and Social Psychology*, *48*(1), 78.

Kaminski, K. S., & Sporer, S. L. (2018). Observer judgments of identification accuracy are affected by non-valid cues: A Brunswikian lens model analysis. *European Journal of Social Psychology*, *48*(1), 47–61.

Kemp, E., Kennett-Hensel, P. A., & Kees, J. (2013). Pulling on the heartstrings: Examining the effects of emotions and gender in persuasive appeals. *Journal of Advertising*, *42*(1), 69–79.

Keshari, P., & Jain, S. (2016). Effect of age and gender on consumer response to advertising appeals. *Paradigm*, *20*(1), 69–82.

Kumkale, G. T., & Albarracín, D. (2004). The sleeper effect in persuasion: A meta-analytic review. *Psychological Bulletin*, *130*(1), 143.

Lariscy, R., & Tinkham, A. W. (1999). The sleeper effect and negative political advertising. *Journal of Advertising*, *28*(4), 13–30.

Lewis, I. M., Watson, B., White, K. M., & Tay, R. (2007). Promoting public health messages: Should we move beyond fear-evoking appeals in road safety? *Qualitative Health Research*, *17*(1), 61–74.

Lindauer, M., Mayorga, M., Greene, J., Slovic, P., Västfjäll, D., & Singer, P. (2020). Comparing the effect of rational and emotional appeals on donation behavior. *Judgment and Decision Making*, *15*(3), 413–420.

Maddux, J. E., & Rogers, R. W. (1980). Effects of source expertness, physical attractiveness, and supporting arguments on persuasion: A case of brains over beauty. *Journal of Personality and Social Psychology*, *39*(2), 235.

McKay-Nesbitt, J., Manchanda, R. V., Smith, M. C., & Huhmann, B. A. (2011). Effects of age, need for cognition, and affective intensity on advertising effectiveness. *Journal of Business Research*, *64*(1), 12–17.

McKenna, F. P., Stanier, R. A., & Lewis, C. (1991). Factors underlying illusory self-assessment of driving skill in males and females. *Accident Analysis & Prevention*, *23*(1), 45–52.

Miller, N., & Campbell, D. T. (1959). Recency and primacy in persuasion as a function of the timing of speeches and measurements. *The Journal of Abnormal and Social Psychology*, *59*(1), 1.

Miller, N., Maruyama, G., Beaber, R. J., & Valone, K. (1976). Speed of speech and persuasion. *Journal of Personality and Social Psychology*, *34*(4), 615.

Mills, J., & Aronson, E. (1965). Opinion change as a function of the communicator's attractiveness and desire to influence. *Journal of Personality and Social Psychology*, *1*(2), 173.

Moons, W. G., Mackie, D. M., & Garcia-Marques, T. (2009). The impact of repetition-induced familiarity on agreement with weak and strong arguments. *Journal of Personality and Social Psychology*, *96*(1), 32.

Moore, D. W. (2004). *Ballot order: Who benefits?* Gallup Poll Tuesday Briefing, April 20th (www.gallop.com).

Olson, J. M., & Cal, A. V. (1984). Source credibility, attitudes, and the recall of past behaviours. *European Journal of Social Psychology*, *14*(2), 203–210.

Ozanne, M., Liu, S. Q., & Mattila, A. S. (2019). Are attractive reviewers more persuasive? Examining the role of physical attractiveness in online reviews. *Journal of Consumer Marketing*, *36*(6), 728–739.

Pelham, B. W., Carvallo, M., & Jones, J. T. (2005). Implicit egotism. *Current Directions in Psychological Science*, *14*(2), 106–110.

Petrocelli, J. V., Seta, C. E., & Seta, J. J. (2023). Lies and bullshit: The negative effects of misinformation grow stronger over time. *Applied Cognitive Psychology*, *37*(2), 409–418.

Petty, R. E., & Cacioppo, J. T. (1979). Issue involvement can increase or decrease persuasion by enhancing message-relevant cognitive responses. *Journal of Personality and Social Psychology*, *37*(10), 1915.

Petty, R. E., & Cacioppo, J. T. (1982). The need for cognition. *Journal of Personality and Social Psychology*, *42*(1), 116–131.

Petty, R. E., Cacioppo, J. T., Petty, R. E., & Cacioppo, J. T. (1986). *The elaboration likelihood model of persuasion* (pp. 1–24). Springer.

Puckett, J. M., Petty, R. E., Cacioppo, J. T., & Fischer, D. L. (1983). The relative impact of age and attractiveness stereotypes on persuasion. *Journal of Gerontology*, *38*(3), 340–343.

Sääksjärvi, M., Hellén, K., & Balabanis, G. (2016). Sometimes a celebrity holding a negative public image is the best product endorser. *European Journal of Marketing*, *50*(3/4), 421–441.

Schimmelpfennig, C., & Hunt, J. B. (2020). Fifty years of celebrity endorser research: Support for a comprehensive celebrity endorsement strategy framework. *Psychology & Marketing*, *37*(3), 488–505.

Small, D. A., Loewenstein, G., & Slovic, P. (2013). Sympathy and callousness: The impact of deliberative thought on donations to identifiable and statistical victims. In *The feeling of risk* (pp. 51–68). Routledge.

Tay, R. S., & Ozanne, L. (2002). Who are we scaring with high fear road safety advertising campaigns? *Asia Pacific Journal of Transport*, *4*, pp. 1–12

Tormala, Z. L., Briñol, P., & Petty, R. E. (2006). When credibility attacks: The reverse impact of source credibility on persuasion. *Journal of Experimental Social Psychology*, *42*(5), 684–691.

Tormala, Z. L., & Petty, R. E. (2004). Source credibility and attitude certainty: A metacognitive analysis of resistance to persuasion. *Journal of Consumer Psychology*, *14*(4), 427–442.

Trampe, D., Stapel, D. A., Siero, F. W., & Mulder, H. (2010). Beauty as a tool: The effect of model attractiveness, product relevance, and elaboration likelihood on advertising effectiveness. *Psychology & Marketing*, *27*(12), 1101–1121.

Walster, E., & Festinger, L. (1962). The effectiveness of "overheard" persuasive communications. *Journal of Abnormal and Social Psychology*, *65*(6), 395–02.

Wathen, C. N., & Burkell, J. (2002). Believe it or not: Factors influencing credibility on the web. *Journal of the American Society for Information Science and Technology*, *53*(2), 134–144.

Werner, C. M., Stoll, R., Birch, P., & White, P. H. (2002). Clinical validation and cognitive elaboration: Signs that encourage sustained recycling. *Basic and Applied Social Psychology*, *24*(3), 185–203.

Wiegman, O. (1985). Two politicians in a realistic experiment: Attraction, discrepancy, intensity of delivery, and attitude change 1. *Journal of Applied Social Psychology*, *15*(4), 673–686.

Witte, K., & Allen, M. (2000). A meta-analysis of fear appeals: Implications for effective public health campaigns. *Health Education & Behavior*, *27*(5), 591–615.

Zajonc, R. B. (1984). The interaction of affect and cognition. *Approaches to Emotion*, *239*, 246.

Chapter 6

Seeing the social world through biased eyes

Social cognition, according to Baron and Branscombe (2014), refers to

> *how we think about the social world, our attempts to understand it and ourselves and our place in it.*

(p. 46)

Sounds straightforward right? Well, not really. The trouble is we have a limited cognitive capacity for processing information and the social world bombards our senses with a huge amount of it. As a result, we have to resort to rules of thumb or "heuristics" to help us in our quest to understand it. How do heuristics help? Taylor (1981) described us as "cognitive misers" as we try to process information using the minimal amount of cognitive resources. Heuristics help as we can apply these automatically, that is with minimal effort and without awareness, freeing up more of our limited cognitive resources for other things.

These heuristics give us an accurate answer most of the time but they are not immune to error. The result is that sometimes our understanding of our social world is a little skewed or not quite in line with reality. In this part of our social psychology adventure, we will look at some of the shortcuts we use, how they influence our understanding of the social world and how in some cases, they may "lead us up the garden path", that is, they may lead us to make errors in our understanding.

USE OF SCHEMAS

One way in which we can quickly process information about the social world is through the use of schemas. A schema is like a suitcase of all the information connected with a particular recurring social situation. Baron et al. 2007 define schemas as:

DOI: 10.4324/9781003396208-6

> *mental frameworks that help us to organise social information and that guide our actions and processing of information relevant to those contexts.*

(p. 54)

Take, for example, a visit to a university canteen. A schema may contain information about what to do in this social setting, for example, that we have to queue to pay for our food. We would expect to see tables and chairs and boards showing what was on offer that day. Or how about a graduation ceremony? You may already have a schema for what happens, in what order, in these social situations. A schema might tell you a bit about how to dress, where you would sit, what normally happens, etc. Schank and Abelson (1975) suggest that we organise such social information of routine activities into a "script" that tells us what to expect in each situation.

The impact of these scripts is that when things happen that are unexpected, they catch our attention and are remembered more easily. Nakamura et al. (1985) demonstrated this with undergraduate students attending a lecture. Their lecturer performed five actions that were considered relevant to a script for a lecture such as pointing to information on the blackboard (remember this was in 1985!), or underlining a word on the blackboard. He also performed five actions that were considered irrelevant to a script for a lecture such as bending a coffee stirrer or walking in and out of a side room. When the students were given a recognition memory test for the actions, they remembered the irrelevant actions better. They also however showed recognition for relevant actions that hadn't actually been performed but were consistent with a script for a lecture. In a similar scenario, Kintsch and Bates (1977) reported better memory for irrelevant statements in a lecture such as jokes or announcements than they did for the lecture material itself!

So how do these schemas help? They help us process information in an efficient way. We don't have to consciously think about all the different elements of a social situation as our schema already leads us to know what to expect and how to behave. Schemas can also be used to help us understand and predict another person's behaviour. A schema might have a collection of attributes that commonly go together. Kelley (1950) illustrated how this works in his warm/cold study. Students were told that a guest lecturer would be taking their class and were given a short biographical description that had been provided. For half of the students, they were told:

People who know him consider him to be a rather cold person, industrious, critical, practical and determined.

For the other half of the students, they were told:

People who know him consider him to be a rather warm person, industrious, critical, practical and determined.

The description of the guest lecturer as being cold led to more negative evaluations whereas the description of him being warm led to him being seen as more considerate of others, more informal, more sociable, more popular and more humorous amongst other positive qualities. This has since been replicated by Widmeyer and Loy (1988). A visiting professor was due to give a lecture. For some students, they were led to believe he was a rather warm person, for some, that he was a rather cold person. Some students thought he was a professor of physical education and some thought he was a professor of social psychology. Being described as warm was sufficient for the visiting professor to be perceived as an effective teacher. Not only that but he was seen to be more sociable and humorous! His background (PE or Social Psychology) had no effect at all.

In these cases, it is possible that our schemas for "cold" people and "warm" people contain other positive attributes that usually go together. When one is activated, so too are the associated attributes. However, as we saw with the lecture study above, schemas can lead us astray. García-Bajos and Migueles (2003) demonstrated how our willingness to accept that certain things happened if they are consistent with our schema for an event, can lead to persistent false memories. After listening to a one-minute account of a mugging incident, students were asked to write down as much as they could remember about the account and were then asked to complete a recognition memory test by indicating whether certain sentences were true or not. The account contained ten behaviours considered to be typical of a mugging incident such as approaching the victim unnoticed and ten behaviours considered to be untypical such as covering the victim's mouth.

In their free recall of the account, students tended to include more typical behaviours than atypical and where errors were made, these were more likely to be the inclusion of typical behaviours that were not actually mentioned but were consistent with their "script" for this event. When it came to the recognition test, the students identified the low typicality statements accurately but when it came to the high typicality statements, they incorrectly recognised almost half of the sentences as having been in the account when they were not. That is, when the information was consistent with their script for such an event, they misremembered having seen or heard that information when they didn't.

Would we be better off without schemas and scripts then? The evidence would suggest not. An inkling of what we might experience without them can be gleaned from the study of individuals with Korsakov's syndrome (Aronson et al., 2014). Korsakov's syndrome is a neurological condition caused largely by alcohol abuse, that affects memory. Individuals diagnosed with this condition find it difficult to make new memories which makes it very difficult to impose meaning on social situations as schemas cannot be constructed or added to. (There is a very good clip from a programme called Dr House that illustrates this well, available on YouTube.) Sacks (2011) described a patient with this diagnosis as having to:

> ... literally make himself (and his world) up every moment.
>
> (p. 110)

So, for all their shortcomings, schemas do seem to be of use.

USE OF METAPHORS

The use of schemas suggests that we understand the social world through its similarity to other experiences. However, Landau et al. (2010) argue that social cognition is also "metaphor-enriched". That is, we often understand the social world through likening social concepts to dissimilar things. For example, we often talk about people in power being "high up in an organisation" or being "at the top". We talk about social climbers as people who are successful in an organisation and talk of people "heading for a fall" if they are losing power. Robinson et al. (2008) demonstrated how these metaphors influence behaviour. They reported that those who considered themselves to be more dominant and powerful were quicker to respond to spatial probes that appeared high on a screen compared to low. Similarly, Schubert (2005) claimed faster reaction times for dominant words when they appeared high on a screen and faster reaction times for submissive words when they appeared lower on a screen. Imagine seeing a pictorial representation of staff at an organisation. The greater the distance between the manager's picture at the top and the subordinates underneath, the greater the power attributed to the manager (Giessner & Schubert, 2007). It even works with divine concepts too. Photographs presented in higher positions on a screen were judged to be of individuals who had a stronger belief in God compared to if they were presented lower on the screen (Meier et al., 2007)!

There is one interesting exception to the rule here. The evolutionary work of Buss (1995) suggests that power and status are desired by females in a male partner. However, this is not the case for males who instead look for faithfulness and youth in a partner. It is interesting to note therefore that when pictures of members of the opposite sex appeared high on a screen, males rated them as less attractive but females rated them as more attractive than when they appeared lower on a screen. When they were presented low on the screen, males rated the pictures as more attractive and the women rated them as less attractive. I know this will fuel a few fires (to use a metaphor!) but it does explain the imaginative title of Meier and Dionne's (2009) article summarising this research: "Downright sexy"!

Of course, we also talk about "feeling low" at times. Meier and Robinson (2006) in fact start their paper with a lyric from a song "It's Been Awhile" by Staind:

It's been a while since I could hold my head up high.

(p. 451)

Their paper asks "Does feeling down mean seeing down?" The answer, from their study, is yes. Individuals experiencing depressive symptoms tended to give preferential attention to lower areas of a screen.

How else might metaphors influence social cognition? Imagine being given a nice mug of hot chocolate to hold (if you don't like hot chocolate, think of an alternative hot drink you do like). Shortly after, you are asked to rate your feelings of friendliness on a scale from 1 (unfriendly) to 5 (very friendly). Do you think it would have any effect? Those holding a hot drink gave an average rating of 3.42. Those holding a cold drink however gave a rating of only 2.5 (Lin & Lin, 2022). This is similar to the results of Williams and Bargh (2008). They conspired to create a situation where participants were asked to hold the confederate's coffee cup for a minute whilst they recorded the participants name, whilst they travelled in the lift to the laboratory. Once participants arrived at the laboratory, they were asked to complete a questionnaire which asked them about impressions

■ **Figure 6.1** Holding a hot drink can boost ratings of friendliness according to Lin and Lin (2022).

of personality. For example, they might read that Person A was intelligent, skilful and industrious and then be asked to rate this person on 10 personality traits. Those individuals who had held a hot cup of coffee were significantly more likely to rate the person as being warm in personality compared to those who held a cup of iced coffee. It isn't just holding hot drinks that works this magic either. Ask participants to sit in a cold or a warm room and you will not be surprised to know that those in the warmer room will report stronger feelings of closeness to you as the experimenter than those in the colder room (IJzerman & Semin, 2009). This is not a one-way relationship. Feeling excluded can lead us to perceive room temperature as colder too (Zhong & Leonardelli, 2008).

Let's take our story outside, to a university campus. You are walking along when a fellow student asks you to participate in a survey about campus issues. You agree and are promptly handed a clipboard. The question you see first is this: How important is it for students to have a say in campus issues? How would you answer? Well, this is really a trick question because the truth is that the weight of the clipboard would influence your response. Don't believe me? Well, Jostmann et al. (2009) demonstrated just this. Participants from a Dutch University were asked to indicate how important it was to them that a university committee would listen to the opinions of students regarding the size of a grant to study abroad. Those holding a heavy clipboard indicated a higher level of importance to the issue than those holding a light clipboard.

When it comes to morality though, the saying "Cleanliness is next to Godliness" might play a role. Liljenquist et al. (2010) asked undergraduate students to undertake a series of tasks contained in a small packet, whilst working in either a room that had been sprayed with (the somewhat unfortunately named) Windex, a citrus cleaning spray or in a room that had not been sprayed. In the packet of tasks, one of the items was a flyer for a charity. Participants were asked whether they would be interested in volunteering for this charity, and asked whether they wanted to donate to it. Those working in the clean-scented room were significantly more likely to both express an interest in volunteering and to donate money.

Schnall et al. (2008) asked participants to wash their hands after watching a brief clip from the film Trainspotting, that was chosen as a means of eliciting disgust. The simple act of washing hands, led to less severe judgements of moral transgressions. Make a work area dirty however and more severe moral judgements follow (Schnall et al., 2008). Metaphors therefore influence our social judgement in a variety of ways, from priming us to evaluate issues differently to constructing a different view of an individual. Priming in itself can make information more readily available for us to apply and it is this that underlies our next rule of thumb or heuristic, the availability heuristic.

THE AVAILABILITY HEURISTIC

Now, I do occasionally like to dip into EastEnders to see how the storyline has developed and, like many soaps, they often cover particular disorders such as eating disorders, bipolar disorder, or panic attacks. One idea is that by covering these issues on a popular soap, it will heighten awareness of this in the general population (Keller & Brown, 2002). A 2008 study provides evidence for this using antidepressant direct-to-consumer advertising. Those who recalled the advertising best tended to overestimate the prevalence of depression compared to those who recalled the advertising least. Frequent advertising, the authors claim, increases the accessibility of information and therefore they are recalled more easily. This has a knock-on effect in terms of diagnosis. Donohue and Berndt (2004) reported a higher diagnosis rate of depression for periods when spending on advertising of antidepressants peaked.

■ **Figure 6.2** Are the diagnoses of doctors free from bias?

What you may be less familiar with, however, is the idea that it also increases awareness of these disorders in health professionals. Weber et al. (1993) reported that the more "available" a possible diagnosis was, the more frequent and earlier doctors generate this with future patients. Specifically, if a similar case has been recently diagnosed, this increases the chance that the same diagnosis will be used in future. Tversky and Kahneman (1973) refer to this rule of thumb as the "availability heuristic". We often make social judgements based on how easily we can recall relevant events or information. If we can recall it easily, then we believe that to be more common or frequent. Aronson et al. (2014) quote a Dr, Dr Marion in saying:

> *Doctors are just like everyone else. We go to the movies, watch TV, read newspapers and novels. If we happen to see a patient who has symptoms of a rare disease that was featured on the previous night's "Movie of the Week", we're more likely to consider that conditions when making a diagnosis.*

(p. 68)

The availability heuristic can also influence our judgements about crime as well as health. Roberts and Doob (1990) conducted three studies to demonstrate the role that the media can have on our perceptions of crime. Newspapers tend to focus on violent crime in their reporting. Graber (1980), for example, identified this skewing of reporting in a content analysis of newspaper reports. Twenty-five percent of all crime reports mentioned were about murder despite this crime making up just 1% of all crimes reported. In Canada, Doob (1985) suggested over 50% of newspaper reports describe violent crime, something that again did not match the actual crime statistics. In one of the studies by Roberts and Doob (1990), visitors to the Ontario Science Centre in Canada were asked to read a summary of a court case, either as reported in a newspaper or as reported in court documents. When asked to then make a judgement about the sentence given, 63% of those who read the newspaper account said the sentence was too lenient. Of those who read the court documents, only 19% did so. When thinking of offenders, salient examples come to mind which are often violent criminals. Because these come to mind easily, we tend to overestimate the prevalence of violent crime and make judgements on this basis.

It isn't just TV that might influence our social judgements however. Diekman et al. (2000) argue that literature can have a similar effect on our judgements by making particular behaviours more readily accessible. They chose to explore the effect of romance novels on safe sex practices. Modern romance novels, they suggest, contain a high level of unsafe sex practices. No surprise then that those who read a lot of these types of books held more negative views towards condom use. Sunstein (2006) suggests that the availability heuristic plays a critical role in attitudes towards climate change. When assessing the risk, individuals look to see if examples of harm can be recalled easily. If they can, people tend to see greater risk than if they can't.

If you want to experience the availability heuristic, try this simple task. Read each name in the list below (Table 6.1) without trying to memorise them necessarily.

Ok, so now, without looking back at the table and actually counting, do you think there were more male names, more female names or an equal balance of male and female names in the list? McKelvie (1995) conducted this study in 1995 and reported the operation of an availability heuristic. When famous women's names were used alongside non-famous men's names, 61.3% said

■ **Table 6.1** Names taken from McKelvie (1995).

1	Ivan Boyarski	Indira Ghandi
2	Margaret Thatcher	Mary Magdalene
3	Gertrude Stein	Mustafa Hussad
4	Tony Leshner	Beatrix Potter
5	Frank Tennant	Jane Austen
6	Harold Stevens	Agatha Christie
7	Lady Macbeth	Scott Stephens
8	Florence Nightingale	Hugo Dean
9	Pete McCoy	Meryll Streep
10	Marilyn Monroe	Dick Tannenbaum
11	Sophia Loren	Steven Thomas
12	Jane Fonda	Bruce Brown
13	James Bloscovitch	Katherine Hepburn

there were more women's names than men. There were in fact equal numbers of male and females' names, just as in our example above. We could try the same experiment but just have famous men's names and non-famous women's names in the table. When McKelvie did this, 50% of his participants said that men's names were more common in the table! Fame increases the availability of the name in memory and this in turn influences our judgments of frequency.

Before we look at our next heuristic, it is worth mentioning the work of Fox (2006) who pointed to a potentially useful trick for lecturers seeking student evaluations … Students studying business at Duke University, were asked to list either 2 or 10 ideas for how their course could be improved before giving their overall evaluation. Those who were asked to list 10 ideas gave significantly more positive evaluations. Why? The availability heuristic was at play! When asked to think of 10 ideas, students struggled to find sufficient instances. The conclusion was therefore that it must have been a pretty good course. Those asked to identify just 2, managed to do so with ease so considered that actually it wasn't such a great course after all. A similar finding was reported by Schwartz who asked students to list either 6 or 12 examples of when they had acted assertively. Those asked to list 6 rated themselves as more assertive than those asked to list 12. Listing 6 was relatively easy leading to the overestimation of how assertive they really were. Kahneman (2011) points to other examples where this has a somewhat paradoxical effect. For example, people believe that they use their bikes less after being asked to recall many rather than few instances of doing so.

THE REPRESENTATIVENESS HEURISTIC

The availability heuristic isn't the only example of a rule of thumb that influences our behaviour. The representativeness heuristic is equally influential. This heuristic is used when we make a judgement about how similar someone or some event is to a prototype or most common exemplar. A prototype is an example that has all the attributes commonly seen in members of a group. Let me explain. The following vignette is from a study by Tversky and Kahneman (1982):

> *Linda is 31 years old, single, outspoken and very bright. She majored in philosophy. As a student, she was deeply concerned with issues of discrimination and social justice and also participated in anti-nuclear demonstrations.*
>
> (p. 11)

Participants were asked to make a judgement about the occupation of Linda. One option was that Linda was a bank teller. A bank teller is someone who handles customer cash. Another option was that she was a bank teller who is active in the feminist movement. Other options included that she was a teacher, a psychiatric social worker or an insurance salesperson. Participants ranked the suggestion that Linda was a feminist bank teller as more probable than just a bank teller. Why? Tversky and Kahneman argued that this is an example of the representativeness heuristic at play. The descriptive elements in the vignette are much more representative of someone who is an active feminist than of a stereotype of a bank teller per se. This was the case even though logically; it is much more likely that Linda is a bank teller than *both* a bank teller *and* a feminist. This was so surprising to the researchers that in Kahneman's (2011) book, he devotes a whole chapter to this calling it "Linda: Less is more"!

The representativeness heuristic also works in clinical settings. Brannon and Carson (2003) asked nurse to read descriptions of patient cases and to generate a diagnosis. In one scenario, the patient had experienced symptoms that suggested a heart attack (pain radiating to the left arm, fast pulse rate, pressure on the chest, shortness of breath, etc.). In half of these cases, the patient was also described as having recently lost their job (a stressor). In the second scenario, the symptoms displayed by the patient were suggestive of a stroke (slurred speech, uneven gait, weakness in one arm, etc.). In half of these cases, the patient had the smell of alcohol on their breath. In the first scenario, all nurses attributed the symptoms to a heart attack when no stressor was mentioned. However, when a job loss was mentioned, 26% attributed the symptoms to stress. In the second scenario, 98% attributed the symptoms to a physical illness. When alcohol was mentioned, 72% attributed the symptoms to drunkenness! The authors claim that the nurses were using the representativeness heuristic to guide their judgement. For example, slurred speech, uneven gait and the smell of alcohol all fit the prototype of a drunken person well. Kulkarni et al. (2019) reported a similar phenomenon using severe trauma cases. The chances of being transferred to a trauma centre were directly linked to the presence of representative characteristics.

Imagine that you are given a choice between accepting a lottery ticket with a random number sequence on it and a lottery ticket with a patterned sequence of numbers on it. For example, the patterned sequence might be 1, 2, 3, 4, 5, 6, 7, 8, 9, and 10 or 5, 10, 15, 20, 25, 30, 35, 40, 45, and 50. Which would you prefer? When Krawczyk and Rachubik (2019) tried this, they reported that most people (70%) chose the ticket with the random numbering on it. One of the most popular reasons for choosing the random number ticket was that participants believed it had a higher chance of winning and that it was "more random". The researchers claimed that this illustrated the use of a representative heuristic, that is the prototype of a lottery ticket is such that it has a selection of random numbers on it.

So, why do we succumb to this heuristic in situations where it actually leads us to erroneous conclusions? Kahneman and Tversky (1973) suggest we ignore base rate information. Base rate information is information that tells us something about the frequency of individuals/events/phenomena in different categories. To illustrate, let's look at Fischoff and Bar-Hillel's example from their 1984 article. They told participants that the information they were going to read about "Frank", was selected from a random sample of 30 engineers and 70 lawyers. In the text, participants learnt that Frank was twice divorced, spent most of the time at the country club where he bemoaned his attempts at having tried to follow in his father's footsteps and that that he regretted the long hours of academic study he had undertaken. They were then asked to make a decision about whether they thought Frank was an engineer or a lawyer. More than 80% decided he was a lawyer. Another group of students then read the same passage but were told that it had been selected from a sample of 70 engineers and 30 lawyers. That is, the base rate had been changed. What happened now to their judgements? In short, nothing. They were still more likely to say that Frank was a lawyer than an engineer. The information provided was more representative of what participants knew about lawyers and this swayed their judgement.

The representativeness heuristic has been implicated in many flawed political decisions and events such as the Arab Spring uprisings (Weyland, 2012), Latin American pension reforms (Weyland, 2005), the Egyptian Presidential Elections (Albek, 2022), and estimates of injury in natural disasters (Stolwijk & Vis, 2021). Carnes and Sadin (2015) suggest that politicians use it to manipulate voter's thoughts about how representative they are of a particular group of voters. For example, they might over-emphasise how difficult their childhood was for them as a way of ensuring they are classified as a member of middle-class voters. They coined the term "mill-worker's son" heuristic to describe this.

THE STATUS QUO HEURISTIC

Do you prefer modern art to the "Old Masters"? The reason I ask is that these questions relate to the status quo heuristic. We prefer situations or objects that have been in existence longer. That doesn't mean things like a bar of chocolate that has slowly rotted at the back of the fridge but if you are told the brand of chocolate has been in existence since 1937, you are more likely to evaluate it positively than if you are told the brand has only been in existence for three years (Eidelman et al., 2010). People tend to be more positive about things that have been in existence for longer. Eidelman et al. demonstrated this with nature (people rated a tree as more pleasurable and enjoyable to look at when it was older), with art (paintings completed in 1905 were rated as more aesthetically pleasing compared to those completed in 2005) and with medical practices (participants rated acupuncture's value more positively if they were told it was a practice that had been around for 2000 years compared to 250 years). Edelman, Pattershall, and Crandall even demonstrated this in terms of degree changes. Students were asked for their opinion about a change to a degree course. In one condition they were told the rule of needing 32 credit hours to graduate had been around for 10 years. In another condition, they were told it has existed for 100 years. The proposal was to change this to a requirement of 38 credit hours. When told the existing requirement had been in place for 10 years, there was a weak preference for keeping things the same. When told it had been in place for 100 years, this difference was extended. The longer things had stayed the same, the more that situation was preferred.

■ **Table 6.2** Evaluations of acupuncture vary according to how long participants are told it has been in existence.

Time that participants were told acupuncture had been in existence for (in years)	Mean evaluation of acupuncture as a technique to relieve pain and restore health (1–9 where 1 is strongly disagree and 9 is strongly agree)	Standard deviation
250	5.16	1.59
500	5.54	1.08
1000	5.71	0.97
2000	6.10	1.32

Data taken from Eidelman et al. (2010).

Warner and Kiddoo (2014) demonstrated how this might influence our views about religious groups. They told their participants one of two things about the Mormon religion. In one condition they were told the religion was relatively old (some of the passages were written in 2200 BC) and in a second condition they were told it was relatively new (it was discovered and translated in 1823). The older participants thought the Mormon faith was, the less prejudice was shown towards individuals following this religion.

The status quo heuristic also influences our view of political candidates. Eidelman and Crandall (2014) asked participants to evaluate a candidate for a Mayoral election in their town. They were shown a photograph and a brief description of the individual. For half of the participants, they were led to believe the candidate was running for a second term of office having held this post already. For the other half of participants, they were led to believe the candidate was running for office for the first time. The candidate who had already been in office was rated as both more attractive and more pleasant!

ANCHORING AND ADJUSTMENT BIASES

These heuristics suggest we process a lot of information automatically, with little conscious awareness. This is, after all, the value of these rules of thumb; to save us cognitive energy. What happens when we encounter a situation where there is a good deal of uncertainty? We often use something that we do know as a starting point and then adjust from there. This is what is known as anchoring and adjustment. Northcraft and Neale (1987) conducted their study in Arizona, USA. Participants visited a property that was for sale. They were given a ten-page document which included information about property sales in the neighbouring area and the listing price of similar property nearby. The actual listing price for the property was $74,900. Participants saw a different listing price in their packs. Some saw $65,900 and others saw $83,900. These figures served as the anchors, giving participants a starting point for their own decisions. What effect did this have? Those who saw a starting price of $65,900 estimated the property was worth $63,571 on average. Those who saw a starting price of $83,900 estimated the same property to be worth $72,196 on average. In other words, the participants adjusted from the initial starting price.

Surely this is just because these participants were students. Estate agents who make valuations all the time may not be susceptible to this anchoring and adjustment. However, Northcraft and Neale demonstrated they were also using this heuristic. Their estimates of value were $67,811 and $75,190 in the same two conditions.

Rather shockingly, anchoring and adjustment also has an influence in the courtroom. Legal experts were given information about a realistic court case and recommended sentences for the culprit. For some experts, they read recommendations for a lenient sentence whereas for others they read recommendations for a longer sentence. The experts were asked to give their own recommendations after reading this information. In cases like this, the legal experts should rely on their experience and knowledge. But this was not the case. When the recommendations they read were for a lenient sentence, the experts themselves recommended a more lenient sentence. Conversely, when they read recommendations for a harsh sentence, they too followed suit and recommended a harsh sentence. What makes this even more concerning is that for one-third of the experts, they had been told that the recommendations they read about had been made by a journalist, someone who has no expertise in criminal cases. For one-third, they were told the recommendations had been made by rolling a dice, something that is down to chance. For the final third, they were told the recommendations had been made by an experienced prosecutor. The source of the recommendations, however, made no difference at all (Englich et al., 2006).

Our use of anchoring and adjustment is so prevalent that participants in Strack and Mussweiler's study were even influenced by a high anchor of 140 years when estimating Mahatma Ghandi's age (1997)! It is worth remembering this heuristic next time you go shopping too as anchoring is known to influence our evaluation of products when looking at the price of products (Biswas & Burton, 1993).

CONTROLLED PROCESSING

We have only touched on a few heuristics in this chapter but hopefully, you can now see how our automatic processing of social information is by no means minimal. We do however engage in controlled processing too. One example of this is our engagement in counterfactual thinking. As Kahneman and Miller (1986) explain, we imagine what might have been if circumstances had been different. We are more likely to engage in this conscious and effortful type of thinking when we experience an event as negative (Aronson et al., 2014).

Medvec et al. (1995) provided a nice illustration of this by studying medallists at the 1992 Summer Olympics in Barcelona. They analysed the emotional reactions of medal winners both at the point where their events ended and when they stood on the podium using videotaped coverage. Undergraduate students were asked to rate the expressed emotion of the athletes. To the researchers' surprise, bronze medallists were rated as appearing happier than silver medallists. Looking at the clips of athletes immediately after their event finished, the mean rating of happiness for the bronze medallists was 7.1 compared to only 4.8 for the silver medallists. When they stood on the podium to collect their medals, the mean rating for happiness of bronze medal winners was 5.7 compared to 4.3 for the silver medallists. Why would someone who finished third look happier than someone who finished second? Medvec et al. claim that these results are explained in terms of counterfactual thinking. For the bronze medallist, they are thinking that they could have come fourth and missed out on a medal completely so they are happy to have won one. For the silver medallist, however, they are thinking that they could have come first but missed out. In support of this, they conducted a second study looking at interviews with the medal winners. Silver medallists were more likely to use statements that referred to the narrow miss of a gold medal using "almost" statements compared to statements that referred to achievements using "at least" wording. This latter type of statement was much more frequently given for bronze medallists.

A similar situation can be observed when it comes to exam results. Medvec and Savitsky (1997) asked students on an Introductory Psychology course to complete a brief questionnaire asking them what grade they had achieved and what they had expected to achieve. They were asked to rate their satisfaction with their grade. So, I don't think any of us would be too shocked to know that students who achieved a higher grade were more satisfied than those who didn't. However, an interesting split occurred for those who achieved marks very close to the cut-off mark between grades. Those who just scraped into a higher category of mark were particularly satisfied. Those who didn't make the higher categories of marks and only just missed it were particularly dissatisfied. Someone achieving a score of 55, for example, may therefore be more satisfied than someone achieving a 59. For Medvec and Savitsky, this demonstrates downward and upward counterfactual thinking. Downward counterfactual thinking leads to thoughts of "at least I ..." achieved this grade whereas upward counterfactual thinking leads to thoughts of "I almost ..." achieved this grade. As Medvec and Savitsky themselves point out, Markman et al. (1993) suggest that upward counterfactual thinking nearly always follows failure experiences whereas downward counterfactual thinking nearly always follows success.

This effect is not restricted to the world of academia or sport. It has also been shown to have an effect in health-related contexts. Tenbrunsel et al. (1996) reported that individuals value decreases in their cholesterol levels more when they cross a boundary such as from above normal to normal than they do decreases within a category even though in both cases this is something to be celebrated.

Increasing controlled processing

One way to increase the chance of controlled processing occurring is to sit individuals in front of a mirror. Dijksterhuis and Van Knippenberg (2000) did just this in a study that required individuals to write an essay arguing against a nuclear testing programme. Before writing the essay, the participants were asked to complete a scrambled sentence task. This task contained words designed to prime stereotypes of politicians. Typically, people see politicians as being "longwinded" in their explanations. Under normal conditions of testing, the participants in Dijksterhuis and Knippenberg's study tended to write longer essays after completing the sentence task compared to if it had contained neutral words unrelated to politician stereotypes. However, seat these same individuals in front of a mirror whilst writing their essay and the effect disappears. The mirror has the effect of increasing self-focus and hence controlled processing.

An alternative is to ask individuals to consider the possibility that their answer may not be right. Lord et al. (1984) asked their participants to make judgements about capital punishment. Following this, they were presented with four bits of information: a one-sentence summary of a research finding, a two-page description of the methodology used in that research, a one-sentence summary of a conflicting finding and a two-page description of the methodology used in that study. They were then asked to report their attitudes towards capital punishment having read this information. For some of the participants, they were explicitly asked to consider whether their judgements would remain the same if the study they were reading about, had produced an outcome supporting the opposite side of the issue from the one it did. This simple instruction was sufficient to reduce belief polarisation (that is, the strengthening of already held beliefs). Lord et al. (1984) suggest that the request to consider opposite or alternative points of view can push us to engage in more controlled reasoning leading to more considered judgements. They quote Oliver Cromwell to enforce the idea that we do not adequately consider alternative possibilities!

There are limits to the amount of control you have!

Whilst these strategies might work to encourage controlled processing, if we try too hard to control our thoughts, it can backfire. For example, if I tell you not to think about pink elephants for the next minute, chances are that you will think about pink elephants more than you otherwise would. The more you try to stop thinking about them, the more you will do so. Wegner (1994) calls these incidents ironic processes of mental control. An operator process attempts to control our thoughts of pink elephants whilst a monitoring process actively searches for these unwanted thoughts to make sure they are being suppressed. If a thought of a pink elephant is detected, the monitoring process brings it to our attention which ironically means we are more likely to think about it than we would otherwise.

Wegner et al. (1987) asked participants to verbalise their stream of consciousness for 5 minutes whilst *not* thinking about a white bear. If they happened to think about a white bear, they had to ring a bell. They simply could not stop thinking about the bear. Even when instructed not to, they indicated thinking about the white bear more than once every minute. In a follow-up task, when asked to do the opposite and actively think about the white bear, they tended to have more thoughts about it than if they had not done the initial suppression task! Wegner referred to this

■ Figure 6.3 If told not to think of a white bear, chances are you will do just that!

as a rebound effect. Such a finding can explain why diets more often fail than succeed. Trying to suppress thoughts of food can make them occur more frequently hence why dieting may lead to over-eating (Polivy & Herman, 1985).

A similar effect is observed with stereotypes. Macrae et al. (1994) provide evidence that suggests telling people not to show prejudice can backfire. Participants were shown a picture of a skinhead and were asked to write briefly about a typical day in the life of the person in the photo. For half of the participants, they were told that stereotypes have been shown to influence our evaluations of others and they should actively try to avoid letting stereotypes influence their writing. For the other half of the participants, no such instruction was given. Once they had finished writing their passage, they were then shown a second photograph. This time it was of a different male skinhead. Once again, participants were asked to construct a passage of writing about a day in the life of the person in the photo but no instructions about stereotyping were given to anyone. Independent raters were asked to rate the written passages in each part of the study, in terms of how stereotypical they were. Consistent with Wegner's ironic processes theory, those who had been asked to actively inhibit stereotypical thoughts in the first part of the study wrote passages that were considered to be far more stereotypical in the second part. As Macrae et al. write:

Out of sight, then, does not necessarily mean out of mind, at least where unwanted thoughts are concerned.

(p. 814)

It might be worth remembering this in cases where you ask someone to keep a secret. Lane et al. (2006) demonstrated that instructing participants not to reveal privileged information on a shape task let to them doing so more than if they were not given this instruction! If you are thinking of bribing someone to give your secret, well, that won't work either. As Lane and Liersch (2012) reported, monetary incentives lead to even more chance of information being leaked.

Hopefully through this chapter you will have picked up the sense that there is an awful lot of processing going on about our social world that we may not even be aware of. We rather like our shortcuts and heuristics (of which there are many more than we can realistically cover in this chapter) as they help conserve our limited cognitive energy and resources. When we process information in an effortful and controlled manner, this takes time. At the time of writing this, the air traffic control automatic system has just failed in UK airports and the amount of time it is taking to manually process information reminds me very much of the key points this chapter aims to make!

REFERENCES

Albek, A. (2022). *The impact of heuristics on political behavior* Egypt's Morsi as a case study*. Authorea Preprints.

An, S. (2008). Antidepressant direct-to-consumer advertising and social perception of the prevalence of depression: Application of the availability heuristic. *Health Communication, 23*(6), 499–505.

Aronson, E., Wilson, T. D., & Akert, R. M. (2014). *Social psychology* (8th ed.). Pearson Education.

Baron, R. A. & Branscombe, N. R., (2014) *Social psychology*. (13th ed.). Pearson.

Baron, R. A., Branscombe, N. R., & Byrne, D. (2007). *Social Psychology: International edition*. 11/E.; Allyn & Bacon.

Biswas, A., & Burton, S. (1993). Consumer perceptions of tensile price claims in advertisements: An assessment of claim types across different discount levels. *Journal of the Academy of Marketing Science, 21*, 217–229.

Brannon, L. A., & Carson, K. L. (2003). Nursing expertise and information structure influence medical decision making. *Applied Nursing Research, 16*(4), 287–290.

Buss, D. M. (1995). Evolutionary psychology: A new paradigm for psychological science. *Psychological Inquiry*, *6*(1), 1–30.

Carnes, N., & Sadin, M. L. (2015). The "Mill Worker's Son" heuristic: How voters perceive politicians from working-class families—And how they really behave in office. *The Journal of Politics*, *77*(1), 285–298.

Diekman, A. B., Gardner, W. L., & McDonald, M. (2000). Love means never having to be careful: The relationship between reading romance novels and safe sex behavior. *Psychology of Women Quarterly*, *24*(2), 179–188.

Dijksterhuis, A., & Van Knippenberg, A. D. (2000). Behavioral indecision: Effects of self-focus on automatic behavior. *Social Cognition*, *18*(1), 55–74.

Donohue, J. M., & Berndt, E. R. (2004). Effects of direct-to-consumer advertising on medication choice: The case of antidepressants. *Journal of Public Policy & Marketing*, *23*(2), 115–127.

Doob, A. N. (1985). The many realities of crime. In *Perspectives in criminal law*. Canada Law Book.

Eidelman, S., & Crandall, C. S. (2014). The intuitive traditionalist: How biases for existence and longevity promote the status quo. In *Advances in experimental social psychology* (Vol. 50, pp. 53–104). Academic Press.

Eidelman, S., Pattershall, J., & Crandall, C. S. (2010). Longer is better. *Journal of Experimental Social Psychology*, *46*(6), 993–998.

Englich, B., Mussweiler, T., & Strack, F. (2006). Playing dice with criminal sentences: The influence of irrelevant anchors on experts' judicial decision making. *Personality and Social Psychology Bulletin*, *32*(2), 188–200.

Fox, C. R. (2006). The availability heuristic in the classroom: How soliciting more criticism can boost your course ratings. *Judgment and Decision Making*, *1*(1), 86–90.

García-Bajos, E., & Migueles, M. (2003). False memories for script actions in a mugging account. *European Journal of Cognitive Psychology*, *15*(2), 195–208.

Giessner, S. R., & Schubert, T. W. (2007). High in the hierarchy: How vertical location and judgments of leaders' power are interrelated. *Organizational Behavior and Human Decision Processes*, *104*(1), 30–44.

Graber, D. A. (1980). *Crime news and the public* (pp. 24–26). Praeger.

IJzerman, H., & Semin, G. R. (2009). The thermometer of social relations: Mapping social proximity on temperature. *Psychological Science*, *20*(10), 1214–1220.

Jostmann, N. B., Lakens, D., & Schubert, T. W. (2009). Weight as an embodiment of importance. *Psychological Science*, *20*(9), 1169–1174.

Kahneman, D. (2011). *Thinking, fast and slow*. Macmillan.

Kahneman, D., & Miller, D. T. (1986). Norm theory: Comparing reality to its alternatives. *Psychological Review*, *93*(2), 136.

Kahneman, D., & Tversky, A. (1973). On the psychology of prediction. *Psychological Review*, *80*(4), 237.

Keller, S. N., & Brown, J. D. (2002). Media interventions to promote responsible sexual behavior. *Journal of Sex Research*, *39*(1), 67–72.

Kelley, H. H. (1950). The warm-cold variable in first impressions of persons. *Journal of Personality*, *18*, 431–439.

Kintsch, W., & Bates, E. (1977). Recognition memory for statements from a classroom lecture. *Journal of Experimental Psychology: Human Learning and Memory*, *3*(2), 150.

Krawczyk, M. W., & Rachubik, J. (2019). The representativeness heuristic and the choice of lottery tickets: A field experiment. *Judgment and Decision Making*, *14*(1), 51–57.

Kulkarni, S. S., Dewitt, B., Fischhoff, B., Rosengart, M. R., Angus, D. C., Saul, M., yealy, D. M., & Mohan, D. (2019). Defining the representativeness heuristic in trauma triage: A retrospective observational cohort study. *PLOS ONE*, *14*(2), e0212201.

Landau, M. J., Meier, B. P., & Keefer, L. A. (2010). A metaphor-enriched social cognition. *Psychological Bulletin*, *136*(6), 1045.

Lane, L. W., Groisman, M., & Ferreira, V. S. (2006). Don't talk about pink elephants! Speakers' control over leaking private information during language production. *Psychological Science*, *17*(4), 273–277.

Lane, L. W., & Liersch, M. J. (2012). Can you keep a secret? Increasing speakers' motivation to keep information confidential yields poorer outcomes. *Language and Cognitive Processes*, *27*(3), 462–473.

Liljenquist, K., Zhong, C. B., & Galinsky, A. D. (2010). The smell of virtue: Clean scents promote reciprocity and charity. *Psychological science*, *21*(3), 381–383.

Lin, M., & Lin, S. C. (2022). A study on the association between physical warmth and social warmth in high school students of Taiwan. Clinical Case Reports International, *6*, 1422.

Lord, C. G., Lepper, M. R., & Preston, E. (1984). Considering the opposite: A corrective strategy for social judgement. *Journal of Personality and Social Psychology*, *47*(6), 1231.

Macrae, C. N., Bodenhausen, G. V., Milne, A. B., & Jetten, J. (1994). Out of mind but back in sight: Stereotypes on the rebound. *Journal of Personality and Social Psychology*, *67*(5), 808.

Markman, K. D., Gavanski, I., Sherman, S. J., & McMullen, M. N. (1993). The mental simulation of better and worse possible worlds. *Journal of Experimental Social Psychology*, *29*(1), 87–109.

McKelvie, S. J. (1995). Bias in the estimated frequency of names. *Perceptual and Motor Skills*, *81*, 1331–1338.

Medvec, V. H., Madey, S. F., & Gilovich, T. (1995). When less is more: Counterfactual thinking and satisfaction among Olympic medalists. *Journal of Personality and Social Psychology*, *69*(4), 603.

Medvec, V. H., & Savitsky, K. (1997). When doing better means feeling worse: The effects of categorical cutoff points on counterfactual thinking and satisfaction. *Journal of Personality and Social Psychology*, *72*(6), 1284.

Meier, B. P., & Dionne, S. (2009). Downright sexy: Verticality, implicit power, and perceived physical attractiveness. *Social Cognition*, *27*(6), 883–892.

Meier, B. P., Hauser, D. J., Robinson, M. D., Friesen, C. K., & Schjeldahl, K. (2007). What's "up" with God? Vertical space as a representation of the divine. *Journal of Personality and Social Psychology*, *93*(5), 699.

Meier, B. P., & Robinson, M. D. (2006). Does "feeling down" mean seeing down? Depressive symptoms and vertical selective attention. *Journal of Research in Personality*, *40*(4), 451–461.

Nakamura, G. V., Graesser, A. C., Zimmerman, J. A., & Riha, J. (1985). Script processing in a natural situation. *Memory & Cognition*, *13*, 140–144.

Northcraft, G. B., & Neale, M. A. (1987). Experts, amateurs, and real estate: An anchoring-and-adjustment perspective on property pricing decisions. *Organizational Behavior and Human Decision Processes, 39*(1), 84–97.

Polivy, J., & Herman, C. P. (1985). Dieting and binging: A causal analysis. *American Psychologist, 40*(2), 193.

Roberts, J. V., & Doob, A. N. (1990). News media influences on public views of sentencing. *Law and Human Behavior, 14*(5), 451–468.

Robinson, M. D., Zabelina, D. L., Ode, S., & Moeller, S. K. (2008). The vertical nature of dominance-submission: Individual differences in vertical attention. *Journal of Research in Personality, 42*(4), 933–948.

Sacks, O. (2011). *The man who mistook his wife for a hat*. Picador.

Schank, R. C., & Abelson, R. P. (1975). Scripts, plans and goals. In *Proceedings of the 4th international joint conference on artificial intelligence. IJCAI* (Vol. 1).

Schnall, S., Benton, J., & Harvey, S. (2008). With a clean conscience: Cleanliness reduces the severity of moral judgments. *Psychological Science, 19*(12), 1219–1222.

Schubert, T. W. (2005). Your highness: Vertical positions as perceptual symbols of power. *Journal of Personality and Social Psychology, 89*(1), 1.

Stolwijk, S., & Vis, B. (2021). Politicians, the representativeness heuristic and decision-making biases. *Political Behavior, 43*(4), 1411–1432.

Sunstein, C. R. (2006). *Infotopia: How many minds produce knowledge*. Oxford University Press.

Taylor, S. E. (1981). The interface between social and cognitive psychology. In J. H. Harvey (Ed.), *Cognition, social behaviour and the environment*. Erlbaum.

Tenbrunsel, A., Wade-Benzoni, K., Messick, D., & Bazerman, M. (1996). *Reducing the dysfunctional effects of standards through the use of multiple standards*. Unpublished manuscript. Northwestern University.

Tversky, A., & Kahneman, D. (1973). Availability: A heuristic for judging frequency and probability. *Cognitive Psychology, 5*(2), 207–232.

Tversky, A., & Kahneman, D. (1982). Evidential impact of base rates. In D. Kahneman, P. Slovic, & A. Tversky (Eds.), *Judgment under uncertainty: Heuristics and biases* (pp. 153–160), Cambridge University Press.

Warner, R. H., & Kiddoo, K. L. (2014). Are the latter-day saints too latter day? Perceived age of the Mormon Church and attitudes toward Mormons. *Group Processes & Intergroup Relations, 17*(1), 67–78.

Weber, E. U., Böckenholt, U., Hilton, D. J., & Wallace, B. (1993). Determinants of diagnostic hypothesis generation: Effects of information, base rates, and experience. *Journal of Experimental Psychology: Learning, Memory, and Cognition, 19*(5), 1151.

Wegner, D. M. (1994). Ironic processes of mental control. *Psychological Review, 101*(1), 34.

Wegner, D. M., Schneider, D. J., Carter, S. R., & White, T. L. (1987). Paradoxical effects of thought suppression. *Journal of Personality and Social Psychology, 53*(1), 5.

Weyland, K. (2005). Theories of policy diffusion lessons from Latin American pension reform. *World Politics, 57*(2), 262–295.

Weyland, K. (2012). The Arab Spring: Why the surprising similarities with the revolutionary wave of 1848? *Perspectives on Politics, 10*(4), 917–934.

Widmeyer, W. N., & Loy, J. W. (1988). When you're hot, you're hot! Warm-cold effects in first impressions of persons and teaching effectiveness. *Journal of Educational Psychology*, *80*(1), 118.

Williams, L. E., & Bargh, J. A. (2008). Experiencing physical warmth promotes interpersonal warmth. *Science*, *322*(5901), 606–607.

Zhong, C. B., & Leonardelli, G. J. (2008). Cold and lonely: Does social exclusion literally feel cold. *Psychological Science*, *19*(9), 838–842.

Chapter 7

Is a pub the best place to visit on a hot day?

Picture this. You've been out for a long walk in the countryside. The sun is scorching hot and you see a pub on the horizon. Your thoughts soon turn to refreshments and what you will order at the bar. But is a pub the best place to be on a hot day? What if it is crowded? In this chapter, we aim to find answers to these questions by exploring 11 different factors that we think make a difference to our decision to engage in anti-social behaviour. As Abraham Lincoln once said, life may not always be a bed of roses. Sometimes the less positive side of our behaviour comes to the fore. So let's embark on our journey through the 11 factors ….

FACTOR 1: TEMPERATURE

When the sun is out, we tend to think of happy times and opportunities to go out and about in the great outdoors. I hate to put a dampener on things but did you also know that hot temperatures are associated with a whole host of rather unpleasant anti-social behaviours? It is no accident that we talk about angry people as getting "hot under the collar".

On the sports field, ambient temperature can have a startling effect on aggressive tendencies. Craig et al. (2016) analysed 2,326 National Football League games. For teams playing in their home stadiums, temperature significantly predicted the number of aggressive penalties awarded. Larrick et al. (2011) analysed data from over 57,000 Major League Baseball games. High temperatures were observed to increase the probability of a pitcher hitting a batter. However, this was only after fellow teammates had been hit by the opposing team. Hot temperatures therefore served to increase retaliation.

It isn't just on the sports field that temperature has an effect. Crime rates are known to be affected by it too. Anderson (1989) analysed data taken from an 1899 study by Dexter that included assaults in New York City from 1891 to 1897 and murders in Denver from 1884 to 1896. It also included the average daily temperature for each month. When Anderson analysed this data, he discovered a strong correlation between assault rate and temperature. In the summer months, the assault rate was about 20 a day compared to about 12.5 a day in the winter months. Harries and Stadler (1983) reported a similar observation using Dallas police reports from March to October 1980. July and August were the hottest months and they also were the months where the highest number of assaults occurred.

Auliciems and DiBartolo (1995) reported a significant association between calls to the police to intervene in domestic violence cases and outside temperature in Brisbane during the year 1992. Carlsmith and Anderson (1979) suggest that the probability of a riot occurring increases monotonically with temperature. They re-analysed data from Baron and Ransberger (1978) covering 102 major riots in the United States between 1967 and 1971. Accounting for the different number of days in the different temperature ranges, they reported a strong linear relationship. Incidentally, you may remember the London riots of 2011. They took place in August when the average temperature was 75°F ....

■ **Figure 7.1** When the temperature rises, so too do aggressive tendencies.

Temperature can influence the level of aggression shown by police also. Vrij et al. (1994) reported an increase in aggressive behaviour towards offenders by police officers when temperatures were high. This was observed in a Fire Arms Training System context where police officers were shown scenarios on a screen and asked to act as they would in reality. Ryan (2020) demonstrated that the effect of temperature has an influence on police activity even in reality. He analysed the traffic stops conducted by the City of Pittsburgh Police Department over 5 years. No surprises for guessing what he found. Consistent with our pattern so far, high temperatures were associated with more issuing of tickets for traffic violations than when temperatures were cooler.

It is a sobering thought that with climate change, our average temperatures are increasing. Miles-Novelo and Anderson (2019) argue that this is likely to produce changes that will increase the likelihood of violent behaviour occurring. This is not just the direct effect on anti-social behaviour but also the indirect effect in terms of food insecurity and economic deprivation. Mares and Moffett (2016) have already documented the link between the effect of climate change on loss of land and failed crops and increased violence in certain countries.

Unfortunately hot temperature has also been shown to affect violent suicides as well as violent behaviour (Maes et al., 1994). In Belgium, Maes et al. compared the average ambient temperature with the incidence of violent suicide between 1979 and 1987. They found a strong association. Higher temperatures combined with an increase in air temperature over a period of a few weeks was a significant predictor of the violent suicide rate. Page et al. (2007), similarly, reported a 5% increase in violent suicide rates with each 1°C rise in temperature above 18°C (64°F). They analysed daily suicide rates in England and Wales between January 1993 and December 2003. In the heatwave that occurred in 1995, the suicide rate itself increased by 46.9%.

Some have argued that the increase in violence on hotter days, particularly towards other people, is simply due to the fact that we are more likely to be out and about and hence in contact with others. The more social contact we have, the more opportunities there are for violence to occur. This is the Routine Activity Theory proposed by Cohen and Felson (1979). However, Stevens et al. (2023) reported a similar association between domestic violence and temperature to that obtained by Auliciems and DiBartolo even when the domestic violence occurrences had taken place inside.

There is also debate about whether the relationship between temperature and violence is linear or curvilinear and if curvilinear, whether this is an inverted U shape curve or a U shape curve. Cohn (1993) suggested that more complaints about domestic violence were received on days when the temperature was moderately high rather than extremely high or extremely low. In fact, Cohn was so confident of this, that he went so far as to develop an equation for predicting domestic violence. Baron and Bell (1976) argue that when the temperature is too extreme, our thoughts turn to escape rather than conflict, something that they discussed as part of their Negative Affect Escape Model.

There is some suggestion for the idea of a curvilinear relationship from a cross-cultural study conducted by Van de Vliert et al. (1999). They examined 136 countries to look at the relationship between ambient temperature and political violence. A mean daytime temperature of approximately 76°F predicted the most violent political actions against and by the governments of those countries, more so than when the temperature was colder or hotter.

Air conditioning plays a big role in reducing the aggressive instincts of over-heated individuals. Harries et al. (1984) identified temperature as affecting aggression in areas considered lower in socioeconomic status that were less likely to have air conditioners. In a study that has as much relevance now as it did when it was first published, Baron (1976) asked a male confederate to drive to an intersection where there were traffic lights on days when the temperature was reliably above 80°F. When the lights turned green, in the control condition, the confederate drove forward. In the experimental conditions, however, he remained stationary, preventing other cars behind him from continuing on their journey. When the temperature was uncomfortably hot (no air-conditioning in the car), drivers honked their horns more quickly at the confederate than when they were in air-conditioned cars.

Kenrick and MacFarlane (1986) conducted a similar study in Phoenix, Arizona. They, too, found a strong relationship between horn-honking and temperature. This was particularly the case for drivers who had their windows open and for male drivers (more about gender and aggression later). Drivers who had air-conditioning were once again relatively unaffected by the ambient temperature.

It is worth noting, for the next family barbeque held on a hot day, that family "disturbances" have been noted to be more prevalent on hotter days too (Rotton & Frey, 1985). What's more, check if the food on the barby isn't too spicy. Batra et al. (2017)

demonstrated that individuals eating spicy food exhibited higher levels of trait aggression, and perceived aggressive intentions in others more readily. Add alcohol into the mix and you have a perfect recipe for aggression. Otrachshenko et al. (2021) reported an increase in violent mortality in a large-scale Russian study but did suggest that lowering vodka consumption may reduce the impact! Which brings us nicely to factor number 2 …

FACTOR 2: ALCOHOL

So, what effect does alcohol have on anti-social behaviour? Taylor and Sears (1988) enlisted 18 male volunteers from Kent State University to try and find an answer. For half of the participants, they administered a drink made of 40% vodka and 60% ginger ale. For the other half, the placebo participants, they administered a drink of ginger ale with 1 cc of vodka on the surface. The participants were asked to complete a reaction time task with another participant seated in a different room. They could select an electric shock with an intensity of anywhere between one and nine to deliver to their opponent IF they were slower than the participant themselves. Participants were informed that an intensity of eight was considered definitely unpleasant. An intensity of nine, however, was labelled "16". This, participants were told, would deliver an electric shock that was twice the intensity that that person had identified as being unpleasant. 28 trials of the task were completed in four sections.

Those intoxicated with the alcoholic drink were significantly more likely to choose to administer the electric shock of intensity "16" than those in the placebo group. Remember that the opponent had not shown any intention to administer any harm to the participants at all and the participants were fully aware of how unpleasant the shock would be.

This is not the full story though because in the same room as the participant were two confederates. They were introduced to the participants as being undergraduates whom another member of faculty had wanted to observe an experiment in progress. During the first block of trials, they remained quietly observant. During the second block, however, they exerted mild pressure on the participant to select higher-intensity shocks. During the third block, they became intensely interested and showed clear disapproval if the participant did not comply with their suggestions to administer high-intensity shocks. In the fourth block, one of the confederates suggested that their influence might interfere with the study and they remained quiet as a result.

For participants in both groups, during block 1, the maximum intensity shock was not selected hardly at all. But introduce a bit of mild pressure from two observers and those who had drunk the alcoholic drink chose this on 18% of the trials. Those in the placebo group didn't select it at all. How about when the pressure increased during block 3? Now, those intoxicated with alcohol administered this shock across 55% of the trials. There was a small increase in the placebo group also but this was insufficient to reach significance. The effect of peer pressure, particularly when this was felt to be strong pressure, really did seem to influence those who had been drinking alcohol. Remove that pressure for the fourth block though and this reduces the effect (the highest intensity was only chosen on 29% of trials for the intoxicated group now).

So, why does alcohol have this effect on aggressive behaviour? Carpenter and Armenti (1972) had previously suggested that alcohol causes hyperactivity in subcortical areas of the brain and this leads to aggression but Taylor and Sears argue for an interaction effect. Situational factors are important. Steele and Josephs (1990) argue for a cognitive explanation in terms of its effects on perception and thought. Alcohol, they claim, causes a restriction of attention. When under the influence, we are less able to attend to weaker cues and focus instead on salient cues. If we perceive a

■ **Figure 7.2** Alcohol myopia: we become less able to attend to weaker cues and instead focus on threat.

threat then we become less able to attend to other cues that might lessen this. They refer to this phenomenon as "Alcohol Myopia".

A nice illustration of this was provided by Zeichner and Pihl (1979). Participants received an auditory tone which was unpleasant, and were told that this was delivered by another participant in another room (it was actually delivered by a computer). To stop the tone, participants could deliver an electric shock as fast as possible. The computer would then deliver a second tone, matched in terms of intensity and duration to the electric shock the participant had just administered. So, if the participant only delivered a brief intensity shock, they would receive only a brief intensity auditory tone in response. Simple, right? Well, it would appear it is only if you are sober. Those participants who had had alcoholic drinks weren't able to pick up on this contingency. They delivered about three times as much shock to their "partner"! Steele and Josephs (1990) suggest that the alcohol myopia may well have led participants to attend to the salient cue of the unpleasant sound whilst obscuring their attention to the contingency. They ended up inadvertently harming themselves as a result!

There is an interesting add-on to this though. If you ask an intoxicated person to engage in a distractor task, the effect of alcohol on aggression is reduced. Using a similar electric shock procedure to the one described above, Giancola and Corman (2007) simultaneously asked participants to also complete a computerised task that required them to remember the sequential order of illumination of four squares on the screen. When experiencing a high-intensity shock themselves, participants were more likely to deliver high-intensity shocks back and particularly so, when they had been given an alcoholic drink. When asked to do the distraction task at the same time, however, this effect was suppressed. It does, the authors suggest, point to the role of alcohol in disrupting our ability to attend to and process information in the short term.

Of course, all of these studies took place in the laboratory. But there is an interesting study that looked at the same issue in a field study, yes, in a pub. Flowe et al. (2011) wanted to see whether hypothetical sexual aggression was associated with alcohol intake if salient cues of a woman's sexual availability were present. The researchers went into five public houses in the United Kingdom and presented willing volunteers with a scenario. The scenario was described as a hypothetical intimate encounter. Participants saw a photograph of a woman wearing either provocative clothing or conservative clothing and were asked to imagine that they had met this person in a nightclub. After talking to the participant and dancing with him, the woman had invited him back to her place. For some of the participants, the woman was described as being sober. For some, she was described as being drunk. Participants were then presented with a line of text at a time, after which they had to say whether they would stop and "call it a day" or remain in the situation. There were 29 lines in total. As the participant progressed through the lines, the activity described became more intimate from kissing all the way through to sexual intercourse. The exceptions were line 12 where the woman displayed signs that she did not want any sexual attention, line 18 where the woman exclaims that she feels uncomfortable and line 23 where she explicitly asks the participant to stop.

Worryingly, 12% remained in the scenario after line 23. For those individuals who had a high level of alcohol in their blood, they were more likely to attend to the clothing of the woman than to her comments in deciding how long to remain in the situation. Twenty-one-point six percent were prepared to stay in the scenario long enough to commit hypothetical sexual aggression when the woman wore revealing clothing compared to only 3.6% when she dressed conservatively. When the woman was described as being drunk, 15.1% were prepared to be sexually aggressive compared to 9.5% when she was portrayed as sober. For Flowe et al, this does indeed suggest that alcohol reduces the ability to attend to and process less salient cues and is a useful warning sign to us all, of the implications this can have.

Now, as you are probably learning through the course of this book, nothing in psychology is ever that straightforward. Laplace et al. (1994) argue that the effect of intoxication on individuals' anti-social behaviour is particularly strong for individuals who have had the least experience with alcohol and DeWall et al. (2010) present evidence to suggest that alcohol has the greatest effect on aggression in heavy men. In their paper, aptly named "The big, the bad and the boozed-up", they argue that there is some truth to the stereotype of the "big, drunk, aggressive guy".

There is quite a twist to the tale. However, research reported by Bègue et al. (2009) points to expectancy effects having a big influence on behaviour. Rather than using electric shock administration as a measure of aggression, they used the Hot Sauce Paradigm. Participants experienced an obnoxious confederate in an early part of the study. Having been told he would have to give his turn to the participant, the confederate was seen to swear, look at the participant in a way that suggested extreme dislike and to question whether he would need to wait longer before leaving the room. The participant was then asked to taste test three glasses of cocktails. For one group of participants, they were informed that the drink tasted like alcohol but it was actually non-alcoholic. For one group of participants, they were informed that the drink contained a moderate amount of alcohol equivalent to 2–3 glasses of vodka. The third group were informed that the drink contained a large amount of alcohol equivalent to 5–6 glasses of vodka.

The participant was then asked to complete some questionnaires. Whilst they did this, the offensive confederate returned and was asked to complete a taste test. This involved eating mashed potato which they themselves had seasoned with salt and hot sauce. They were then asked to season a second plate of mashed potato ready for the participant to eat. On leaving the room after this, the confederate kicked the legs of the chair the participant was sitting on and exclaimed that the dish would blow their head off. How unpleasant.

On completing the questionnaires, the participant was taken to a different room where they were given a bowl of mashed potato and given the opportunity to season it with salt and hot sauce as they liked. After this, they were given the bowl of excessively seasoned mash that the confederate has prepared for them. The final task was to prepare a bowl of mash for the offensive confederate to eat. Whilst doing this, a second confederate came in and incited revenge as an option!

Well, contrary to what you might be expecting, the amount of alcohol actually consumed made very little difference. However, there was a very strong relationship between the amount of alcohol the participant *thought* they had consumed and how much salt and hot sauce they added to the confederate's dish! In other words, it was the belief that they had consumed alcohol that was the important factor! Lang et al (1975) reported a similar effect. Participants who believed they had consumed alcohol were more aggressive than those who believed they had consumed a non-alcoholic drink regardless of how much alcohol they had actually consumed. Marlatt and Rohsenow (1981) refer to this as the "think-drink" effect. When we expect that alcohol will make us more aggressive, chances are it will.

Even seeing advertisements for alcohol can be enough to prompt individuals to see another person as behaving in a more hostile manner (Bartholow & Heinz, 2006). Such advertisements increase the accessibility of aggressive thoughts and with them, the chance of anti-social behaviour occurring.

FACTOR 3: ANONYMITY

So, why else might a pub not be the best place to be on a hot day? A study by Diener et al. (1976) gives us a clue. Over 1,000 children who were out on Halloween night trick-or-treating were secretly observed. In 27 different homes, a bowl of candy bars and a bowl of coins were visible on a table just inside the front door. Each child was told they could take one sweet from the bowl whilst the homeowner went back to work in another room. Some children were asked for their name and where they lived. When the children's identities remained anonymous, more stealing occurred. Twenty-one percent stole either sweets, money or both when anonymous and alone and 57% did so when anonymous and in a group. When the children's identities were made salient, only 7.5% stole when alone and 20.8% did so when in a group. Anonymity, particularly when in a group, does seem to increase the chance of anti-social behaviour being displayed.

The strength of this factor was illustrated by Mann (1981). He studied 21 separate cases of attempted suicide where crowds of

■ **Figure 7.3** Does anonymity increase anti-social behaviour?

people were present. In each case, an individual threatened to jump from a bridge or building. Not only did warmer temperatures predict crowd baiting (where the crowd jeers), but the size of the crowd did too. Getting lost in a crowd and losing that sense of personal identity lead to more anti-social behaviour.

You might already be wondering how this applies in more modern contexts. You may well be aware of the issues with anti-social behaviour online. When we use the internet anonymously, we are likely to show less restraint. Suler (2004) refers to this as the online disinhibition effect. An example was provided by Lapidot-Lefler and Barak (2012). They studied the incidence of what is called flaming behaviour. This is anti-social communication such as swearing, making threatening comments, and using hostile language. They asked participants to engage in a discussion online revolving around a social dilemma. When individual identity was made more salient by enforcing eye contact using a webcam, flaming behaviour reduced. The authors claim that an online sense of un-identifiability fuels anti-social behaviour.

FACTOR 4: CROWDING

We are more likely to feel a sense of anonymity when we are in a large group according to Festinger et al. (1952). And this brings us to our next factor, crowding. Just imagine if your research required you to visit six nightclubs, six times for two hours at a time. Well, that was exactly the case for Macintyre and Homel (1997). The nightclubs in question were in Queensland, Australia. The more crowded the venue, the more violent incidents occurred, even when levels of drunkenness were controlled. (Think about this in Fresher's Week for sure!)

The idea that crowding could be an important factor in predicting anti-social behaviour is not new. Calhoun (1962) demonstrated this using rats as his participants. The more rats they introduced into a fixed-size enclosure; the more aggressive incidents occurred. When the enclosure became very crowded, some became "delinquent". They mounted any rat they encountered, infant mortality rose to 96% in some areas of the enclosure (with cannibalism rife) and some stopped building nests altogether. Incidentally, Calhoun actually sought the agreement of a neighbour to build a rat enclosure in woodland at the back of his garden. What he ended up with, was a "rat city" spanning a quarter of an acre (Ramsden & Adams, 2009). Be thankful for good neighbours.

Even in the home, there is evidence that crowding can trigger aggressive incidents. Gove et al. (1979) pointed to the increased opportunity for conflict resulting from crowded living conditions. Ruback and Pandey (1992) took their study outdoors and studied the effect of crowding on aggression in India. They interviewed passengers who took rides on three-wheeled auto rickshaws. These have room for eight people to sit but this does mean that the passengers are then in constant physical contact with their neighbouring passengers. They can accommodate nine but this does require the ninth person to find a tiny portion of seat or to stand and crouch down. There was significantly more yelling that occurred when the auto rickshaw was more crowded, passengers rated their fellow travellers and the driver more negatively and considered the rickshaw to be less clean and more noisy.

UK prisons have come under the spotlight in recent years due to overcrowding. Considering the link between crowding and anti-social behaviour, it is probably not surprising that in 2016, one of the biggest prison riots broke out at Birmingham Prison. Lawrence and Andrews (2004) studied 79 prison inmates from a medium to high-security prison. As well as asking them to share their subjective feelings about crowding and their personal space preferences, the researchers also collected data on general well-being, stress and perceptions of aggression. Crowding was associated with increases in stress and arousal and a decline in well-being. In line with the research we have already mentioned, experiences of crowding in the prison were associated with a greater likelihood of perceiving an event as aggressive and involving hostile others. Martin et al. (2012), studying overcrowding in prisons in the United States, reported a similar effect on correctional officers with a strong relationship between overcrowding in prisons and stress in those responsible for keeping order in them. The name of their paper says it all "They can take us over any time they want".

It isn't just prisons where this effect is seen. However, Nijman and Rector (1999) collated reports of all verbal and physical aggressive incidents that took place on two closed psychiatric wards between February and December 1996. As the number of patients on the ward increased, so too did the number of incidents reported. However, Nijman and Rector do suggest that it may be psychological space that is more important than physical space that is, having privacy. When a courtyard was added to one of the wards, the effect on incidents was not significant. Ng et al. (2001) suggested that verbal aggression was particularly associated with crowding in psychiatric inpatient units in New Zealand.

It is important to acknowledge here though that gender does make a difference. Brown and Grunberg (1995) studied the effects of crowding in rats and noticed that it had a stress effect on males but a calming effect for females. In fact, Taylor et al. (2000) point to a personal communication from Stern and McClintock (1998) to suggest that having lots of people around actually increases longevity for female rats. Those housed in groups of five with other female rats lived, on average, 40% longer than those housed in isolation. (Would be interesting to see what the outcome would be if the other four were male ….). Taylor et al. (2000) suggest that under any conditions of stress, for females, a "tend and befriend" mechanism predominates whilst for men it is more akin to a "fight or flight" response. This brings us nicely to the next factor in our journey, gender.

FACTOR 5: GENDER

To what extent does gender make a difference? Well, if we believe the statistics, it makes quite an impact. Males are more violent than females in pretty much every culture (Kassin et al., 2016). Males are more likely to behave aggressively but are also more likely to be a target for aggressive behaviour from others (Harris, 1994). According to the Office for National Statistics, in the year ending March 2022, 93% of convicted murderers in the United Kingdom were male and 72% of victims were male.

But as usual in psychology, this paints far too simplistic a picture of males as aggressors and women as pacifiers. When the type of aggression has been explored in more detail, some interesting patterns emerge. Björkqvist et al. (1992) asked:

> *Do girls manipulate and boys fight?*
>
> (p. 117)

The answer to which was a resounding yes. Physical aggression was more likely to occur in males than in females who are much more likely to engage in indirect forms of aggression. Indirect forms of aggression could be things such as excluding an individual from a group or manipulating the social network of a person. It could be malicious gossip and spreading rumours. Österman et al. (1998) identified a similar pattern cross-culturally, in Finland, Poland, Israel, and Italy.

These gender differences appear to begin early. Ostrov and Keating (2004) observed children at preschool. The children were put into groups of three and given a picture of either Winnie-the-Pooh,

Big Bird, or Elmo to colour in. They were given one jumbo coloured crayon and two jumbo white crayons and told that they had 3 minutes to work on the picture. An hourglass was used to give the children an idea of how long they had left. Measures of aggression included verbal aggression (insults, name-calling), physical aggression (hitting, pushing), relational aggression (excluding others from the activity, spreading rumours or secrets), and non-verbal aggression (mean faces, intrusive pointing). Non-verbal aggression came top of the list when it came to frequency but in terms of relational aggression, girls were significantly more likely to engage in this sort of behaviour than boys. In terms of physical aggression, boys showed a trend to deliver this more often but were significantly more likely to be on the receiving end of this type of aggressive behaviour.

Archer (2004) conducted meta-analyses of research exploring sex differences in aggression and the difference in indirect aggression, he argues, disappears by late adolescence/early adulthood. Both men and women can be verbally abusive and yell when provoked. Bettencourt and Miller (1996) similarly suggest that when provoked, any gender differences disappear and Graves (2007) actually points to an increase in physical aggression in women.

One contributing factor to this later finding may well be what Hawley et al. (2007) refer to, in the title of their book, as:

The bright side of bad behaviour.

Demonstrating aggression, especially when combined with relationship-boosting actions, can elevate an individual's status. They may gain access to rewards or become popular with peers.

However, as in all things, balance is called for. White and Kowalski (1994) suggest that aggressive women are seen as socially deviant and pathological compared to aggressive men. Reidy et al. (2009) enlisted the help of 64 male volunteers to take part in a study of aggressive behaviour. They completed a questionnaire designed to measure the extent to which they endorsed a traditional masculinity. They were then asked to take part in a competitive reaction time task against an opponent seated in an adjacent room. Regardless of winning or losing, participants had the opportunity to deliver an electric shock to their opponent (who, unbeknown to them, was fictitious). Their opponent had a similar opportunity. Before beginning this task, the participants heard what they believed was their opponent, responding to questions via an intercom system. It was, in reality, a pre-recording of an actress giving these responses. For some participants, they were led to believe that their opponent was someone who adhered to traditional female gender roles. For some, they were led to believe that this was someone who did not conform to these roles at all. One of the additional things they overheard was their opponent having their pain tolerance measured. The task then began. Over the course of 30 trials, participants received 12 shocks in total from their opponent.

The degree to which participants endorsed traditional masculinity related strongly to the amount of aggression displayed. Those considered "hypermasculine" (conforming strongly to traditional male roles) demonstrated more extreme aggression towards an opponent who did not endorse traditional femininity. The results, the authors suggest, may be relevant to understanding domestic violence and the degree to which traditional gender role beliefs may play a part.

According to White and Kowalski (1994) aggressiveness in men is something that has been implicated in explaining men's success in competitive environments whether this is the workplace or the sports field. Women on the other hand have traditionally been seen as unsuited for competitive roles as this is not part of the traditional feminine stereotype. Such stereotypes have their roots in evolutionary explanations of behaviour and Björkqvist (2018) has suggested that both physical and indirect aggression give evolutionary advantages. So, it is to this factor that we now turn.

FACTOR 6: EVOLUTION

According to evolutionary explanations, anti-social behaviour, such as aggression, can have an adaptive function (Archer, 2009). For example, it can increase access to resources. Buss and Shackelford (1997) argue that aggression, in our ancestral past, was a means of obtaining access to life-supporting resources such as freshwater or food. Daly and Wilson (1988) report that in situations of high-resource conflict, such as where an inheritance goes to one sibling only, homicide amongst brothers is more likely. They also identified a trend for male killers to be poor and unmarried that is lacking in resources.

But it doesn't just have to be physical resources. Aggression can also increase access to potential mates. Archer (2009) points to the work of Brown et al. (2007) who studied aggressive behaviour in house crickets. Those given no access to females for 4 days were more aggressive to other males subsequently than those who had daily access. Daly and Wilson (1988) argue that

■ **Figure 7.4** Aggression may well have an adaptive function.

aggressive behaviour gives those who are unlikely to reproduce a better chance of doing so. Griskevicius et al. (2009) asked participants to read a story. For one-third of the participants, the story was about meeting a very attractive person, having a romantic dinner together and a meaningful conversation. For one-third, the story was about starting a new job and finding out they are in competition with two other individuals of the same sex as themselves. For the final third, the story concerns loss of a wallet whilst at home. Following this story (which was presented as a test of memory), participants were asked to imagine being at a party when someone they know carelessly spills their drink on them and doesn't apologise. They were then asked to rate their response using eight items on an aggression questionnaire such as rating how likely they would be to hit the person, how likely they would be to talk behind their back, and how likely they would be to exclude them from a social group.

Consistent with the idea of aggression as an adaptive behaviour for securing mates, when participants were given a motive to compete for status (from the stories) with individuals who were the same sex as themselves, they were more likely to show aggression towards the person who spilled their drink on them. However, men became more directly aggressive (e.g. pushing them) but women became more indirectly aggressive (e.g. excluding the person from a group). However, in a second study, the authors did show that having a female audience did induce men to control their aggressive instincts. For male participants who read the courtship story, they were more likely to be directly aggressive when they were asked to imagine an audience of other men had observed the drink spillage incident. However, when the audience was female, this effect was attenuated. Clearly, it is not good to be seen as aggressive when trying to create a romantic good impression.

The drive to secure access to mates could, Smith (2007) suggests, be at the root of human warfare. He argues that engaging in aggressive acts can be a way of raising status, which in turn increases the chance of reproductive success. Chang et al. (2011) provide evidence consistent with this view. Heterosexual males were shown photos of either attractive or unattractive opposite-sex people taken from a Chinese online rating site (the mind boggles!) and were asked to estimate the age of the people in the photographs. They were then asked to complete a questionnaire which quizzed them on their opinions towards war or trade conflicts with other countries. Those shown pictures of attractive opposite-sex individuals were more likely to endorse aggressive attitudes towards hostile countries than those who were shown pictures of unattractive opposite-sex individuals. Not only that, but they were quicker to process war scenes or war-related words after. The authors referred to this phenomenon as the mating-warring association. Females, however, showed no such effect.

According to evolutionary theory (Griskevicius et al., 2009), being seen as dominant and aggressive can work in men's favour when it comes to reproduction. Women see such traits as being advantageous for offspring. Buss and Shackelford (1997) point to the finding that across cultures, where homicide occurs, it is much more likely that men are the killers, with other males their victims. Aggression can, of course, lead to harm and for women, this can be a costly price to pay. Voland (1998) suggests that the lack of a mother can significantly reduce a child's chances of reaching adulthood, hence the difference in direct aggression between the sexes.

Vandello and Bosson (2013) suggest that male aggression is a way of maintaining a sense of "manhood". When asked to engage in a task that required the braiding of hair of a female mannequin, male participants subsequently chose to do a punching task more often than a puzzle task, compared to male participants who had had the same task presented as a rope strengthening task (Bosson et al., 2009). The struggle to maintain a sense of manhood also has a role to play in cultures of honour. And that brings us to factor number 7.

FACTOR 7: CULTURE

One thing we learnt from factor 6 was that aggression can be a way of elevating status for males. Aggression therefore can be a way of broadcasting to others one's toughness. Fessler et al. (2014) refer to this idea as the "Crazy Bastard Hypothesis". If our reputation is damaged, aggression is used to restore it. Historically, work in this area has focused on the cultural norms of aggression in the North and South of the United States. In the South, traditional herding communities were susceptible to cattle theft. The legal system was felt to be insufficient to enforce laws so individuals learnt to stand up for themselves and to defend their territory using violent means (Vandello et al., 2008). In the North, agricultural communities dominated and these instead, were more co-operative. Even though times have moved on, a cultural lag exists where the values of maintaining honour are still pervasive. For example, Vandello and Cohen (2008) identify continuing North-South differences in actual serious violence.

Vandello et al. (2008) asked undergraduate students at campuses in the North and South to complete a short questionnaire concerning attitudes towards aggression. The questionnaire contained short scenarios that respondents were asked to imagine themselves in and what they would do in that situation. Those from the South were more likely to see other men as being aggressive and more likely to report fighting themselves if they saw their peers as being violent. That is, they were more likely to see aggression as the norm.

Cohen and Nisbett (1997) wanted to demonstrate the cultural differences between North and South in a field study. They sent letters to 921 companies all over the United States. In the letters, an applicant enquired about employment following a relocation to the area. In some of the letters, the applicant confessed to having been convicted of manslaughter. This was presented as a situation where the applicant's fiancee was having an affair with someone, whom the applicant then got into a fight with and killed. It was being presented as a case of preserving honour. In the other half of the letters, the applicant confessed to having been convicted of theft of a motor vehicle. The name and contact details were given for a response. Sure enough, the letters where the applicant confessed to a manslaughter conviction were treated more positively by companies based in the South. The tone of letters was sympathetic in a quarter of all letters received compared to none received from companies based in the North.

In the laboratory, the difference was even stronger. Cohen et al. (1996) asked participants to complete a questionnaire, pointing them in the direction of a table which was positioned at the end of a narrow hallway. On their way there, they encountered a person (a confederate) working at a filing cabinet with the drawer open. They had to close the drawer to let the participant pass. On the return journey back along the hallway, the confederate again had to shut the drawer to let the participant pass. They slammed it this time and as the participant passed, they bumped their shoulder and called them an "arsehole". As the participant continued their journey along the hallway, another confederate appeared around the corner and headed down the hallway, heading straight for the participant. Cohen et al. refer to this part of the study as "the chicken game" as the measure taken was how close the confederate got before the participant "chickened out" and moved.

As you might have guessed by now, the Southerners who had been insulted waited a lot longer before moving out of the way. Not only that but also the insult caused a rise in cortisol levels (associated with stress) and were more likely to believe that the insult had somehow damaged their reputation or status. For Northern participants, the insult had little effect.

Aggression is, it appears, construed as necessary for self-protection in Southern cultures. It is therefore not surprising that Southerners are more likely to own and use guns to protect their territory than those in the North (Cohen & Nisbett, 1994). [However, more recently, Felson and Pare (2010) suggest that this is less to do with a culture of honour than it is a culture of gun ownership].

It isn't just Southern cultures though. Any culture where legal systems are deemed not to be able to enforce the law can develop such honour cultures. Restrepo (2015) studied professional hockey players in Canada. Those raised in cultures where law enforcement officials were a long way from town, were more likely to be aggressive in games as measured by penalty minutes.

How about cultures where there are no legal enforcers? The Yanomamö tribe in Venezuela are considered to be one of the most aggressive tribal societies in the world. Chagnon (1988), for example, suggests that 30% of males in this tribe die as a result of being killed by someone either in their own tribe or from an external tribe. In contrast, Robarchek and Robarchek (1992) suggest that the Semai tribes of Malaysia are one of the most peaceful. Such tribes tend to rely on co-operation for survival and have little external threats (Aronson et al., 2014).

FACTOR 8: MEDIA

In Western cultures, one of the most hotly debated factors when it comes to anti-social behaviour is the media. As Bushman and Anderson (2001) state:

> *Modern society is exposed to a massive dose of violent media.*
>
> (p. 477)

Does this trigger aggression? According to Anderson and Bushman (2001), the effect of violent media on aggression is larger than the effects of calcium intake on bone mass or lead exposure on IQ. Gibson et al. (2016) reported a significant effect of watching relational aggression (e.g. withdrawal of friendship) in surveillance reality TV clips. Having watched such clips, participants were then asked to write an essay which was either positively or negatively evaluated by a confederate. In the final part of the study, they were asked to participate in a reaction time task. If their opponent lost, they could deliver a pretty unpleasant noise to them – think scratching nails against a blackboard or a loud siren. The average intensity of the noise delivered was 4.67 for those who had watched the reality TV that included relational aggression compared to only 2.98 for those who watched a family surveillance reality TV programme that contained little or no violence.

This is a pattern seen in other studies also. For example, in Liebert and Baron's seminal 1972 study, children aged between 5 and 9 years were shown a 3.5-minute excerpt from either "The Untouchables" or from a sports programme. In the Untouchables excerpt, there was a chase, two scenes where characters were fighting, two shootings, and a knifing. In the sports programme excerpt, there were scenes of athletes competing in various sporting activities such as hurdle races and high jumps. Children were then taken to a separate room and sat in front of a metal box that had a red button and a green button on it. Under the red button was the word "hurt" and under the green button was the word "help". The box had wires coming through it which appeared to go into another room. Children were told that when a white light on the box came on, this meant that a child in the next room was turning a handle as part of a game. If the participant themselves pressed the green button, this would make the handle easier to turn. If they pressed the red button, it would make the handle hot meaning the other child would have to let go of it. Every time the white light came on, they had to press a button. They could press

■ Table 7.1 Mean total duration of aggressive responses in all groups.

	5–6 years		8–9 years	
	Boys	Girls	Boys	Girls
Untouchables	9.65	8.98	12.50	8.53
Sports	6.86	6.50	8.50	6.27

Data taken from Liebert and Baron (1972).

it for a short time to help or hurt a little, or a longer time to help or hurt more.

As Table 7.1 illustrates, those who had watched the Untouchables excerpt were more likely to display an aggressive response by pressing the red "hurt" button for longer than those who watched the sports excerpt. This was particularly the case for the older boys. The Untouchables excerpt also led to a higher level of aggressive play after. Aggressive play was considered to have occurred if children chose to play with the toy gun, toy knife or chose to assault the doll. Bear in mind the limited exposure to televised violence in this study – this certainly provides food for thought.

This sort of effect seems to be robust not just across time but across cultures. Anderson et al. (2017) examined the relationship between media violence and aggression in seven countries (China, Croatia, Germany, Japan, Romania, Australia, and the United States) and reported finding a significant effect even after factors that could impact this such as abusive parenting had been accounted for. It is important to note that this is not about exposing individuals to adult violence in television programmes. Children's cartoons have been shown to have a disproportionate amount of violence in them (Gerbner, 1972). Gerbner stated:

the average cartoon hour in 1967 contained more than three times as many violent episodes as the average adult dramatic hour.

(p. 36)

Consistent with previous findings, Hassan and Daniyal (2013) reported a 33% increase in violent behaviour in children after watching cartoons. Rideout et al. (2010) suggest that by 2010, children between the ages of 8 and 18 were spending an average of 8.5 hours everyday accessing media. Given the rise in social media platforms and access to media on mobile phones, it would not be surprising if this had risen further.

Why might violence in the media be so damaging? One idea proposed by Drabman and Thomas (1974), amongst others, is that repeated exposure to violent media may desensitise individuals to violence in everyday life. They showed a clip from a cowboy film (Hopalong Cassidy) to third and fourth graders (8–10 years). The clip contained a number of violent events such as fistfights and shootings. Following this, the participants were asked to monitor the behaviour of two younger children in an adjacent room, whom they could see on a monitor screen. These younger children became involved in an altercation which ended in a fight. How long did the participants wait before calling for help? If they had watched the cowboy film, a lot longer than if they hadn't watched any film at all! Of those who did not see a film, 58% notified the experimenter before the younger children began to fight physically. Of those who saw Hopalong Cassidy, only 17% did so. Drabman and Thomas believe that a desensitisation process was at work. If we see violence in the media enough, we begin to think this is normative and when it occurs in real-life, we no longer consider this to be surprising. Mrug et al. (2015) demonstrated that young adults show lower increases in blood pressure if exposed regularly to TV and movie violence compared to those with less exposure suggesting a reduced emotional reactivity to violence.

It may also lead to less prosocial behaviour. Bushman and Anderson (2009) asked participants to watch either a violent movie (The Ruins, 2008) or a nonviolent movie (Nim's Island, 2008). On leaving the theatre, they saw a young woman drop a pair of crutches. As her ankle was bandaged up, she struggled to pick them up. Bushman and Anderson measured how long it took for participants to offer help. Those who had just watched the violent movie took 26% longer to help. Bushman and Anderson called their paper "Comfortably numb", pointing to the desensitising effect of violent media.

Of course, it is possible that people who have aggressive tendencies seek out violent media more than those who don't. But, as Slater et al. (2003) suggest, this can lead to a downward spiral whereby the violent media reinforces violent behaviour and the violent behaviour reinforces the desire to seek out violent content.

There is, of course, a whole burgeoning literature exploring the effect of violent videogames on behaviour but for our purposes, we are not going to embark on that area here as it is vast. However, Garnham (2022) does offer an overview of this area. Before we leave the factor of media though, it is worth noting that books have also been implicated in the link between violent content and aggression/violence. Even as far back as Chaucer's time, the Canterbury Tales are replete with verbal aggression (Jucker, 2000).

Tatar (1987) examined the fairy tales written by the Brothers Grimm. These fairy tales have been in existence since 1812 but were originally considered to be German folklore not intended for children. Seven edits later, and in 1857, Wilhelm Grimm published a more child-friendly version. However, even then the fairy tales included tales of starving children to death. In Snow White, Tatar points to the rather graphic request of the stepmother for her lungs and liver. In Cinderella, the stepsisters cut off their heels and toes to fit their feet into the glass slipper. Not exactly the best of bedtime reading.

Davies et al. (2004) analysed a compilation of 25 nursery rhymes for episodes of violence. Forty-one percent were considered to be violent in some way, with some including law-breaking behaviour or animal abuse. "Rock-A-Bye baby", for example is centred around a baby in a cradle, falling from a tree in strong winds and in "Oranges and Lemons" one line reads "Here comes a chopper to chop off your head". Davies et al. suggest that nursery rhymes contain a higher percentage of accidental and aggressive violence than television programmes and the frequency of violence is 11 times higher than that in TV viewing. It remains to be seen whether these have the same effect on violent behaviour as other forms of media.

FACTOR 9: PROVOCATION

Nursery rhymes certainly couldn't be blamed for what happened to Charles Barkley in a New York bar in 1997. Charles, a professional basketball player, was unfortunate enough to have a glass of water thrown at him as he waited for his drink at the bar. In response, he got hold of the culprit, Jorge Lugo and threw him through a plate glass window (Griskevicius et al., 2009). The provocation of the spilt water was sufficient for Barkley to react in a violent manner. Clearly, the intention to spill water over Charles was intentional. This does make a difference as when provocation is unintentional, most do not reciprocate (Kremer & Stephens, 1983).

However, when provocation is intentional, it can turn us into very anti-social individuals indeed. Provocation can be something as simple as receiving harsh criticism or having sarcastic remarks aimed at us. Anything that threatens our reputation in the eyes of others seems to be particularly sensitive (Griskevicius et al., 2009).

Baron (1988) invited participants to develop an advertisement campaign for a new product, a shampoo. They were told that their ideas would be evaluated by an accomplice who would also provide feedback. For half of the participants, they were given constructive feedback. The comments were non-threatening and considerate in tone. For the other half, they were given what Baron referred to as "destructive feedback". This referred to factors about the participant that had led to poor performance such as lack of effort, sometimes suggested getting someone else to do it and pointed to the weakness of the whole campaign plan. Participants then completed a questionnaire asking them to indicate how they would respond to the criticism using five measures such as making excuses or leaving the room. They were asked how they would handle future conflicts with the accomplice. The last part of the study involved the participant and accomplice having to decide how to split a 10-million-pound budget between them, with the participant representing the print media unit and the accomplice representing the television unit. The accomplice began by suggesting 8 million was given to his unit and made only two concessions after.

Destructive criticism led to feelings of anger and to a greater desire to compete rather than collaborate with the accomplice in future encounters. When distributing the money, however, those who had received the destructive criticism made more concessions to the accomplice. Whilst this might seem like they were being generous, Baron claims this was a "concede now but even the score later" strategy.

Provocation can provide a justification for aggression according to Bettencourt and Miller (1996). When provocation is used, gender differences in aggression are greatly reduced. Nobody likes to be provoked!

FACTOR 10: FRUSTRATION

Cast your mind back to the last time you stood in a queue. It might have been to pay for something, it might have been to board a bus or a train, and it might have been a queue to gain entry to an entertainment venue. Imagine how you might have felt if someone had jumped the queue after you had been waiting for some time. Chances are you would have felt frustrated. Which brings us nicely to our penultimate factor. Dollard et al.

■ **Figure 7.5** Beware the queue jumpers (or rather beware the rest of the queue!) "Queue" by hktang.

(1939) proposed the frustration-aggression hypothesis. If we are prevented from making progress towards a goal, we experience frustration. This in turn can lead to an increase in aggression. Sometimes, oftentimes, we cannot take out that aggression on the source of frustration so we may displace it onto someone or something else. Indeed, Harris (1974) actually did study queue jumpers. When people pushed in a queue to pay, an aggressive response was triggered but the closer a participant was to the checkout, the greater the aggressive response.

We don't need to look too far to find more recent evidence to support Dollard. Mazza et al. (2020), for example, suggest that the increased frustration and agitation experienced as a result of the COVID-19 pandemic was a critical factor in the incidence of domestic violence at that time. In a different medical context, Efrat-Treister et al. (2020) identified frustration as a key factor in explaining increased aggression towards staff in a large hospital emergency department after patients were required to wait for many hours to be seen. Brown et al. (2001) studied passengers on a British ferry heading across the channel to France. In a paper aptly named "Life on the Ocean Wave", Brown et al. reported a study conducted at a time when French fishing boats had blockaded the port causing journeys to be cancelled. Passengers were asked to complete a "European Survey" whilst in the ferry terminal. This included some measures of aggressive attitudes towards France. For example, one vignette involved an insult being delivered to a French person who had accidentally spilled coffee, and another involved a petition against the number of French tourists in Canterbury. Passengers were asked to say the extent to which they endorsed the hostile behaviours. This study was repeated 5 days later to give a comparison. Those experiencing cancellations due to the blockade expressed more aggressive attitudes and showed a significantly less positive orientation towards French people compared to those who travelled without obstruction. For example, they were more likely to endorse the insult delivered to the French person who accidentally spilt their coffee.

The power of frustration is so robust that Adachi and Willoughby (2011) raise the possibility that violent video games cause aggression not because of the violence but because of the frustration that they cause.

The story is not quite that straightforward. However, there are some conditions that do make a difference. Kulik and Brown (1979) demonstrated that it is unexpected frustration that leads to increased aggression. They recruited students to engage in a task designed to bring in donations for a charity. Students had to phone complete strangers to ask them to donate. If successful, they would get commission. For half of the students, they were led to believe that they would be successful and hence, gain a large amount of commission. This was because they were given a list of people who were likely to donate and which had a 60–65% success rate. For the other half, they were led to believe that they would find it tough. They were given a success-rate list of 10–15%. The task was rigged so that no donations were received. Those who had high expectations of success demonstrated more aggression, both in their verbal responses to the strangers but also in terms of their behaviours such as slamming the receiver down. This was, however, only true for those whose potential donors gave "illegitimate" reasons for not donating such as believing that charities were a "rip-off".

This does suggest that modifications are needed to Dollard's original hypothesis and Berkowitz (1989) provided these. According to Berkowitz, frustration is an unpleasant experience that creates uncomfortable feelings. It is these that lead to aggression, not the frustration itself. We do take account of the situation rather it being a direct causal relationship. To illustrate, imagine your efforts to solve a problem are thwarted by an individual.

However, the reason is that their hearing aid stopped working. Would you still feel the same need to aggress? According to Burnstein and Worchel (1962), no. Frustration does not always lead to aggression.

Some have argued that releasing pent-up frustration reduces aggression. Freud (1933) termed this "catharsis". Is there any truth to the idea that "letting off steam" helps? Not really. Anderson et al. (2003) reported that listening to songs with aggressive lyrics actually increased aggression. Over the course of a season, high school footballers showed an increase in hostility rather than a decline (Patterson, 1974) and Bushman (2002) pointed to the increase in aggression when participants were asked to hit a punch bag whilst ruminating about the person who had angered them. The same individuals were later more likely to administer a loud blast of noise to the person who had angered them. As Bushman himself writes:

> *Doing nothing at all was more effective than venting anger.*
>
> (p. 724)

FACTOR 11: EXCITATION

So that brings us to our last factor, excitation. If a pub is not the best place to go on a hot day then maybe the gym would be better. After all, many are air-conditioned and if you choose the right one, they may not be too crowded either. But wait! Because of Zillman and Bryant's study is anything to go by, this too may not be ideal.

Participants were asked to take part in a simplified battleship game. Each time their opponent missed; the participant could deliver feedback of an intensity of their choosing. This could be nice, as in the removal of an unpleasant noise or nasty as in the delivery of an unpleasant noise. Their opponent, in the adjacent room, was being taught a strategy against which the participant would have to defend themselves. Whilst they were waiting for the opponent, they were asked to perform a task for 1 minute whilst being shown some slides. For half of the participants, they were asked to pedal an exercise bike for 1 minute but for the other half, they were asked to put their hands into an opaque box and thread small discs that were there, onto a plastic-coated wire.

After 1 minute, they were asked some simple questions about the contents of the slides before starting the game. During the game, unbeknown to the participant, the location of their battleship was known and after a predetermined number of guesses, it was hit. They then heard their opponent speak to the experimenter over the intercom. Half of the participants heard their opponent ask how many trials it took them. For the other half, they heard their opponent insult them. They then waited for the opponent again for six minutes and the second game began. Guess who was more aggressive in terms of the feedback given? Yes, those who were both provoked but had also been asked to pedal the exercise bike. The residual excitation in combination with provocation had enhanced aggressive impulses. A person who is experiencing a high level of arousal or excitation, Zillman and Bryant claim, can be more readily provoked into behaving aggressively.

Zillman (1979) developed this idea into the excitation-transfer model. When we experience a high level of excitation, this can be transferred to other situations we find ourselves in. Schachter and Singer (1962) demonstrated this in a laboratory situation. Arousal caused by an injection of adrenaline led to aggression when a person who was waiting with a participant became hostile. However, for those who had the effects of adrenaline explained to then, this did not occur. In the former case, the arousal was transferred to the situation, leading to aggressive intent.

This may explain why aggression is associated so often with sport. Sivarajasingam et al. (2005) studied Welsh international rugby and football matches that took place between 1995 and 2002. On Sundays, when these matches were being played, admissions to Cardiff hospitals for domestic violence increased significantly. Somewhat ironically, aggression is more often associated with supporters of winning teams than losing teams. Moore et al. (2007) suggests that when a team loses, this decreases happiness but that's about it. Winning doesn't increase happiness, but it does increase aggressive tendencies. Moore's work involved male rugby football fans attending matches at the Millennium stadium in Cardiff. The more aggressive they felt, the more they intended to drink after. It was not celebration but aggression that predicted drinking behaviour. Given what we know about the effect of alcohol on aggression, this suggests an inflammatory situation. Perhaps the garden is the best place to spend time after all!

REFERENCES

Adachi, P. J., & Willoughby, T. (2011). The effect of video game competition and violence on aggressive behavior: Which characteristic has the greatest influence? *Psychology of Violence*, *1*(4), 259.

Anderson, C. A. (1989). Temperature and aggression: ubiquitous effects of heat on occurrence of human violence. *Psychological bulletin, 106*(1), 74.

Anderson, C. A., & Bushman, B. J. (2001). Effects of violent video games on aggressive behavior, aggressive cognition, aggressive affect, physiological arousal, and prosocial behavior: A meta-analytic review of the scientific literature. *Psychological Science, 12*(5), 353–359.

Anderson, C. A., Carnagey, N. L., & Eubanks, J. (2003). Exposure to violent media: The effects of songs with violent lyrics on aggressive thoughts and feelings. *Journal of Personality and Social Psychology, 84*(5), 960.

Anderson, C. A., Suzuki, K., Swing, E. L., Groves, C. L., Gentile, D.A., Prot, S., Lam, C. P., Sakamoto, A., Horiuchi, Y., Krahé, B., Jelic, M., Liuqing, W., Toma, R., Warburton, W. A., Zhang, X. M., Tajima, S., Qing, F., & Petrescu, P. (2017). Media violence and other aggression risk factors in seven nations. *Personality and Social Psychology Bulletin, 43*(7), 986–998.

Archer, J. (2004). Sex differences in aggression in real-world settings: A meta-analytic review. *Review of General Psychology, 8*(4), 291–322.

Archer, J. (2009). Does sexual selection explain human sex differences in aggression? *Behavioral and Brain Sciences, 32*(3–4), 249–266.

Aronson, E., Wilson, T. D., & Akert, R. M. (2014). *Social psychology* (8th ed.). Pearson Education.

Auliciems, A., & DiBartolo, L. (1995). Domestic violence in a subtropical environment: Police calls and weather in Brisbane. *International Journal of Biometeorology, 39*, 34–39.

Baron, R. A. (1976). The reduction of human aggression: A field study of the influence of incompatible reactions 1. *Journal of Applied Social Psychology, 6*(3), 260–274.

Baron, R. A. (1988). Negative effects of destructive criticism: Impact on conflict, self-efficacy, and task performance. *Journal of Applied Psychology, 73*(2), 199.

Baron, R. A., & Bell, P. A. (1976). Aggression and heat: The influence of ambient temperature, negative affect, and a cooling drink on physical aggression. *Journal of Personality and Social Psychology, 33*(3), 245.

Baron, R. A., & Ransberger, V. M. (1978). Ambient temperature and the occurrence of collective violence: The "long, hot summer" revisited. *Journal of Personality and Social Psychology, 36*(4), 351.

Bartholow, B. D., & Heinz, A. (2006). Alcohol and aggression without consumption: Alcohol cues, aggressive thoughts, and hostile perception bias. *Psychological Science, 17*(1), 30–37.

Batra, R. K., Ghoshal, T., & Raghunathan, R. (2017). You are what you eat: An empirical investigation of the relationship between spicy food and aggressive cognition. *Journal of Experimental Social Psychology, 71*, 42–48.

Bègue, L., Subra, B., Arvers, P., Muller, D., Bricout, V., & Zorman, M. (2009). A message in a bottle: Extrapharmacological effects of alcohol on aggression. *Journal of Experimental Social Psychology, 45*(1), 137–142.

Berkowitz, L. (1989). Frustration-aggression hypothesis: Examination and reformulation. *Psychological Bulletin, 106*(1), 59.

Bettencourt, B., & Miller, N. (1996). Gender differences in aggression as a function of provocation: A meta-analysis. *Psychological Bulletin, 119*(3), 422.

Björkqvist, K. (2018). Gender differences in aggression. *Current opinion in psychology*, *19*, 39–42.

Björkqvist, K., Lagerspetz, K. M., & Kaukiainen, A. (1992). Do girls manipulate and boys fight? Developmental trends in regard to direct and indirect aggression. *Aggressive Behavior*, *18*(2), 117–127.

Bosson, J. K., Vandello, J. A., Burnaford, R. M., Weaver, J. R., & Arzu Wasti, S. (2009). Precarious manhood and displays of physical aggression. *Personality and Social Psychology Bulletin*, *35*(5), 623–634.

Brown, W. D., Chimenti, A. J., & Siebert, J. R. (2007). The payoff of fighting in house crickets: Motivational asymmetry increases male aggression and mating success. *Ethology*, *113*(5), 457–465.

Brown, K. J., & Grunberg, N. E. (1995). Effects of housing on male and female rats: Crowding stresses males but calms females. *Physiology & Behavior*, *58*(6), 1085–1089.

Brown, R., Maras, P., Masser, B., Vivian, J., & Hewstone, M. (2001). Life on the ocean wave: Testing some intergroup hypotheses in a naturalistic setting. *Group Processes & Intergroup Relations*, *4*(2), 81–97.

Burnstein, E., & Worchel, P. (1962). Arbitrariness of frustration and its consequences for aggression in a social situation. *Journal of Personality*, *30*, 528–541.

Bushman, B. J. (2002). Does venting anger feed or extinguish the flame? Catharsis, rumination, distraction, anger, and aggressive responding. *Personality and social psychology bulletin*, *28*(6), 724–731.

Bushman, B. J., & Anderson, C. A. (2001). Media violence and the American public: Scientific facts versus media misinformation. *American Psychologist*, *56*(6–7), 477.

Bushman, B. J., & Anderson, C. A. (2009). Comfortably numb: Desensitizing effects of violent media on helping others. *Psychological Science*, *20*(3), 273–277.

Buss, D. M., & Shackelford, T. K. (1997). From vigilance to violence: Mate retention tactics in married couples. *Journal of Personality and Social Psychology*, *72*(2), 346.

Calhoun, J. B. (1962). Population density and social pathology. *Scientific American*, *206*(2), 139–149.

Carlsmith, J. M., & Anderson, C. A. (1979). Ambient temperature and the occurrence of collective violence: a new analysis. *Journal of personality and social psychology*, *37*(3), 337.

Carpenter, J. A., & Armenti, N. P. (1972). Some effects of ethanol on human sexual and aggressive behavior. In *The biology of alcoholism: Volume 2: Physiology and behavior* (pp. 509–543). Springer US.

Chagnon, N. A. (1988). Life histories, blood revenge, and warfare in a tribal population. *Science*, *239*(4843), 985–992.

Chang, L., Lu, H. J., Li, H., & Li, T. (2011). The face that launched a thousand ships: The mating-warring association in men. *Personality and Social Psychology Bulletin*, *37*(7), 976–984.

Cohen, L. E., & Felson, M. (1979). Social change and crime rate trends: A routine activity approach. *American Sociological Review*, *44*(4), 588–608.

Cohen, D., & Nisbett, R. E. (1994). Self-protection and the culture of honor: Explaining southern violence. *Personality and Social Psychology Bulletin*, *20*(5), 551–567.

Cohen, D., & Nisbett, R. E. (1997). Field experiments examining the culture of honor: The role of institutions in perpetuating norms about violence. *Personality and Social Psychology Bulletin, 23*(11), 1188–1199.

Cohen, D., Nisbett, R. E., Bowdle, B. F., & Schwarz, N. (1996). Insult, aggression, and the southern culture of honor: An "experimental ethnography". *Journal of Personality and Social Psychology, 70*(5), 945.

Cohn, E. G. (1993). The prediction of police calls for service: The influence of weather and temporal variables on rape and domestic violence. *Journal of Environmental Psychology, 13*(1), 71–83.

Craig, C., Overbeek, R. W., Condon, M. V., & Rinaldo, S. B. (2016). A relationship between temperature and aggression in NFL football penalties. *Journal of Sport and Health Science, 5*(2), 205–210.

Daly, M., & Wilson, M. (1988). Evolutionary social psychology and family homicide. *Science, 242*(4878), 519–524.

Davies, P., Lee, L., Fox, A., & Fox, E. (2004). Could nursery rhymes cause violent behaviour? A comparison with television viewing. *Archives of Disease in Childhood, 89*(12), 1103–1105.

DeWall, C. N., Bushman, B. J., Giancola, P. R., & Webster, G. D. (2010). The big, the bad, and the boozed-up: Weight moderates the effect of alcohol on aggression. *Journal of Experimental Social Psychology, 46*(4), 619–623.

Diener, E., Fraser, S. C., Beaman, A. L., & Kelem, R. T. (1976). Effects of deindividuation variables on stealing among Halloween trick-or-treaters. *Journal of Personality and Social Psychology, 33*(2), 178.

Dollard, J., Doob, L., Miller, N., Mowrer, O., & Sears, R. (1939). *Frustration and aggression*. Yale University Press.

Drabman, R. S., & Thomas, M. H. (1974). Does media violence increase children's toleration of real-life aggression? *Developmental Psychology, 10*(3), 418.

Efrat-Treister, D., Moriah, H., & Rafaeli, A. (2020). The effect of waiting on aggressive tendencies toward emergency department staff: Providing information can help but may also backfire. *PLOS One, 15*(1), e0227729.

Felson, R. B., & Pare, P. P. (2010). Gun cultures or honor cultures? Explaining regional and race differences in weapon carrying. *Social Forces, 88*(3), 1357–1378.

Fessler, D. M., Tiokhin, L. B., Holbrook, C., Gervais, M. M., & Snyder, J. K. (2014). Foundations of the crazy bastard hypothesis: Nonviolent physical risk-taking enhances conceptualized formidability. *Evolution and Human Behavior, 35*(1), 26–33.

Festinger, L., Gerard, H. B., Hymovitch, B., Kelley, H. H., & Raven, B. (1952). The influence process in the presence of extreme deviates. *Human Relations, 5*(4), 327–346.

Flowe, H. D., Stewart, J., Sleath, E. R., & Palmer, F. T. (2011). Public house patrons' engagement in hypothetical sexual assault: A test of alcohol myopia theory in a field setting. *Aggressive Behavior, 37*(6), 547–558.

Freud, S. (1933). *New introductory lecture on psychoanalysis*. Norton.

Garnham, W. A. (2022). *Applied psychology for foundation year: Key ideas for foundation courses*. Routledge.

Gerbner, G. (1972). Symbolic functions. *Television and Social Behavior: Media Content and Control, 72*(9057), 28.

Giancola, P. R., & Corman, M. D. (2007). Alcohol and aggression: A test of the attention-allocation model. *Psychological Science, 18*(7), 649–655.

Gibson, B., Thompson, J., Hou, B., & Bushman, B. J. (2016). Just "harmless entertainment"? Effects of surveillance reality TV on physical aggression. *Psychology of Popular Media Culture*, *5*(1), 66.

Gove, W. R., Hughes, M., & Galle, O. R. (1979). Overcrowding in the home: An empirical investigation of its possible pathological consequences. *American Sociological Review*, 59–80.

Graves, K. N. (2007). Not always sugar and spice: Expanding theoretical and functional explanations for why females aggress. *Aggression and Violent Behavior*, *12*(2), 131–140.

Griskevicius, V., Tybur, J. M., Gangestad, S. W., Perea, E. F., Shapiro, J. R., & Kenrick, D. T. (2009). Aggress to impress: Hostility as an evolved context-dependent strategy. *Journal of Personality and Social Psychology*, *96*(5), 980.

Harries, K. D., & Stadler, S. J. (1983). Determinism revisited: Assault and heat stress in Dallas, 1980. *Environment and Behavior*, *15*(2), 235–256.

Harries, K. D., Stadler, S. J., & Zdorkowski, R. T. (1984). Seasonality and assault: Explorations in inter-neighborhood variation, Dallas 1980. *Annals of the Association of American Geographers*, *74*(4), 590–604.

Harris, M. B. (1974). Mediators between frustration and aggression in a field experiment. *Journal of Experimental Social Psychology*, *10*(6), 561–571.

Harris, M. B. (1994). Gender of subject and target as mediators of aggression 1. *Journal of Applied Social Psychology*, *24*(5), 453–471.

Hassan, A., & Daniyal, M. (2013). Impact of television programs and advertisements on school going adolescents: A case study of Bahawalpur city, Pakistan. *Bulgarian Journal of Science and Education Policy (BJSEP)*, *7*(1), 26–37.

Hawley, P. H., Little, T. D., & Rodkin, P. C. (Eds.). (2007). *Aggression and adaptation: The bright side to bad behavior*. Lawrence Erlbaum Associates Publishers.

Jucker, A. H. (2000). Slanders, slurs and insults on the road to Canterbury: Forms of verbal aggression in Chaucer's Canterbury Tales. In: Taavitsainen I, Navalainen T, Pahta P and Rissanen M (eds) *Placing Middle English in Context (Topics in English Linguistics 35)*. Mouton de Gruyter, pp. 369–389.

Kassin, S., Fein, S., & Markus, H. R. (2016). *Social psychology*. Cengage Learning.

Kenrick, D. T., & MacFarlane, S. W. (1986). Ambient temperature and horn honking: A field study of the heat/aggression relationship. *Environment and Behavior*, *18*(2), 179–191.

Kremer, J. F., & Stephens, L. (1983). Attributions and arousal as mediators of mitigation's effect on retaliation. *Journal of Personality and Social Psychology*, *45*(2), 335.

Kulik, J. A., & Brown, R. (1979). Frustration, attribution of blame, and aggression. *Journal of Experimental Social Psychology*, *15*(2), 183–194.

Lang, A. R., Goeckner, D. J., Adesso, V. J., & Marlatt, G. A. (1975). Effects of alcohol on aggression in male social drinkers. *Journal of Abnormal Psychology*, *84*(5), 508.

Lapidot-Lefler, N., & Barak, A. (2012). Effects of anonymity, invisibility, and lack of eye-contact on toxic online disinhibition. *Computers in Human Behavior*, *28*(2), 434–443.

Laplace, A. C., Chermack, S. T., & Taylor, S. P. (1994). Effects of alcohol and drinking experience on human physical aggression. *Personality and Social Psychology Bulletin*, *20*(4), 439–444.

Larrick, R. P., Timmerman, T. A., Carton, A. M., & Abrevaya, J. (2011). Temper, temperature, and temptation: Heat-related retaliation in baseball. *Psychological Science*, *22*(4), 423–428.

Lawrence, C., & Andrews, K. (2004). The influence of perceived prison crowding on male inmates' perception of aggressive events. *Aggressive Behavior: Official Journal of the International Society for Research on Aggression*, *30*(4), 273–283.

Liebert, R. M., & Baron, R. A. (1972). Some immediate effects of televised violence on children's behavior. *Developmental Psychology*, *6*(3), 469.

Macintyre, S., & Homel, R. (1997). Danger on the dance floor: A study of interior design, crowding and aggression in nightclubs. *Policing for Prevention: Reducing Crime, Public Intoxication and Injury*, *7*(1), 91–113.

Maes, M., De Meyer, F., Thompson, P., Peeters, D., & Cosyns, P. (1994). Synchronized annual rhythms in violent suicide rate, ambient temperature and the light-dark span. *Acta Psychiatrica Scandinavica*, *90*(5), 391–396.

Mann, L. (1981). The baiting crowd in episodes of threatened suicide. *Journal of Personality and Social Psychology*, *41*(4), 703.

Mares, D. M., & Moffett, K. W. (2016). Climate change and interpersonal violence: A "global" estimate and regional inequities. *Climatic Change*, *135*, 297–310.

Marlatt, G. A., & Rohsenow, D. J. (1981). The think-drink effect. *Psychology Today*, *15*, 60–93.

Martin, J. L., Lichtenstein, B., Jenkot, R. B., & Forde, D. R. (2012). "They can take us over any time they want" correctional officers' responses to prison crowding. *The Prison Journal*, *92*(1), 88–105.

Mazza, M., Marano, G., Lai, C., Janiri, L., & Sani, G. (2020). Danger in danger: Interpersonal violence during COVID-19 quarantine. *Psychiatry Research*, *289*, 113046.

Miles-Novelo, A., & Anderson, C. A. (2019). Climate change and psychology: Effects of rapid global warming on violence and aggression. *Current Climate Change Reports*, *5*, 36–46.

Moore, S. C., Shepherd, J. P., Eden, S., & Sivarajasingam, V. (2007). The effect of rugby match outcome on spectator aggression and intention to drink alcohol. *Criminal Behaviour and Mental Health*, *17*(2), 118–127.

Mrug, S., Madan, A., Cook, E. W., & Wright, R. A. (2015). Emotional and physiological desensitization to real-life and movie violence. *Journal of Youth and Adolescence*, *44*, 1092–1108.

Ng, B., Kumar, S., Ranclaud, M., & Robinson, E. (2001). Ward crowding and incidents of violence on an acute psychiatric inpatient unit. *Psychiatric Services*, *52*(4), 521–525.

Nijman, H. L., & Rector, G. (1999). Crowding and aggression on inpatient psychiatric wards. *Psychiatric Services*, *50*(6), 830–831.

Österman, K., Björkqvist, K., Lagerspetz, K. M., Kaukiainen, A., Landau, S. F., Frączek, A., & Caprara, G. V. (1998). Cross-cultural evidence of female indirect aggression. *Aggressive Behavior: Official Journal of the International Society for Research on Aggression*, *24*(1), 1–8.

Ostrov, J. M., & Keating, C. F. (2004). Gender differences in preschool aggression during free play and structured interactions: An observational study. *Social Development, 13*(2), 255–277.

Otrachshenko, V., Popova, O., & Tavares, J. (2021). Extreme temperature and extreme violence: Evidence from Russia. *Economic Inquiry, 59*(1), 243–262.

Page, L. A., Hajat, S., & Kovats, R. S. (2007). Relationship between daily suicide counts and temperature in England and Wales. *The British Journal of Psychiatry, 191*(2), 106–112.

Patterson, A. H. (1974). Hostility catharsis: A naturalistic quasi-experiment. *Proceedings of the Division of Personality and Society Psychology, 1*(1), 195–197.

Ramsden, E., & Adams, J. (2009). Escaping The laboratory: The rodent experiments of john b. Calhoun & Their cultural influence. *Journal of Social History, 42*, 761–792.

Reidy, D. E., Shirk, S. D., Sloan, C. A., & Zeichner, A. (2009). Men who aggress against women: Effects of feminine gender role violation on physical aggression in hypermasculine men. *Psychology of Men & Masculinity, 10*(1), 1.

Restrepo, P. (2015). *The Mounties and the origins of peace in the Canadian prairies*. MIT.

Rideout, V. J., Foehr, U. G., & Roberts, D. F. (2010). *Generation M 2: Media in the lives of 8- to 18-year-olds*. Henry J. Kaiser Family Foundation.

Robarchek, C. A., & Robarchek, C. J. (1992). A comparative study of Waorani and Semai. In J. Silverberg & J. Patrick Gray (Eds.), *Aggression and Peacefulness in Humans and Other Primates*, eds J. Silverberg and J. P. Gray. Oxford University Press, 189–213.

Rotton, J., & Frey, J. (1985). Air pollution, weather, and violent crimes: Concomitant time-series analysis of archival data. *Journal of Personality and Social Psychology, 49*(5), 1207.

Ruback, R., & Pandey, J. (1992). Very hot and really crowded: Quasi-experimental investigations of Indian "Tempos. *Environment and Behavior, 24*, 5257–5554.

Ryan, M. E. (2020). The heat: Temperature, police behavior and the enforcement of law. *European Journal of Law and Economics, 49*, 187–203.

Schachter, S., & Singer, J. (1962). Cognitive, social, and physiological determinants of emotional state. *Psychological Review, 69*(5), 379.

Sivarajasingam, V., Moore, S., & Shepherd, J. P. (2005). Winning, losing, and violence. *Injury Prevention, 11*(2), 69–70.

Slater, M. D., Henry, K. L., Swaim, R. C., & Anderson, L. L. (2003). Violent media content and aggressiveness in adolescents: A downward spiral model. *Communication Research, 30*(6), 713–736.

Smith, D. L. (2007). *The most dangerous animal: Human nature and origins of war*. St. Martin's.

Steele, C. M., & Josephs, R. A. (1990). Alcohol myopia: Its prized and dangerous effects. *American Psychologist, 45*(8), 921.

Stern, K., & McClintock, M. K. (1998). Regulation of ovulation by human pheromones. *Nature, 392*(6672), 177–179.

Stevens, H. R., Graham, P. L., Beggs, P. J., & Hanigan, I. C. (2023). No retreat from the heat: Temperature-related risk of violent assault is increased by being inside. *International Journal of Urban Sciences, 28*, 1–16.

Suler, J. (2004). The online disinhibition effect. *Cyberpsychology & Behavior*, *7*(3), 321–326.

Tatar, M. (1987). *The hard facts of the Grimms' Fairy Tales*. Princeton University Press.

Taylor, S. E., Klein, L. C., Lewis, B. P., Gruenewald, T. L., Gurung, R. A., & Updegraff, J. A. (2000). Biobehavioral responses to stress in females: Tend-and-befriend, not fight-or-flight. *Psychological Review*, *107*(3), 411.

Taylor, S. P., & Sears, J. D. (1988). The effects of alcohol and persuasive social pressure on human physical aggression. *Aggressive Behavior*, *14*(4), 237–243.

Van de Vliert, E., Schwartz, S. H., Huismans, S. E., Hofstede, G., & Daan, S. (1999). Temperature, cultural masculinity, and domestic political violence: A cross-national study. *Journal of Cross-Cultural Psychology*, *30*(3), 291–314.

Vandello, J. A., & Bosson, J. K. (2013). Hard won and easily lost: A review and synthesis of theory and research on precarious manhood. *Psychology of Men & Masculinity*, *14*(2), 101.

Vandello, J. A., & Cohen, D. (2008). Culture, gender, and men's intimate partner violence. *Social and Personality Psychology Compass*, *2*(2), 652–667.

Vandello, J. A., Cohen, D., & Ransom, S. (2008). US Southern and Northern differences in perceptions of norms about aggression: Mechanisms for the perpetuation of a culture of honor. *Journal of Cross-Cultural Psychology*, *39*(2), 162–177.

Voland, E. (1998). Evolutionary ecology of human reproduction. *Annual Review of Anthropology*, *27*(1), 347–374.

Vrij, A., Van der Steen, J., & Koppelaar, L. (1994). Aggression of police officers as a function of temperature: An experiment with the fire arms training system. *Journal of Community & Applied Social Psychology*, *4*(5), 365–370.

White, J. W., & Kowalski, R. M. (1994). Deconstructing the myth of the nonaggressive woman: A feminist analysis. *Psychology of Women Quarterly*, *18*(4), 487–508.

Zeichner, A., & Pihl, R. O. (1979). Effects of alcohol and behavior contingencies on human aggression. *Journal of Abnormal Psychology*, *88*(2), 153.

Zillman, D. (1979). *Hostility and aggression*. Erlbaum.

Chapter 8

Soft drinks, President Obama and the reduction of prejudice

"Stereotypes", "prejudice", and "discrimination" – these are all terms that we hear a lot in the media. But what do these terms mean? Aronson et al. (2014) distinguish between them in terms of whether they are affective, behavioural, or cognitive in nature. Stereotypes, for example, represent the cognitive component (the beliefs about a group and the qualities they possess). Prejudice represents the affective component (how we feel about those in a group) and discrimination represents the behavioural component (how we act in response to others in a group). Stereotypes can lead to prejudice. Esses et al. (1993), for example, reported a positive correlation between stereotypes (beliefs) and prejudice (feelings) towards social groups and issues. Similarly, prejudice can lead to discrimination. Pereira et al. (2010) demonstrated a link between prejudicial feelings towards immigrants and behavioural opposition to immigration.

It is important to note, however, that stereotypes in themselves can help us to make sense of the world by allowing generalisations. They are not always negative and can be true to some extent. For example, the older we get, the frailer we get. The difficulty arises when we over-generalise, something that Myers and Twenge (2016) refer to as the 10% problem. For example, Greitemeyer (2009) asked "Are singles what we think?" and reported a stereotype of single people as being less extraverted and agreeable, less conscientious and physically attractive and more neurotic than those in relationships.

STEREOTYPES OF GENDER

Let's do a quick thought experiment. Close your eyes and imagine what this person might look like: a professor of physics. Now, imagine what a kind nurse might look like. Chances are, that in the

DOI: 10.4324/9781003396208-8

first instance, you imagined a male and in the second a female. I may be wrong but according to Eagly and Sczesny (2009) stereotypes of gender roles are very pervasive with women being seen as suitable for support roles and men for leadership roles. Fiske et al. (2018) identified warmth and competence as traits that we use when evaluating others. However, there is a tendency, they report, for women to be seen as high on warmth but for men to be the reverse. This view of women is similar to the view of other low status, non-threatening groups. Eagly and Mladinic (1994) dubbed this the "Women are wonderful" effect. The emphasis on warmth leads to more positive feelings towards women compared to men.

However, it is not all sweetness and roses. In terms of competence, women tend to be seen as low in competence compared to men. This can have implications in the workplace. Heilman et al. (2004) asked undergraduate students to participate in a study of personnel decision-making. They were given an information pack containing details of the position being advertised which was an Assistant Vice-President for sales in an aircraft company. The responsibilities included not only training and supervising more junior staff but also keeping on top of industry trends in product development (e.g. engine assemblies, fuel tanks). In addition, the details of ten potential employees were included. Of the ten, only two were women. Participants could see a check mark against three of the potential employees that they were being asked to review. One was a woman and the other two men. The second of the two men was used to try and disguise the nature of the study and data was not used from this review. A sheet containing information about each person's background and status currently in the organisation was provided. This indicated whether they had evidenced clear success in their roles or whether they were about to have their appraisal. The descriptions were used for the female half the time and the male half the time. When there was some ambiguity about success, women were seen as significantly less competent than men. When there was clear evidence of success, women were seen as equally competent but they were liked less and were considered hostile.

How about when women become mothers? According to Cuddy et al. (2004), mothers who work, trade their perceived competence for perceived warmth. This has negative implications as people report less interest in the recruitment or career development of these individuals as a result. For working men who become fathers, the same does not apply. They gain in perceptions of warmth but perceived competence remains stable. Joshi et al. (2015) conducted a huge meta-analysis of over 100 studies, pooling data from over 370,000 employees. Salary bonuses and promotions were found to be 14 times larger for males than that predicted from performance data.

Does this mean that women are less likely to achieve higher positions of leadership within organisations? Not necessarily. Women are more likely to be appointed to board positions when a company is in a state of crisis than when things are going well (Bruckmüller et al., 2014). The authors gathered data from all FTSE 100 companies that had appointed a woman to their board of directors in 2003. They then gathered data from all FTSE 100 companies that had appointed a man to a similar role in the same year. Would you believe it? Those appointing a man to this role were significantly more likely to have had a relatively stable performance on the stock market over the previous year than those appointing a woman. Ryan and Haslam (2005) referred to this as the "glass cliff".

Where women are seen to be successful on a male-related task, such performance is more often attributed to luck than to talent, the reverse of what happens for men (Deaux & Emswiller, 1974). When men are successful on a female-related task though, it is skill and talent that continues to dominate attributions.

■ **Figure 8.1** Gender stereotypes can influence job decisions as in Ryan and Haslam's glass cliff metaphor.

Even in education, stereotypes about gender can play a big role in student evaluations. Teacher behaviours tend to be rated more highly when the teacher is identified by a male as opposed to a female name (MacNell et al., 2015) and science students tend to be seen as less talented when female as opposed to male (Leslie et al., 2015). The pervasiveness of gender stereotypes extends even to the media. Take a look at how men and women are depicted in the media. Chances are that you will find:

> *there is a pronounced tendency to represent men with their faces and women with their bodies.*
>
> (Archer et al., 1983, p. 727)

This is thought to represent stereotypes that emphasise qualities associated with the face, for men such as personality and intellect. We know from Schwarz and Kurz (1989) that if an individual is evaluated with a high degree of facial prominence, they are likely to be rated as more intelligent, assertive and ambitious. For women, however, it is physical attractiveness that is emphasised instead, hence the focus on the body. It is interesting to note that male politicians are represented with higher facial prominence than female politicians according to Konrath and Schwarz (2007). They aptly named their paper "Do male politicians have big heads?"

It is not just gender where pervasive stereotypes exist. Cuddy et al. (2005) report consistent stereotyping of the elderly across six non-US countries. Elderly people are stereotyped as being both warm but incompetent, not too dissimilar from the stereotype of women mentioned earlier. Similar to what we saw with gender stereotypes, when individuals behave in a way that does not fit with the stereotype, we tend to like them less. Undergraduates were presented with information about an individual named George. George was described as a 71-year-old retired plumber who is physically active, playing golf, and going for long walks. In one condition, the students were also told that George had recently experienced some memory problems and had to spend 30 minutes looking for his keys (high incompetence). In another condition, they were instead told that George prides himself on his perfect memory although last week he spent 30 minutes looking for his keys (low incompetence). When rating George's personality, the students rated him as warmer when he was perceived to be high in incompetence. That is, they rewarded stereotypical consistent behaviour.

It is important to note that stereotypes do not just influence the judgement of observers of others but can affect individuals who are subject to these stereotypes. Spencer et al. (2016) refer to this effect as stereotype threat. Negative stereotypes about an individual's group can cause them to be worried about being judged negatively as a result. To illustrate this, Spencer et al. (1999) asked students who were good at maths to complete a difficult maths test. Women underperformed compared to men. When told that the test was one that did not show gender differences, women performed equally as well as men. Steele et al. (2002) believed this demonstrated the effect of stereotype threat that is the stereotype about women being less talented at maths compared to men causing a detriment in performance. Steele and Aronson (1995) used a similar paradigm with students of white and black African American origin. A test of verbal ability was used. According to Steele and Aronson, the stereotype threat here is related to negative stereotypes about the intellectual ability of African Americans. When told that the test was a test of verbal ability, black participants performed a full standard deviation lower than white participants. When told that the test was a test of problem solving and no relationship to verbal ability, there was no difference in performance of the two groups. The idea that stereotype threat was at play here was further suggested when participants were asked to complete a pre-test involving 80 incomplete words. Of the 80 words, ten could be completed to form stereotype-related words and five could be completed to form self-doubt related words. When African American participants were expected to take the verbal ability task, they completed the words to form stereotype relevant and self-doubt related words more often than white participants.

WHY DO WE USE STEREOTYPES?

Given the potential of stereotypes to negatively affect behaviour, why do we use them? One idea is that it helps us to conserve cognitive effort (Bodenhausen, 1993). Human beings are "cognitive misers" (Fiske & Russell, 2010). We try to expend as little effort as possible due to the overwhelming demand on our limited cognitive ability. Not surprisingly then, many of these stereotypes are automatically triggered as we try to make sense of the world around us. Particularly in ambiguous situations, this can lead us to jump to unwarranted conclusions. Payne (2001) primed participants with pictures of either black or white faces on a computer screen. They were then asked to classify a picture as a gun or as a tool as quickly as possible. Those exposed to black faces in the priming part of the task were not only faster at identifying guns compared to those exposed to white faces but

■ Figure 8.2 Scrooge isn't the only miser if we believe Fiske and Russell (2010).

were also more likely to make errors in identifying tools as guns too. Similarly Eberhardt et al. (2004) reported that participants needed less perceptual information to identify crime-relevant objects when they had been primed with black as opposed to white faces. What this tells us is that although stereotypes function to give us a framework for organising information about people that means we can understand our social world more easily, the downside to this is we often lose accuracy (Corcoran & Mussweiler, 2010).

One attempt to illustrate the accuracy problem is the illusory correlation theory (Hamilton & Gifford, 1976). According to this theory, we have a tendency to associate distinctive things that co-occur. For example, if a particularly unusual behaviour occurs, and a particular group of individuals are considered to be less frequently occurring in society, then we tend to associate the two. How might this lead to stereotypes? If an individual has less contact with a person from a minority group, they have fewer opportunities to observe their behaviour. Negative behaviours are less common than positive behaviours. Hence, we are more likely to associate negative behaviours with individuals from minority groups. Both are infrequent and hence distinctive and therefore we associate the two.

Hamilton and Gifford presented participants with 39 statements, some of which described desirable behaviours. Eighteen of these statements were described as being true of individuals from Group A and nine as being true of individuals from Group B. Some of the statements described undesirable behaviours. Eight of these were described as being true of individuals from Group A and four of individuals from Group B. Although less statements related to Group B individuals overall, the ratio of desirable to undesirable behaviours was similar. When later asked to estimate the number of statements about each group that mentioned undesirable behaviours, they overestimated the number for Group B. When asked to decide what traits described members of each group, you've guessed it – Group B came out worse with more undesirable traits associated with its members. The stereotypes, caused by illusory correlations, led to prejudicial attitudes.

This heuristic-based way of thinking about social categories requires less energy than the self-control needed to overcome them. Gailliot et al. (2009) wanted to find out what happened when participants were given a sugary drink to consume before taking part in a task that required them to write about a stigmatised individual, a gay man. The sugary drink appeared to reduce the number of homosexual stereotypes used in the essay and reduced the number of remarks considered to be prejudicial (See Table 8.1). Glucose appeared to provide the energy needed to self-regulate their responses. One word of warning however. Alcohol, whilst containing sugar, is not going to help much at all (although you may already have guessed that from a previous chapter!). Bartholomew and Allison (2006) found alcohol to be a disrupter of the ability to stop responding in a stereotypical fashion!

We may not necessarily be aware of the cognitive processing that determines stereotypes. DeSteno et al. (2004), for example, points to the way that emotional states can exacerbate stereotypical judgments automatically. New York City residents were asked to take part in a judgement task. They had to estimate the frequency of different events. On the basis of their results, they were told they were either in the group "over-estimators" and

■ **Table 8.1** Mean number (and SD) of stereotypes used about homosexuals in the essays written by participants according to experimental condition.

Condition	Mean	Standard deviation
Sucrose	1.66	2.06
Control	2.97	2.06

Data taken from Gailliot et al. (2009).

given a blue wristband or the group "under-estimators" and given a red wristband. They were shown a word (good or bad in meaning) for 200 ms, followed by a picture of a member of either their group or the other "out-group" for 200 ms before a grey "mask" covered the screen. Participants had to then say whether the picture related to their group or the out-group. In the next part of the study, participants were asked to recall and write about a memory from their past that made them feel angry, sad, or emotionally neutral. They were then asked to repeat the priming task with the words and photos.

Those who had been asked to recall an event from their past that made them angry were significantly slower to associate positive compared to negative attributes with the out-group. Anger, the authors claim, is associated with conflict and aggression and hence triggers us not just to activate stereotypes but to show prejudice in evaluating out-groups more negatively.

WE FAVOUR OUR OWN

Feeling positively about the groups that we belong to is something that Social Identity Theory proposes (Tajfel & Turner, 1978; Tajfel et al., 1979). This tendency can lead us to express favouritism towards members of our own groups and to demonstrate prejudice to out-groups. Allen and Wilder (1979) presented participants with pairs of slides, one showing a painting by Klee and one showing a painting by Kandinsky. Participants declared which one they preferred. After this part of the study, participants were told that they were being placed into a group based on which artist they preferred (although in reality this was random) and were asked to complete a questionnaire giving their opinions about political and social issues. Participants were then asked to make predictions about what other individuals either from their own group or the other group would say about these questions. You can probably guess what happened. Yes, those in their own group were considered to have more similar opinions to their own, even though they had no idea who these people were. Moreover, when Tajfel asked participants to decide how to allocate money to individuals, they showed a distinct in-group favouritism, awarding their own group more.

What happens when a member of our in-group behaves in a socially undesirable way or is seen to be unsuccessful? According to Miller (2009), we distance ourselves from them. Miller calls this "Cutting Off Reflected Failure" or CORF. If a member of our in-group behaves in a socially desirable or successful way, however, we seek

■ **Figure 8.3** People supporting Barack Obama in the 2008 presidential campaign showed BIRG according to Miller (2009).

to promote our connection with them. Miller called this "Basking In Reflected Glory" or BIRG. In both cases, we are motivated to seek a positive identity from the membership of groups we are in. Miller studied the effect of the 2008 presidential election campaign outcome on attitudes and behaviour. Not only did those supporting the successful candidate (Obama) display signs supporting his campaign for longer after the election but those who had supported the losing candidate (McCain) decreased their ratings of him whilst Obama supporters increased their ratings of him. CORF was particularly strong for those low in self-esteem.

PREJUDICE AND THREAT

So why are we more likely to show prejudice to out-group members? One idea is that it is fuelled by feelings of threat. Das et al. (2009) found a link between news about terrorism and prejudicial attitudes. Hearing about a terrorist attack led to an increase in death-related thoughts which in turn increased prejudicial attitudes towards out-group members. Choma et al. (2015) found a similar relationship between viewing footage of events from the 9/11 disaster and increased prejudice towards out-groups. Landau et al. (2004) claimed that the increased threat caused an increase in identification with the US nation and representatives of it such as George Bush.

Branscombe and Wann (1994) demonstrated the threat factor in their "Rocky" study. In one condition, participants saw Rocky, an American boxer, beat a Russian opponent. In condition 2, they saw Rocky lose to a Russian opponent. The more highly people identified as American, the more prejudice they demonstrated towards the Russian in condition 2. In this condition, their national identity had been threatened. Shepherd et al. (2018) suggest that a similar scenario lays behind prejudice towards immigrant groups. They compared the effect of telling white British participants either that immigrants would outnumber British people living in Britain in the next 40 years (threat condition) or that the proportion of immigrants in the United Kingdom will remain unchanged (control condition). Those in the threat condition were more likely to show a willingness to engage in collective action against immigration and to show prejudice in their evaluation of immigrants.

Schmitt et al. (2007) used a different illustration of prejudice to illustrate the power of threat. They studied attitudes towards same-sex marriage in heterosexual individuals. At the time of their study, this was considered to present a threat to the distinctiveness of heterosexual identity for many. Participants were asked to say whether they favoured a same-sex law that would provide couples with all the rights and benefits provided to heterosexual married couples. The only difference between the two conditions was whether the same-sex law was referred to as a same-sex marriage law or a same-sex civil union law.

Merely sharing the label of marriage was sufficient to increase fear for group identity in heterosexuals and hence reduce the number who declared they would support the implementation of the law.

It is no accident that hate crimes increase as minorities are seen to gain political power. Branscombe et al. (2007) points to the example of increased equality initiatives in the United States. Increases in racism were seen in their study, when white Americans who identified with their racial group were questioned about privileges associated with their race. Such questioning can evoke justification of existing differences the authors claim.

PREJUDICE AND SCARCE RESOURCES

One reason why this may occur is due to limited resources. This is the idea behind Realistic Conflict Theory proposed by LeVine and Campbell (1972). In any situation where resources are limited and competition for these arises, hostility will develop. These situations often lead to what is known as zero sum outcomes where one group "wins" and another group "loses". There are plenty of examples in the literature of how this may manifest itself. For example, Butz and Yogeeswaran (2011) reported an increase in prejudice against Asian Americans following the presentation of information about how competition for scarce resources was increasing due to economic decline. Similarly, Filindra and Pearson-Merkowitz (2013) demonstrated how pessimism about the future of a state's economy correlates with support for "restrictionist" immigration policy. This is not a new idea. As far back as 1961, Sherif was conducting a field study to demonstrate this in action. Boys attending a summer camp were divided into two groups, the "Rattlers" and the "Eagles". The groups competed against each other to win limited resources such as medals, trophies, and even a pocket knife. Such competition led to hostility that quickly escalated to the extent that the opposing group's flag was burned, they broke into each other's cabins and overturned beds and fought. The only thing that seemed to counter this was when members of both groups had to work together to achieve superordinate goals, that is goals that required them to cooperate.

Some people may be more driven to show prejudice than others if we believe Adorno et al.'s theory of the Authoritarian Personality (1950). The theory arose from the observation that those who appeared to hold hostile attitudes towards Jewish people tended to also hold hostile attitudes towards other minority groups. Adorno believed that prejudice towards out-groups was the result of having overpowering parents who endorsed harsh discipline. Having such parents led to the displacing of hostility onto weaker sources as it was impossible to express this to the parents themselves.

PREJUDICE AND IGNORANCE

Not everyone agrees however. Allport proposed a different idea, the contact hypothesis. According to Allport (1954), prejudice is linked to a lack of contact with out-groups. This leads to a lack of knowledge of their beliefs and values. Zajonc (1968) suggested that the more we see someone the more we like them (the mere exposure effect). Allport believes the same may be true when it comes to prejudice. Deutsch and Collins (1951) studied what happened in two different housing developments, one in New York City and one in Newark, New Jersey. In New York City, the public housing development was desegregated with people of different racial origins living as neighbours. In Newark, the housing development was segregated. What difference did this make to prejudicial attitudes? According to the authors, those in segregated housing held stronger prejudicial attitudes. Lack of knowledge of out-groups led to fear and a strengthening of differences. Similarities were more easily overlooked. For those in the de-segregated housing, they held much more positive attitudes towards their neighbours, regardless of race. Quinton (2019) demonstrated this in a study exploring attitudes towards international students at the University at Buffalo, SUNY in the United States. Greater socialisation with international students correlated with a reduction in negative attitudes towards them.

So is more connection and interaction the key? Not necessarily. Pettigrew et al. (2011) remind us that negative contact can enhance prejudice and Pettigrew and Tropp (2006) found contact to be effective only if friendships are formed with out-group members. Emotional ties are important and friendships often promote cooperation and working towards common goals. Friendships also have another positive contribution to make in reducing prejudice. Paolini et al. (2004) suggest that if friends of ours are friends with members of an out-group, this can also reduce our own prejudice. They studied prejudicial attitudes between Catholics and Protestants in Northern Ireland. Not only did having a friend in the opposing religious group promote the reduction of prejudice against that group but knowing someone from your own group who had a friend in the opposing religious group also had the same effect. For example, if a Catholic individual's friend was good pals with at least one Protestant, this was sufficient to reduce prejudice in the Catholic individual themselves. Wright et al. (1997) refer to this as the extended contact hypothesis. Knowing that members of groups we identify with have positive interactions with members of out-groups reduces prejudicial attitudes in us.

Given that simple awareness that a friend has positive interactions with a member of an "out-group" is sufficient to reduce prejudice, Crisp and Turner (2009) posited that simply imagining contact with an out-group might be sufficient to have the same effect. Turner and Crisp (2010) asked participants to imagine talking to an elderly stranger. They were then asked to complete some semantic-differential scales to measure their attitudes towards elderly people. Semantic-differential scales have opposing traits listed such as warm-cold and positive-negative. Participants asked to imagine contact showed more positive attitudes towards the elderly than those who were asked to imagine an outdoor scene. In a second study, they asked non-Muslim individuals to imagine meeting a Muslim individual for the first time. They were asked to imagine a positive, relaxed, and comfortable meeting. Again, imagined contact led to more positive attitudes towards Muslim individuals compared to those asked to simply think about Muslims. This effect seems to span across a variety of groups. If a heterosexual man is asked to imagine discussing a novel they are reading with a homosexual man sitting next to them on a train, again any prejudicial attitudes are reduced (Turner et al., 2007).

Given the impact of even imagined contact with out-group members, it is worth pointing out that this has implications beyond simple friendships. Plant et al. (2009) identified the "Obama Effect". High levels of exposure to Barack Obama during his presidential campaign reduced both anti-Black stereotyping and implicit prejudice in a student population. Having a positive exemplar impacted individuals' ability to think of other positive exemplars and this in turn reduced implicit prejudice.

A MORE SUBTLE FORM?

So, does this spell an end for prejudice and its behavioural manifestation, discrimination? Unfortunately, not. Harber (1998) believes that discrimination, following prejudicial attitudes is just becoming less subtle. White students studying at Stanford University were asked to give feedback on two essays, one of which, they were told, had been written by a black student and one written by a white student. Although they focused on different content, the essays were of comparable length, quality, and structure. Despite this, the essay believed to have been written by a black student was rated much more favourably, more positive comments were given about the content and fewer negative comments were given. Summary comments given at the end of the feedback were significantly more supportive when participants believed the author of the essay was black. The implications of this sort of reverse discrimination (Pincus, 2003) can be far-reaching. As Harber writes:

Inflated praise and insufficient criticism may dissuade minority students from striving toward greater achievement levels and may misrepresent the level of effort and mastery that academic and professional advancement entail.

(p. 627)

In addition, just because people don't express prejudicial attitudes, doesn't mean they don't hold them. Monin and Miller (2001) point to the increasing social anxiety associated with the possibility of being labelled as either sexist or racist. Snyder et al. (1979) asked participants to evaluate a movie. They can choose which movie to watch. Two monitors, separated by a screen, are used to display the different movies. A confederate is already sitting in front of each monitor. One of the confederates is from a stigmatised minority group (e.g. disabled or black). The other is from a majority group. Because different movies are showing on each screen, participants feel more comfortable to sit next to the majority group member rather than the stigmatised minority group member. However, when the same movie is playing on both monitors, participants feel more uncomfortable to do so. Why? Because now it would reflect clearly the wish to avoid the stigmatised other.

Monin and Miller (2001) wanted to investigate what would happen if participants were given an opportunity to establish themselves as a non-prejudiced individual initially. Students from Princeton University were asked to state their agreement or disagreement with five sexist statements about women such as "Most women are better off at home taking care of the children". For one third of participants, the statements began with "most", for another third, they began with "some" and for the final third, they did not have any statements to evaluate at all. All participants were then asked to read three vignettes which required them to make a decision about who to offer a stereotypically male job to. For example, they were asked to imagine being the manager of a small cement company looking to recruit a client to visit building sites. Male participants who evaluated statements that used the word "most", and did so negatively were more likely to suggest that a job was better suited to a male than those who saw the word "some" in the statements. It was as though the chance to demonstrate their lack of prejudice had given them free reign to express discriminatory behaviour afterwards. Morin and Miller refer to this as "moral credentialing". The more confident an individual is that they are unprejudiced, the less they are concerned about whether future behaviour can be construed as prejudiced.

One way that such moral credentialing can occur is through engaging in a small but positive behaviour towards a member of a minority group This "tokenism" was neatly demonstrated in a study of begging behaviour by Dutton and Lennox (1974). Participants were given false information that suggested their physiological reactions indicated that they held negative views about the individuals they saw presented in the slides. On their way to collect their payment for the study, they then met a beggar who was either black or white. Two days later, the participants were asked to complete a questionnaire asking if they would donate their time to help an interracial campaign. Those who had donated to the black beggar, were significantly less likely to offer help with the campaign. Providing token help initially reduced their willingness to provide more help later on.

Rosenfield et al. (1982) argues that this may be too simplistic a view however. In a similar set up to Dutton and Lennox, they presented participants with similarly false information about their physiological responses to interracial social scenes. On going to collect payment for their role in the study, they encountered a confederate who either asked them to spare some change for food or asked them to sign a petition. On returning to the laboratory, participants completed a questionnaire asking if they would be willing to engage in volunteer work and if so, to what extent they could get involved. Some of the activities pertained to general causes (e.g. Mental Health Week) and some to black causes (e.g. Black Awareness Symposium). In terms of willingness to donate money, 82% did so when the beggar (or "panhandler" as they called the person) was black. Only 45% did so when the beggar was white. However, those who had donated money to the black beggar were significantly less likely to then volunteer to help black causes after. This was not the case when they had been asked to sign a petition by a black person. The token gesture to the beggar, Rosenfield et al. argue, created a negative impression of black individuals and hence reinforced negative stereotypes. Tokenism only occurs when the initial encounter reinforces negative stereotypes.

Even if we put tokenism aside, subtle forms of discrimination can still be observed. Norton et al. (2006) presented participants with photographs on a computer screen. The photographs varied in terms of race, age, gender, colour of the background, hair

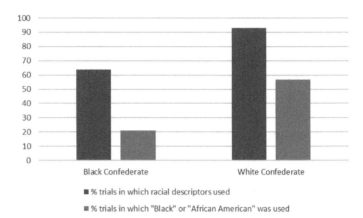

■ **Figure 8.4** What happens when someone is asked to describe a black or a white confederate? Data taken from Norton et al. (2006), study 2.

colour, and facial expression. The sorting task required them to categorise each photo, for example, as white or black if race were the category. In the hypothetical task, they were asked to imagine they were performing the sorting task and were asked to rank the dimensions in terms of how quickly they thought they could categorise exemplars. White participants underestimated the speed with which they could categorise photos by race by overestimated the speed with which they could categorise gender. Black participants were able to make much more accurate estimates of their categorisation speed. White participants, they argue, were trying to ensure they appeared unprejudiced in terms of race.

In a second study, Norton and colleagues employed participants to take part in what they called the political correctness game. Participants were paired with a confederate whom they believed to be another participant. In one condition, the confederate was white and in another the confederate was black. The study was fixed so that the participant was always the questionner. The answerer was given a six-page booklet and was asked to open this. On each page was one photograph. The job for the questionner was to ask as few yes/no questions as possible to identify the photograph the answerer was looking at. When the confederate was white, participants were significantly more likely to mention race in their questions compared to when the confederate was black. The result of this was to make participants less efficient at the task when paired with a black confederate as they failed to use an efficient strategy. It also led to other unexpected consequences. Independent raters judged participants who avoided mentioning race to appear more unfriendly.

SO, WHERE TO NEXT?

Where does this leave our story of prejudice? Will we ever eliminate it? I'm going to leave you with a controversial claim to ponder on. According to Bloom (2016), prejudice is natural. It only becomes harmful when we do not use our judgement and empathy to temper it.

> *We have gut feelings, instincts, emotions, and they affect our judgments and our actions for good and for evil, but we are also capable of rational deliberation and intelligent planning, and we can use these to, in some cases, accelerate and nourish our emotions, and in other cases staunch them. And it's in this way that reason helps us create a better world.*
>
> (Paul Bloom, 2016)

REFERENCES

Adorno, T. W., Frenkel-Brunswik, E., Levinson, D., & Sanford, N. (1950). *The authoritarian personality*. New York: W. W. Norton

Allen, V. L., & Wilder, D. A. (1979). Group categorization and attribution of belief similarity. *Small Group Behavior*, *10*(1), 73–80.

Allport, G. W. (1954). *The nature of prejudice*. Perseus Books.

Aronson, E., Wilson, T. D., & Akert, R. M. (2014). *Social psychology* (8th ed.). Pearson Education.

Archer, D., Iritani, B., Kimes, D. D., & Barrios, M. (1983). Face-ism: Five studies of sex differences in facial prominence. *Journal of Personality and Social Psychology*, *45*(4), 725.

Bartholomew, K., & Allison, C. J. (2006). An attachment perspective on abusive dynamics in intimate relationships. In M. Mikulincer & G. S. Goodman (Eds.), *Dynamics of romantic love: Attachment, caregiving, and sex* (pp. 102–127). The Guilford Press

Bloom, P. (2016). *Against empathy: The case for rational compassion*. Harper Collins.

Bodenhausen, G. V. (1993). Emotions, arousal, and stereotypic judgments: A heuristic model of affect and stereotyping. In D. M. Mackie & D. L. Hamilton (Eds.), *Affect, cognition, and stereotyping* (pp. 13–37). New York: Academic.

Branscombe, N. R., Schmitt, M. T., & Schiffhauer, K. (2007). Racial attitudes in response to thoughts of White privilege. *European Journal of Social Psychology*, *37*(2), 203–215.

Branscombe, N. R., & Wann, D. L. (1994). Collective self-esteem consequences of outgroup derogation when a valued social identity is on trial. *European Journal of Social Psychology*, *24*(6), 641–657.

Bruckmüller, S., Ryan, M. K., Rink, F., & Haslam, S. A. (2014). Beyond the glass ceiling: The glass cliff and its lessons for organisational policy. *Social Issues and Policy Review*, *8*(1), 202–232.

Butz, D. A., & Yogeeswaran, K. (2011). A new threat in the air: Macroeconomic threat increases prejudice against Asian Americans. *Journal of Experimental Social Psychology, 47*(1), 22–27.

Choma, B. L., Charlesford, J. J., Dalling, L., & Smith, K. (2015). Effects of viewing 9/11 footage on distress and islamophobia: A temporally expanded approach. *Journal of Applied Social Psychology, 45*(6), 345–354.

Corcoran, K., & Mussweiler, T. (2010). The cognitive miser's perspective: Social comparison as a heuristic in self-judgements. *European Review of Social Psychology, 21*(1), 78–113.

Crisp, R. J., & Turner, R. N. (2009). Can imagined interactions produce positive perceptions?: Reducing prejudice through simulated social contact. *American Psychologist, 64*(4), 231.

Cuddy, A. J., Fiske, S. T., & Glick, P. (2004). When professionals become mothers, warmth doesn't cut the ice. *Journal of Social Issues, 60*(4), 701–718.

Cuddy, A. J., Norton, M. I., & Fiske, S. T. (2005). This old stereotype: The pervasiveness and persistence of the elderly stereotype. *Journal of Social Issues, 61*(2), 267–285.

Das, E., Bushman, B. J., Bezemer, M. D., Kerkhof, P., & Vermeulen, I. E. (2009). How terrorism news reports increase prejudice against outgroups: A terror management account. *Journal of Experimental Social Psychology, 45*(3), 453–459.

Deaux, K., & Emswiller, T. (1974). Explanations of successful performance on sex-linked tasks: What is skill for the male is luck for the female. *Journal of Personality and Social Psychology, 29*(1), 80.

DeSteno, D., Dasgupta, N., Bartlett, M. Y., & Cajdric, A. (2004). Prejudice from thin air: The effect of emotion on automatic intergroup attitudes. *Psychological Science, 15*(5), 319–324.

Deutsch, M., & Collins, M. E. (1951). *Interracial housing: A psychological evaluation of a social experiment.* University of Minnesota Press.

Dutton, D. G., & Lennox, V. L. (1974). Effect of prior "token" compliance on subsequent interracial behavior. *Journal of Personality and Social Psychology, 29*(1), 65.

Eagly, A. H., & Mladinic, A. (1994). Are people prejudiced against women? Some answers from research on attitudes, gender stereotypes, and judgments of competence. *European Review of Social Psychology, 5*(1), 1–35.

Eagly, A. H., & Sczesny, S. (2009). *Stereotypes about women, men, and leaders: Have times changed?* American Psychological Association.

Eberhardt, J. L., Goff, P. A., Purdie, V. J., & Davies, P. G. (2004). Seeing black: Race, crime, and visual processing. *Journal of Personality and Social Psychology, 87*(6), 876.

Esses, V. M., Haddock, G., & Zanna, M. P. (1993). Values, stereotypes, and emotions as determinants of intergroup attitudes. In D.M. Mackie, D.L. Hamilton (Eds.), *"Affect, Cognition, and Stereotyping: Interactive Processes in Group Perception"*, Academic Press, pp. 137–166.

Filindra, A., & Pearson-Merkowitz, S. (2013). Together in good times and bad? How economic triggers condition the effects of intergroup threat. *Social Science Quarterly, 94*(5), 1328–1345.

Fiske, S. T., Cuddy, A. J., Glick, P., & Xu, J. (2018). A model of (often mixed) stereotype content: Competence and warmth respectively follow from perceived status and competition. In S. Fiske (Ed) *Social cognition* (pp. 162–214). Routledge.

Fiske, S. T., & Russell, A. M. (2010). Cognitive processes. In *The SAGE handbook of prejudice, stereotyping and discrimination*. Sage (pp. 115–130).

Gailliot, M. T., Peruche, B. M., Plant, E. A., & Baumeister, R. F. (2009). Stereotypes and prejudice in the blood: Sucrose drinks reduce prejudice and stereotyping. *Journal of Experimental Social Psychology*, *45*(1), 288–290.

Greitemeyer, T. (2009). Stereotypes of singles: Are singles what we think? *European Journal of Social Psychology*, *39*(3), 368–383.

Hamilton, D. L., & Gifford, R. K. (1976). Illusory correlation in interpersonal perception: A cognitive basis of stereotypic judgments. *Journal of Experimental Social Psychology*, *12*(4), 392–407.

Harber, K. D. (1998). Feedback to minorities: Evidence of a positive bias. *Journal of Personality and Social Psychology*, *74*(3), 622.

Heilman, M. E., Wallen, A. S., Fuchs, D., & Tamkins, M. M. (2004). Penalties for success: Reactions to women who succeed at male gender-typed tasks. *Journal of Applied Psychology*, *89*(3), 416.

Joshi, A., Son, J., & Roh, H. (2015). When can women close the gap? A meta-analytic test of sex differences in performance and rewards. *Academy of Management Journal*, *58*(5), 1516–1545.

Konrath, S. H., & Schwarz, N. (2007). Do male politicians have big heads? Face-ism in online self-representations of politicians. *Media Psychology*, *10*(3), 436–448.

Landau, M. J., Solomon, S., Greenberg, J., Cohen, F., Pyszczynski, T., Arndt, J., & Cook, A. (2004). Deliver us from evil: The effects of mortality salience and reminders of 9/11 on support for President George W. Bush. *Personality and Social Psychology Bulletin*, *30*(9), 1136–1150.

Leslie, S. J., Cimpian, A., Meyer, M., & Freeland, E. (2015). Expectations of brilliance underlie gender distributions across academic disciplines. *Science*, *347*(6219), 262–265.

LeVine, R. A., & Campbell, D. T. (1972). *Ethnocentrism: Theories of conflict, ethnic attitudes, and group behaviour*. Wiley.

MacNell, L., Driscoll, A., & Hunt, A. N. (2015). What's in a name: Exposing gender bias in student ratings of teaching. *Innovative Higher Education*, *40*, 291–303.

Miller, C. B. (2009). Yes we did! Basking in reflected glory and cutting off reflected failure in the 2008 presidential election. *Analyses of Social Issues and Public Policy*, *9*(1), 283–296.

Monin, B., & Miller, D. T. (2001). Moral credentials and the expression of prejudice. *Journal of Personality and Social Psychology*, *81*(1), 33.

Myers, D. G., & Twenge, J. M. (2016) *Social psychology* (12th ed.). McGraw-Hill.

Norton, M. I., Sommers, S. R., Apfelbaum, E. P., Pura, N., & Ariely, D. (2006). Color blindness and interracial interaction: Playing the political correctness game. *Psychological Science*, *17*(11), 949–953.

Paolini, S., Hewstone, M., Cairns, E., & Voci, A. (2004). Effects of direct and indirect cross-group friendships on judgments of Catholics and Protestants in Northern Ireland: The mediating role of an anxiety-reduction mechanism. *Personality and Social Psychology Bulletin*, *30*(6), 770–786.

Payne, B. K. (2001). Prejudice and perception: The role of automatic and controlled processes in misperceiving a weapon. *Journal of Personality and Social Psychology*, *81*(2), 181.

Pereira, C., Vala, J., & Costa-Lopes, R. (2010). From prejudice to discrimination: The legitimizing role of perceived threat in discrimination against immigrants. *European Journal of Social Psychology, 40*(7), 1231–1250.

Pettigrew, T. F., & Tropp, L. R. (2006). A meta-analytic test of intergroup contact theory. *Journal of Personality and Social Psychology, 90*(5), 751.

Pettigrew, T. F., Tropp, L. R., Wagner, U., & Christ, O. (2011). Recent advances in intergroup contact theory. *International Journal of Intercultural Relations, 35*(3), 271–280.

Pincus, F. L. (2003). *Reverse discrimination: Dismantling the myth*. Lynne Rienner Publishers.

Plant, E. A., Devine, P. G., Cox, W. T., Columb, C., Miller, S. L., Goplen, J., & Peruche, B. M. (2009). The Obama effect: Decreasing implicit prejudice and stereotyping. *Journal of Experimental Social Psychology, 45*(4), 961–964.

Quinton, W. J. (2019). Unwelcome on campus? Predictors of prejudice against international students. *Journal of Diversity in Higher Education, 12*(2), 156.

Rosenfield, D., Greenberg, J., Folger, R., & Borys, R. (1982). Effect of an encounter with a black panhandler on subsequent helping for blacks: Tokenism or confirming a negative stereotype? *Personality and Social Psychology Bulletin, 8*(4), 664–671.

Ryan, M. K., & Haslam, S. A. (2005). The glass cliff: Evidence that women are over-represented in precarious leadership positions. *British Journal of Management, 16*(2), 81–90.

Schmitt, M. T., Lehmiller, J. J., & Walsh, A. L. (2007). The role of heterosexual identity threat in differential support for same-sex civil unions' versus marriages. *Group Processes & Intergroup Relations, 10*(4), 443–455.

Schwarz, N., & Kurz, E. (1989). What's in a picture? The impact of face-ism on trait attribution. *European Journal of Social Psychology, 19*(4), 311–316.

Shepherd, L., Fasoli, F., Pereira, A., & Branscombe, N. R. (2018). The role of threat, emotions, and prejudice in promoting collective action against immigrant groups. *European Journal of Social Psychology, 48*(4), 447–459.

Snyder, M. L., Kleck, R. E., Strenta, A., & Mentzer, S. J. (1979). Avoidance of the handicapped: An attributional ambiguity Analysis. *Journal of Personality and Social Psychology, 37*(12), 2297.

Spencer, S. J., Logel, C., & Davies, P. G. (2016). Stereotype threat. *Annual Review of Psychology, 67*, 415–437.

Spencer, S. J., Steele, C. M., & Quinn, D. M. (1999). Stereotype threat and women's math performance. *Journal of Experimental Social Psychology, 35*(1), 4–28.

Steele, C. M., & Aronson, J. (1995). Stereotype threat and the intellectual test performance of African Americans. *Journal of Personality and Social Psychology, 69*(5), 797.

Steele, C. M., Spencer, S. J., & Aronson, J. (2002). Contending with group image: The psychology of stereotype and social identity threat In M. P. Zanna (Ed.), *Advances in Experimental Social Psychology* (Vol. 34, pp. 379–440). Academic Press, Inc.

Tajfel, H., & Turner, J. C. (1978). Intergroup behavior. *Introducing Social Psychology*, *401*, 466.

Tajfel, H., Turner, J. C., Austin, W. G., & Worchel, S. (1979). An integrative theory of intergroup conflict. *Organizational Identity: A Reader*, *56*(65), 9780203505984–16.

Turner, R. N., & Crisp, R. J. (2010). Imagining intergroup contact reduces implicit prejudice. *British Journal of Social Psychology*, *49*(1), 129–142.

Turner, R. N., Crisp, R. J., & Lambert, E. (2007). Imagining intergroup contact can improve intergroup attitudes. *Group Processes & Intergroup Relations*, *10*(4), 427–441.

Wright, S. C., Aron, A., McLaughlin-Volpe, T., & Ropp, S. A. (1997). The extended contact effect: Knowledge of cross-group friendships and prejudice. *Journal of Personality and Social Psychology*, *73*(1), 73.

Zajonc, R. B. (1968). Attitudinal effects of mere exposure. *Journal of Personality and Social Psychology*, *9*(2p2), 1.

Chapter 9

Do groups make the best decisions?

WHAT IS "A GROUP" AND WHY DO WE FORM THEM?

What do we mean by a group? Cartwright and Zander (1968) defined a group as consisting of three or more people interacting with each other. A group, they suggest, consists of individuals who are interdependent. Why do we form groups? To find one possible answer, I am going to ask you to cast your mind back to your ancestral past because that is where Leary and Baumeister (1995) believe an answer lies. In those times, it made sense to be in a group so that you could ensure survival. You would be able to hunt together, to grow food more successfully, and to find mates and reproduce. Because of the importance of belonging to survival, people act in a way that ensures they will be socially accepted in groups and are alert to any signs of rejection (Pickett & Gardner, 2005).

Rejection is a cold feeling, quite literally. Zhong and Leonardelli (2008) asked undergraduates to recall a time when they felt either excluded or included. They were then asked to estimate the temperature of the room. Those who recalled feeling excluded estimated the temperature of the room to be three degrees lower than those who recalled feeling included. In a second study, participants took part in a virtual ball-tossing exercise. This was presented on the computer and participants were led to believe that they were playing with three other participants. In the exclusion condition, participants received the ball twice but then were excluded from the remaining throws. In the control condition, participants received the ball at points throughout the exercise. Following this, they were asked to complete a marketing survey which asked them to rate how much they wanted five different products: a hot drink, hot soup, an apple, crackers, or a drink. Those in the exclusion condition desired the hot drink and hot soup significantly more than those in the control condition. People's social experience, Zhong and Leonardelli claim, is intimately bound up with physical perception.

However, Brewer (2007) argues that we have an opposing need also which is to feel distinctive from others who do not belong to our group. It is one reason why Brewer believes we are drawn to small groups. Groups that are small give us a sense of belonging but also make us feel special and distinctive.

GROUPS HELP US PERFORM BETTER

Let me introduce you to the League of American Wheelmen. What? Yes, the League of American Wheelmen. This was an organisation that in the late 1800s ran cycling competitions in the United States. Not only that but also, they kept record books in which they recorded average speeds. Enter Triplett, a social psychologist who was interested in these record books because they suggested that cyclists who were racing against the clock tended to achieve slower times than those who raced alongside

■ **Figure 9.1** Triplett noticed that cyclists racing alongside others cycled faster than those racing against the clock.

others. This sparked an idea for Triplett. He brought girls and boys into the laboratory and gave them a really interesting task. Well, that might be distorting the truth a little. He asked them to wind a fishing reel which caused a small flag to move round a circuit. A small social facilitation effect was found with children performing faster when with others. (It is worth noting, however, that Stroebe (2012) re-analysed Triplett's data and reported the effect disappeared when two left-handed children's data were eliminated.)

This effect is now well replicated. Michaels et al. (1982) demonstrated this with students playing pool in the students union. Good pool players improved their potting performance by 9% in the presence of an audience! Zanbaka et al. (2004) even demonstrated social facilitation of a learned response using a virtual human!

In fact the effect holds up to scrutiny in other species too. Zajonc et al. (1969), for example, studied the behaviour of cockroaches. They constructed a runway task which consisted of a straight corridor with a bright light at one end and a darkened box at the other. In one condition, a cockroach was placed in the runway and the time taken to run to the darkened box was measured. In a different condition, other roaches were placed in plexiglass boxes lining the runway. Would the presence of a roach audience make any difference? According to Zajonc et al., yes, it did. The cockroach ran faster! Zajonc et al. suggested that the presence of the audience energised the dominant response in the cockroach, enhancing his running prowess.

It isn't just cockroaches though. Ants excavate more soil when with 1 or 2 other ants than when working alone (Chen, 1937), tadpoles swim faster when with others than when alone (Punzo, 1992), and chickens eat more grain when with others (Bayer, 1929). Bayer's study was particularly striking as he found that when hens were fed separately one day and in a group of four the next, they showed a 96% increase in the amount of food eaten in groups! A word of warning here too. Evidence suggests the same pattern applies for humans. Clendenen et al. (1994) reported that regardless of how many others were present, people eat more when with others than when alone. When it comes to dessert, being with friends rather than strangers can push us to consume significantly more! Ruddock et al. (2021) suggest that this could be an evolutionary strategy to ensure fitness. It is a way of sharing resources with others whilst at the same time ensuring you get what you need to sustain you.

BUT ONLY WHEN THE TASK IS SIMPLE

However, the picture may be a little more complicated than we are making out. Let's return to Zajonc's cockroach. Zajonc et al. also wanted to see what happened when the cockroach was placed in a maze as opposed to a runway. This is a more complex task as it is not immediately apparent which direction the cockroach should go. Does the presence of the roach audience make a difference now? Yes, but this time they slowed him down. The maze represents a more complex task and, on such tasks, groups can hinder our performance.

Returning to the pool players in the students union, Michaels et al. reported that it was only those whose performance was already good that showed social facilitation effects. Those who were poor players actually did even worse. Alone they average 36% of their shots being potted but with an audience, this dropped to 25%. Just in case you are wondering, it also works for food. Where food is unpalatable, social facilitation effects don't work (Pliner & Mann, 2004).

Is it just the complexity of the task that is relevant? One proposal is that it is the presence of others who are evaluating our performance that matters, not just their mere presence (Cottrell, 1972). Cottrell wanted to see what happened when a confederate in the room with a participant was blindfolded. Did social facilitation occur? No. According to Cottrell, no evaluation could occur. Worringham and Messick (1983) provided evidence to support

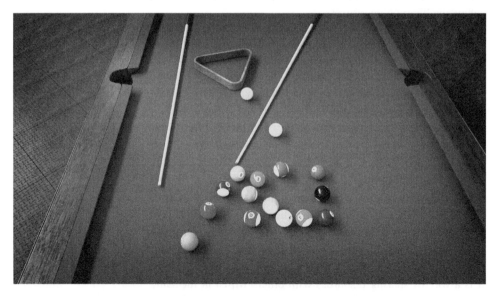

■ **Figure 9.2** The effect of an audience on pool players differs according to their experience.

Cottrell's idea. They measured the running speed of 36 runners whilst running along a path. Some did not encounter anyone else during their run. Some saw a woman sitting on the grass, at about the halfway point, with her back to them. Some saw the woman sitting facing them as they ran past. Who ran the fastest, do you think? Yes, you may have guessed from our story so far that it was the runners who were watched by the observer.

Mullen (1986) identified a similar effect with stutterers. As audience size increased, so did the amount of stuttering observed. The presence of others, Mullen claims, increases self-attention. Carver and Scheier (1981) suggest something similar, that is, that the presence of others causes us to focus our attention inward. If the task is a complex one, this can cause problems. Baron (1986) proposed a cognitive theory to explain this. When in the presence of others, we have to manage a greater amount of distraction. It is difficult for us to attend to the others present and to focus our attention on our individual performance. This conflict leads to more arousal which impacts our performance.

Wells and Skowronski (2012) demonstrated this in a study of golfers on the 2009 PGA Tour. When evaluation pressure was at its peak, in the final rounds, the more likely a player was to choke under pressure. This was especially the case if the player was close to the lead on the tournament board. Evaluation might not be an issue if the person doing this is familiar and well-liked. Gardner and Knowles (2008) provided an intriguing piece of evidence that suggests that having a favourite TV character displayed on your computer screen can cause social facilitation even on novel tasks. (But note: if it is not a favourite character, it doesn't work!)

WHEN IS A LOAF NOT A LOAF?

It looks as though groups can promote good performance at least when we are engaged in simple tasks. So, are groups good for us? The answer is, it depends. One of the factors it depends on is group size. I suspect you will have heard of a game called Tug-of-War. Two teams compete to pull a thick rope to their side of a marker. It is a test of strength. Back in 1913, Ringelmann [who Brown and Pehrson (2019) inform us, was an agricultural engineer], decided to conduct a study using a similar idea. He wanted to measure the force exerted by students in pulling on a rope. As part of this task, Ringelmann varied the size of the teams pulling on the rope. They were clearly strong students. When alone they pulled around 85 kg and in groups, this increased. When in a group of seven, for example, they pulled 450 kg. Hold on you might say. 450 is not seven times 85… Yes, Ringelmann noticed that too. In fact, the bigger the group got, the less force each individual exerted!

Latané et al. (1979) decided to demonstrate this effect in a laboratory study. Participants were seated in a semi-circle with up to five other participants. They were told that their task was twofold – to make noise and to judge noise. On each of 36 yelling or 36 clapping trials, the performers had to perform the required action for 5 seconds whilst observers had to listen. Both performers and observers were then asked to estimate the magnitude of the sound made. In line with Ringelmann's observation, the more people present, the lower the average sound made by each individual. When in a group of two, performance dropped to 71% of what they did as individuals. In groups of four, this dropped further to 51% and in groups of six, this dropped to 40%! This effect has since come to be known as "Social Loafing" (see Simms & Nichols, 2014 for a review).

The tendency to loaf is stronger in men than in women if Karau and Williams' meta-analysis is to be believed and culture also seems to make a difference (Karau & Williams, 1993). Collectivist, Eastern cultures tend to show less loafing than individualist, Western cultures. Gabrenya et al. (1983), for example, reported that Chinese graduate students showed the opposite trend to Latané, Williams, and Harkins' US students, increasing their efforts to 114% of their individual effort when with another person.

So, how do we eradicate or at least minimise the chance of social loafing occurring? One idea proposed by Williams et al. (1981) is to ensure that individual contributions to a task are monitored. Employment organisations have made use of this by encouraging the posting of individual performance to promote future performance (Lount & Wilk, 2014). Lount and Wilk suggest that doing this leads to better performance of groups because it enables social comparison between employees and consequently eradicates social loafing. Harkins and Jackson (1985) point to the importance of being able to compare individual performance with others' performance in the group as critical. There is an interesting aside to this. Schroeder et al. (2016) demonstrated how, as group size increases, if individual performance is not monitored, individuals tend to over-claim the role that they played to the group outcome. "Many hands make overlooked work" as the title of their paper reminds us.

A second idea was proposed by Kerr et al. (2007). Make sure the task is challenging so that an individual sees their contribution to the group as being essential. Worchel et al. (1998) similarly pointed to the importance of feeling you are an important part of a group to productivity.

WHEN GROUPS GO BAD

One reason why individual monitoring is important is that it also prevents deindividuation occurring. Deindividuation describes a situation where individuals lose their sense of individual identity and become absorbed in the norms of the group they are in (Festinger et al., 1963). Individuals do not believe they are being monitored as individuals.

Take the example of lynch mobs. Leader et al. (2007) identified a trend for more atrocities to be committed as the group size increased. Individuals were rendered more anonymous in the bigger groups. A similar message was shared by Mann (1981). Mann studied 21 different examples of someone threatening to jump from a bridge or building. As the crowd size grew, so did the likelihood of crowd baiting, where the crowd encourage the person to take the plunge. Silke (2003) studied 500 violent attacks that had occurred in Northern Ireland. Two hundred and six of these (41%) involved offenders who wore disguises of some description to mask their identity. These same individuals were found to have attacked more people, to have attacked them more violently, and to have engaged in more vandalism than those who were not disguised. These are quite extreme examples of course. But anything that increases a sense of anonymity works in increasing anti-social behaviour. Zhong et al. (2010) suggest that even wearing dark sunglasses can be sufficient to promote selfish behaviour and cheating is much more likely to occur when lights are dimmed.

■ **Figure 9.3** Sunglasses have a dark side too!

Group norms do make a difference however. Johnson and Downing (1979) asked individuals to supposedly administer shocks to another participant who made an error on a learning task. In one condition, participants were asked to wear a robe resembling those worn by members of the Ku Klux Klan. In another condition, they were asked to wear a nurse's uniform. When wearing the latter, shock levels administered were reduced compared to those wearing the robe. Johnson and Downing claim this illustrates the importance of situational factors in deindividuated behaviour.

To reduce deindividuation, the key is to ensure self-awareness is heightened. Sentyrz and Bushman (1998) gave college students the opportunity to taste cream cheese spreads. Some were full fat, some were reduced fat, and some were no-fat versions. In one condition, a large mirror was present. The effect of this was to reduce eating of the full-fat, less healthy option. Self-awareness was increased resulting in a more socially desirable behaviour occurring. Diener and Wallbom (1976) gave participants an anagram task to complete. In one condition, the self-aware condition, they were seated in front of a mirror listening to a recording of their own voice. In the other condition, the non-self-aware condition, they were seated at the side of a mirror and listened to a recording of someone else's voice. Raising self-awareness was sufficient to reduce cheating on the task. Only 7% did so in the self-aware condition compared to a whopping 71% in the non-self-aware condition!

DO GROUPS MAKE BETTER DECISIONS?

You may have seen a TV programme called "Who wants to be a millionaire?" In this quiz show, contestants have to answer a number of multiple-choice questions. If they get stuck, they have some helpful options they can use such as calling an expert or asking the audience. Which do you think is the most helpful of these? Surowiecki (2004) wanted to find out. Call an expert? The correct answer was given 65% of the time. Ask the audience? The correct answer was given 91% of the time! As Surowiecki writes:

> ... *chasing the expert is a mistake, and a costly one at that. We should ... ask the crowd.*
>
> (p. xv)

IT'S GOOD TO SHARE

However, for groups to make better decisions, it is important for members to share information effectively. As Watson et al. (1998) suggest, sometimes groups do not make best use of the knowledge of individual members. Actual productivity does not always align with potential productivity (Littlepage & Silbiger, 1992). Steiner (1972) referred to this as process loss. This is more likely to occur in groups where expertise is not recognised (Libby et al., 1987). Bottger (1984) asked groups of middle-level managers and graduate students to complete a problem-solving task, the NASA moon problem. Individuals who monopolised discussion in terms of the quantity of contributions were often mis-perceived to be the most influential but this did not necessarily lead to the best solutions. Those who had more expertise to share were more influential in determining success. To avoid process loss, therefore, groups need to ensure that the expertise of members is identified and exploited.

The benefit of recognising what each member brings to a task was nicely illustrated in a study reported by Stasser and Titus (1985). Participants were given information about potential candidates for the role of student president. In one condition, individuals were given the same information to read which clearly pointed to Candidate A as the best candidate. Candidate A had eight positive qualities but only four negative qualities whereas Candidates B and C had equal numbers of each. They were then asked to discuss, in groups of four, what their decision was. In a second condition, each of the four individuals were given slightly different information. They all had information which pointed to the same four negative qualities of candidate A but they each had unique information about two positive qualities of the individual. If the knowledge possessed by individual members was effectively exploited, the group should see that Candidate A had eight positive qualities and four negative and so, was the best candidate. However, this was not what happened. Instead, the group members focused on the shared information (the negative qualities) and rejected candidate A. Sharing of information is more important than just what you know.

It is possible to get groups to focus more on unshared info (often referred to as hidden profiles). Mojzisch and Schulz-Hardt (2010) recommend group members to not share their initial preferences at the outset but instead to pool the information they have first. Wittenbaum and Park (2001) suggest giving enough time in discussions for information to be shared and Stasser et al. (1995) advocate giving group members specific responsibility for certain types of information and ensuring that the group is aware of this from the outset.

DON'T ROCK THE BOAT!

Why do groups sometimes get a bad press then? When we are in a group, the desire to maintain solidarity within the group dominates. We may be too concerned with not upsetting the other members of our group than we are in reaching a good decision. Janis (1972) calls this "groupthink". Let's take a look at how this works.

Myers and Twenge (2016) give the example of the sinking of the Titanic. Captain Edward Smith was a renowned sea Captain with 38 years of experience. He made the decision to continue sailing the ship at full speed despite no less than four warnings about possible icebergs. The ship had been marketed as unsinkable and therefore Edward (and his crew) believed it was invulnerable. Indeed, the number of lifeboats had been cut from 64 to 16 so as not to spoil the view. Who needs lifeboats on an unsinkable ship? The crew dismissed the information being relayed from the lookout, so much so that the telegraph operator didn't bother to pass on the last and most complete iceberg warning. The result was the death of just under 1500 people.

This is not an isolated case of groupthink. In 2003, the US Space Shuttle, Columbia, was launched. Prior to this, an engineer, Rodney Rocha had made multiple requests to managers at NASA to look at satellite images of Columbia whilst it was in space on a previous mission. During that mission, foam had

■ **Figure 9.4** Did "groupthink" play a role in the sinking of the Titanic?

been seen breaking off and hitting an area of the shuttle where heat-shielding tiles were located. Rodney's requests were ignored. The result was that on the subsequent launch in 2003, all seven crew members lost their lives when the Columbia exploded (Dimitroff et al., 2005). What is particularly damning about this is that 18 years earlier, groupthink had been a big contributing factor to the space shuttle Challenger accident (Esser & Lindoerfer, 1989).

According to Aronson et al. (2014), there are certain conditions that make groupthink more likely. It is most likely to occur when a group is highly cohesive, isolated from contrary opinions, and when a leader makes their wishes known in a directive manner. People may not voice contrary views (self-censorship) because they are afraid of ruining the group's morale or because they fear being criticised by others. This was evidenced in the decisions made by President Lyndon Johnson and his Tuesday lunch group in the Vietnam War (Myers et al., 2010). Despite receiving numerous warnings from government intelligence experts and US allies about the unlikely success of the decision, Johnson and his policy makers made the decision to escalate the war in Vietnam. The result? Over 58k US and more than million Vietnamese lives were lost. The group was keen to suppress dissent and support the leader but clearly when a leader promotes an idea and doesn't listen to any opposition, defective decisions may be made. The cohesiveness of the group takes precedent, particularly when facing a threat as positive feelings are maintained.

Groupthink has been implicated in other political decisions such as the decision to invade Iraq (McClellan, 2008), the decision to invade Cuba in 1961 (Janis, 1982) and even the events that occurred at Pearl Harbour in 1941 (Myers et al., 2010). In all of these situations, there are key attributes of the group that lead to groupthink (Janis & Mann, 1977). There is an illusion of invulnerability and unanimity for example. Such groups hold excessive optimism that they will succeed. If people raise misgivings, they are quickly and thoroughly rebuffed and ridiculed. The pressure to conform is strong. Groups subject to groupthink are often closed minded, discounting any contrary opinions by justifying their group decisions and overestimating their strength. Schulz-Hardt et al. (2000) argue that groups do prefer to hear and discuss supporting information rather than anything that challenges the status quo. Johnson's team, for example, spent a disproportionate amount of time defending their decision rather than analysing prior decisions.

EXTREME DECISIONS AND RISKY SHIFTS

Groupthink is clearly a dangerous characteristic of some groups. But it isn't the only one. There is a tendency for groups to make decisions that are more extreme than the initial inclination of its members (Brown, 1965). Moscovici and Zavalloni (1969) call this "group polarisation".

Imagine that you are asked to interview potential job applicants. Would group discussion help or hinder your decision-making? Palmer and Loveland (2008) asked participants to rate the performance of lecturers. Compared to their ratings before group discussion, their decision-making showed a strong polarisation effect after it. The evaluation of each lecturer's performance became more polarised and extreme.

Imagine instead that you are managing a number of projects that are considered to be failing. You have to decide whether to invest more money in these in the hope of preventing further loss. Would you? This is a scenario that is all too common in industry. Whyte (1993) asked business students to put themselves in this position. Seventy-two percent said they would when questioned individually but in groups, this escalated to a whopping 94%!

Bekafigo et al. (2019) asked students who did not initially support Donald Trump in the 2016 Presidential campaign, to watch a series of videos of him talking about his views on a range of political issues. They were asked to rate their support for Trump on each issue. Following this, they were given the opportunity to discuss their views for two hours with a group. Guess what happened? Yes, their views became even more extreme in opposition to Trump than before the discussion. One suggestion is that group polarisation occurs as a result of hearing more persuasive arguments in support of their original point of view. This is known as the persuasive arguments theory (Burnstein and Vinokar, 1977).

Brauer et al. (2001) asked French students to read information about the behaviour of a group of adolescents who had spent a week at a youth camp. Seventy-two percent of behaviours were stereotypically selfish or cowardly and 25% were counter-stereotypic. When the students had an opportunity to discuss their impressions of the target group with others, group polarisation occurred with more stereotypical perceptions being reported.

Typically we like to associate with people who are like us. Given what we now know about group polarisation, you will be able

■ **Figure 9.5** The risky shift phenomenon has implications for delinquency. "LAPD Gang Investigation Arrest.jpg" by Chris Yarzab.

to anticipate what effect this may have on our initial attitudes and opinions. Lykken (1997) points to the implications for gang delinquency:

> ... the mischief they get into as a team is likely to be more than merely double what the first would do on his own ...
>
> (p. 263)

Veysey and Messner (1999) suggest that unsupervised peer groups are the strongest predictor of a neighbourhood's victimisation rate. They analysed data from 238 British neighbourhoods. Dishion et al. (1999) suggest that putting delinquents' together ends up promoting "deviancy training" in which polarisation of already delinquent attitudes occurs.

The internet is a hotbed for polarisation to occur thanks to the way that relevant content is pushed towards users based on complicated algorithms. Chen and Chen (2012) claim that the longer people spend in Dark Web forums, the more violent their messages appear to be. Mølmen and Ravndal (2023) claim that polarisation of thinking is one factor that contributes towards the radicalisation of far right terrorism on the internet. We seek out contact from people who are like us and in so doing, may inadvertently end up engaging in the process of polarisation.

Lazer et al. (2009), for example, claim that we tend to select blog posts to read that reinforce rather than challenge our viewpoints. However, we do not always seem aware of the polarising effect of the group. Keating et al. (2016) asked participants to take part in a 15-minute discussion about whether Barack Obama or George Bush was the better president. After discussion, participants were asked to state not only their opinions at that point but also to recall the opinions that they expressed before the discussion. What did they find? In line with expectation, the discussion led to polarisation of attitudes with more extreme views reported after. When asked to recall their pre-discussion attitudes, participants completely overestimated how extreme they had been. We really do not seem to be aware of how much effect a group has on us.

One example of how group polarisation can affect decision-making is the willingness of a group to adopt a more risky solution. Stoner (1961) presented participants with "decision dilemmas". These required participants to make a decision about how much risk a character should take. Here is one example of Stoner's decision dilemmas:

> *Mr A is an electrical engineer who is married and has one child, has been working for a large electronics corporation since graduating from college five years ago. He is assured of a lifetime job with a modest, though adequate salary and liberal pension benefits on retirement. On the other hand, it is very unlikely that his salary will increase much before he retires. While attending a convention, Mr A is offered a job with a small, newly founded company with a highly uncertain future. The new job would pay more to start and would offer the possibility of a share in the ownership of the company if the company survived the competition of the larger firms. Imagine that you are advising Mr A. Listed below are several probabilities or odds of the new company proving financially sound. Please check the lowest probability that you would consider acceptable to make it worthwhile for Mr A to take the new job:*
>
> - *The chances are 1 in 10 that the company would prove financially sound.*
> - *The chances are 3 in 10 that the company would prove financially sound.*
> - *The chances are 5 in 10 that the company would prove financially sound.*

- *The chances are 7 in 10 that the company would prove financially sound.*
- *The chances are 9 in 10 that the company would prove financially sound.*
- *Place a check here if you think that Mr A should not take the new job, no matter what the probabilities.*

(p. 84).

Having made an individual judgement, participants were then asked to discuss their estimates in a group with up to five other people. Stoner was quite amazed to find that when in a group, the estimates became more risky! This is more likely to happen when individuals are in peer groups and occurs more often in adolescents (Gardner & Steinberg, 2005). Indeed, Moscovici and Zavalloni (1969) reported a strengthening of initial negative attitudes towards the United States and positive attitudes towards President de Gaulle in a group of French students after discussion.

CAN GROUPS EVER MAKE BETTER DECISIONS?

It is worth noting, however, that risky shifts are more likely to occur when the initial opinions of the individual group members are towards risk at the beginning of the discussion. How about if the initial opinions are towards caution? In these situations, Stoner (1961) suggests, we are likely to see a "cautious shift", that is, the group is more likely to become risk-averse after discussion than they were initially. Sunstein (2000) points to a number of examples where cautious shifts have been demonstrated including the decision to marry and the decision to board a plane despite severe abdominal pain.

Abrams et al. (2006) asked participants to take part in a series of betting tasks, either whilst sober or after drinking sufficient alcohol to give them a blood alcohol concentration of 0.08%. The performance of individuals versus groups was compared. As you might predict, the risks that individuals were prepared to take individually were greater when intoxicated but when they were in a group, this was not the case at all. A similar message was given by Hopthrow et al. (2014) in a study of decision-making after alcohol consumption. Participants were initially asked to respond to a dilemma about driving after drinking. They were then placed into groups of 4–6 people and were asked to discuss the same dilemma. Who was the most cautious? Why, the groups were. Everyone was initially cautious but the groups were even more so. What made this study particularly interesting was the effect of alcohol consumption. For intoxicated individuals, they were willing to take more risks. However, for groups, the reverse was true. As Brown and Pehrson (2019) suggest:

> ... being in a group "protected" drinkers somewhat from making risky and, in this context, dangerous decisions about getting behind the wheel of a car.
>
> (p. 149)

It seems that groups can be valuable after all when it comes to making decisions. This is certainly the opinion of Sanders and Warnick (1982). They presented participants with a video of a criminal incident. They were later asked to complete a questionnaire that asked them to describe what they had seen, to describe the criminal and to predict their ability to identify the criminal in a line-up. They were then asked to do just that. In one condition, individuals did this without any interaction. In a second condition, the group condition, participants watched the video and then discussed their thoughts with others in their groups before responding. Group discussion had a positive effect on accuracy – both in terms of individuals' eyewitness reconstructions and in terms of the completeness of the reports given.

Nijstad et al. (2006) argue that when it comes to creative thinking, group discussion is more useful when it takes place in smaller groups. When a group is too big, production blocking can occur, where people forget their ideas whilst waiting to speak. Individuals may engage in social loafing and they may be an unwillingness to share ideas that are a little unusual. There is also a suggestion from Paulus and Korde (2014) that generating ideas individually first and only then taking these to the group works best but in later articles, they argue that alternating individual and group brainstorming is optimal (Korde & Paulus, 2017). Make a group aware of the importance of sharing information and the potential of bias and good problem-solving can result. Myers and Twenge (2016) give the example of scientists predicting the summer minimum Arctic Sea ice level. Individually, their predictions ranged from 2.5 million to 5.6 million square kilometres. Average their responses, however, and this almost matched the actual result reported (4.8 million).

So what happens if there isn't a group available to discuss your ideas with? Certainly, where factual questions are concerned, the suggestion would be to ask yourself the same question on different occasions. Vul and Pashler (2008) claim:

> *You can gain about 1/10th as much from asking yourself the same question twice as you can from getting a second opinion from someone else but if you wait three weeks the benefit of re-asking yourself the same question rises to ⅓ the value of a second opinion.*
>
> (p. 646)

It is no accident therefore that they called their paper "Measuring the crowd within"!

REFERENCES

Abrams, D., Hopthrow, T., Hulbert, L., & Frings, D. (2006). "Groupdrink"? The effect of alcohol on risk attraction among groups versus individuals. *Journal of Studies on Alcohol, 67*(4), 628–636.

Aronson, E., Wilson, T. D., & Akert, R. M. (2014). *Social psychology* (8th ed.). Pearson Education.

Baron, R. S. (1986). Distraction-conflict theory: Progress and problems. *Advances in Experimental Social Psychology, 19,* 1–40.

Bayer, E. (1929). Beitrage zur Swelkomponententheorie des Hungers. *Zeitschrift fur Psychologie, 122,* 1–54.

Bekafigo, M. A., Stepanova, E. V., Eiler, B. A., Noguchi, K., & Ramsey, K. L. (2019). The effect of group polarization on opposition to Donald Trump. *Political Psychology, 40*(5), 1163–1178.

Bottger, P. C. (1984). Expertise and air time as bases of actual and perceived influence in problem-solving groups. *Journal of Applied Psychology, 69*(2), 214.

Brauer, M., Judd, C. M., & Jacquelin, V. (2001). The communication of social stereotypes: The effects of group discussion and information distribution on stereotypic appraisals. *Journal of Personality and Social Psychology, 81*(3), 463.

Brewer, M. B. (2007). The importance of being we: Human nature and intergroup relations. *American Psychologist, 62*(8), 728.

Brown, R. (1965). *Social psychology*. Free Press.

Brown, R., & Pehrson, S. (2019). *Group processes: Dynamics within and between groups*. John Wiley & Sons.

Burnstein, E., & Vinokur, A. (1977). Persuasive argumentation and social comparison as determinants of attitude polarization. *Journal of Experimental Social Psychology, 13*(4), 315–332.

Cartwright, D., & Zander, A. (1968). *Group dynamics* (3rd ed.). Peterson.

Carver, C. S., & Scheier, M. F. (1981). The self-attention-induced feedback loop and social facilitation. *Journal of Experimental Social Psychology, 17*(6), 545–568.

Chen, H., & Chen, H. (2012). Improvised explosive devices (IED) on dark web. In Hsinchun, C., Ramesh, S., & Stefan, V. (Eds). Dark Web Exploring and Data Mining the Dark Side of the Web., 319–339.

Chen, S. C. (1937). Social modification of the activity of ants in nest-building. *Physiological Zoology, 10*(4), 420–436.

Clendenen, V. I., Herman, C. P., & Polivy, J. (1994). Social facilitation of eating among friends and strangers. *Appetite, 23*(1), 1–13.

Cottrell, N. B. (1972). Social facilitation. In C. G. McClintock (Ed.), *Experimental social psychology* (pp. 185–236). Holt.

Diener, E., & Wallbom, M. (1976). Effects of self-awareness on antinormative behavior. *Journal of Research in Personality, 10*(1), 107–111.

Dimitroff, R. D., Schmidt, L. A., & Bond, T. D. (2005). Organizational behavior and disaster: A study of conflict at NASA. *Project Management Journal, 36*(2), 28–38.

Dishion, T. J., McCord, J., & Poulin, F. (1999). When interventions harm: Peer groups and problem behavior. *American Psychologist, 54*(9), 755.

Esser, J. K., & Lindoerfer, J. S. (1989). Groupthink and the space shuttle challenger accident: Toward a quantitative case analysis. *Journal of Behavioral Decision Making, 2*(3), 167–177.

Festinger, L., Pepitone, A., & Newcomb, T. M. (1963). Some consequences of de-individuation in a group. In N. J. Smelser, & W. T. Smelser (Eds.), *Personality and social systems* (pp. 125–135). John Wiley & Sons.

Gabrenya, W. K. Jr, Latané, B., & Wang, Y. E. (1983). Social loafing in cross-cultural perspective: Chinese on Taiwan. *Journal of Cross-Cultural Psychology, 14*(3), 368–384.

Gardner, M., & Steinberg, L. (2005). Peer influence on risk taking, risk preference, and risky decision making in adolescence and adulthood: An experimental study. *Developmental Psychology, 41*(4), 625.

Gardner, W. L., & Knowles, M. L. (2008). Love makes you real: Favorite television characters are perceived as "real" in a social facilitation paradigm. *Social Cognition, 26*(2), 156–168.

Harkins, S. G., & Jackson, J. M. (1985). The role of evaluation in eliminating social loafing. *Personality and Social Psychology Bulletin, 11*(4), 457–465.

Hopthrow, T., Randsley de Moura, G., Meleady, R., Abrams, D., & Swift, H. J. (2014). Drinking in social groups. Does 'groupdrink' provide safety in numbers when deciding about risk? *Addiction, 109*(6), 913–921.

Janis, I. L. (1972). *Victims of groupthink: A psychological study of foreign-policy decisions and fiascoes*. Houghton Mifflin.

Janis, I. L. (1982). *Groupthink*. Houghton Mifflin.

Janis, I. L., & Mann, L. (1977). Emergency decision making: A theoretical analysis of responses to disaster warnings. *Journal of Human Stress, 3*(2), 35–48.

Johnson, R. D., & Downing, L. L. (1979). Deindividuation and valence of cues: Effects on prosocial and antisocial behavior. *Journal of Personality and Social Psychology, 37*(9), 1532.

Karau, S. J., & Williams, K. D. (1993). Social loafing: A meta-analytic review and theoretical integration. *Journal of Personality and Social Psychology, 65*(4), 681.

Keating, J., Van Boven, L., & Judd, C. M. (2016). Partisan underestimation of the polarizing influence of group discussion. *Journal of Experimental Social Psychology, 65*, 52–58.

Kerr, N. L., Messé, L. A., Seok, D. H., Sambolec, E. J., Lount, R. B. Jr, & Park, E. S. (2007). Psychological mechanisms underlying the Köhler motivation gain. *Personality and Social Psychology Bulletin, 33*(6), 828–841.

Korde, R., & Paulus, P. B. (2017). Alternating individual and group idea generation: Finding the elusive synergy. *Journal of Experimental Social Psychology*, *70*, 177–190.

Latané, B., Williams, K., & Harkins, S. (1979). Many hands make light the work: The causes and consequences of social loafing. *Journal of Personality and Social Psychology*, *37*(6), 822.

Lazer, D., Pentland, A., Adamic, L., Aral, S., Barabasi, A. L., Brewer, D., Christakis, N., Contractor, N., Fowler J, Gutmann, M., Jebara, T., King, G., Macy, M., Roy, D., & Van Alstyne, M. (2009). Social science. Computational social science. *Science*, *323*(5915), 721–723.

Leader, T., Mullen, B., & Abrams, D. (2007). Without mercy: The immediate impact of group size on lynch mob atrocity. *Personality and Social Psychology Bulletin*, *33*(10), 1340–1352.

Leary, M. R., & Baumeister, R. F. (1995). The need to belong. *Psychological Bulletin*, *117*(3), 497–529.

Libby, R., Trotman, K. T., & Zimmer, I. (1987). Member variation, recognition of expertise, and group performance. *Journal of Applied Psychology*, *72*(1), 81.

Littlepage, G. E., & Silbiger, H. (1992). Recognition of expertise in decision-making groups: Effects of group size and participation patterns. *Small Group Research*, *23*(3), 344–355.

Lount, R. B. Jr, & Wilk, S. L. (2014). Working harder or hardly working? Posting performance eliminates social loafing and promotes social laboring in workgroups. *Management Science*, *60*(5), 1098–1106.

Lykken, D. T. (1997). The American crime factory. *Psychological Inquiry*, *8*(3), 261–270.

Mann, L. (1981). The baiting crowd in episodes of threatened suicide. *Journal of Personality and Social Psychology*, *41*(4), 703.

McClellan, S. (2008). *What happened: Inside the Bush White House and Washington's culture of deception*. Public Affairs.

Michaels, J. W., Blommel, J. M., Brocato, R. M., Linkous, R. A., & Rowe, J. S. (1982). Social facilitation and inhibition in a natural setting. *Replications in Social Psychology*, *2*, 21–24.

Mojzisch, A., & Schulz-Hardt, S. (2010). Knowing others' preferences degrades the quality of group decisions. *Journal of Personality and Social Psychology*, *98*(5), 794.

Mølmen, G. N., & Ravndal, J. A. (2023). Mechanisms of online radicalisation: How the internet affects the radicalisation of extreme-right lone actor terrorists. *Behavioral Sciences of Terrorism and Political Aggression*, *15*(4), 463–487

Moscovici, S., & Zavalloni, M. (1969). The group as a polarizer of attitudes. *Journal of Personality and Social Psychology*, *12*(2), 125.

Mullen, B. (1986). Stuttering, audience size, and the other-total ratio: A self-attention perspective 1. *Journal of Applied Social Psychology*, *16*(2), 139–149.

Myers, D., Abell, J., & Sani, F. (2010). *Social psychology*. McGraw-Hill Education, pp. 157–200.

Myers, D. G., & Twenge, J. M. (2016) *Social psychology*. (12th ed.), McGraw-Hill.

Nijstad, B. A., Stroebe, W., & Lodewijkx, H. F. (2006). The illusion of group productivity: A reduction of failures explanation. *European Journal of Social Psychology*, *36*(1), 31–48.

Palmer, J. K., & Loveland, J. M. (2008). The influence of group discussion on performance judgments: Rating accuracy, contrast effects, and halo. *The Journal of Psychology, 142*(2), 117–130.

Paulus, P. B., & Korde, R. (2014). How to get the most creativity and innovation out of groups and teams. In K. Thomas, & J. Chan (Eds.), *Handbook of research on creativity*. Edward Elgar Publishing.

Pickett, C. L., & Gardner, W. L. (2005). The social monitoring system: Enhanced sensitivity to social cues as an adaptive response to social exclusion. In K. D. Williams, J. P. Forgas, & W. von Hippel (Eds.), *The social outcast: Ostracism, social exclusion, rejection, and bullying* (pp. 213–226). Psychology Press.

Pliner, P., & Mann, N. (2004). Influence of social norms and palatability on amount consumed and food choice. *Appetite, 42*(2), 227–237.

Punzo, F. (1992). Socially facilitated behavior in tadpoles of *Rana catesbeiana* and *Rana heckscheri* (Anura: Ranidae). *Journal of Herpetology, 26*(2), 219–222.

Ringelmann, M. (1913). Research on animate sources of power: The work of man. *Annales de l'Institut National Agronomique* 12 (2), 1–40.

Ruddock, H. K., Brunstrom, J. M., & Higgs, S. (2021). The social facilitation of eating: why does the mere presence of others cause an increase in energy intake? *Physiology & Behavior, 240*, 113539.

Sanders, G. S., & Warnick, D. H. (1982). Evaluating identification evidence from multiple eyewitnesses. *Journal of Applied Social Psychology, 12*(3), 182–192.

Schroeder, J., Caruso, E. M., & Epley, N. (2016). Many hands make overlooked work: Over-claiming of responsibility increases with group size. *Journal of Experimental Psychology: Applied, 22*(2), 238.

Schulz-Hardt, S., Frey, D., Lüthgens, C., & Moscovici, S. (2000). Biased information search in group decision making. *Journal of Personality and Social Psychology, 78*(4), 655.

Sentyrz, S. M., & Bushman, B. J. (1998). Mirror, mirror on the wall, who's the thinnest one of all? Effects of self-awareness on consumption of full-fat, reduced-fat, and no-fat products. *Journal of Applied Psychology, 83*(6), 944.

Silke, A. (2003). Deindividuation, anonymity, and violence: Findings from Northern Ireland. *The Journal of Social Psychology, 143*(4), 493–499.

Simms, A., & Nichols, T. (2014). Social loafing: A review of the literature. *Journal of Management Policy and Practice, 15*(1), 58.

Stasser, G., Stewart, D. D., & Wittenbaum, G. M. (1995). Expert roles and information exchange during discussion: The importance of knowing who knows what. *Journal of Experimental Social Psychology, 31*(3), 244–265.

Stasser, G., & Titus, W. (1985). Pooling of unshared information in group decision making: Biased information sampling during discussion. *Journal of Personality and Social Psychology, 48*(6), 1467.

Steiner, I. D. (1972). *Group process and productivity* (pp. 393–422). Academic Press.

Stoner, J. A. F. (1961). *A comparison of individual and group decisions involving risk*. Doctoral dissertation, Massachusetts Institute of Technology.

Stroebe, W. (2012). The truth about Triplett (1898), but nobody seems to care. *Perspectives on Psychological Science, 7*(1), 54–57.

Sunstein, C. R. (2000). Deliberative trouble? Why groups go to extremes. *The Yale Law Journal*, *110*(1), 71–119.

Surowiecki, J. (2004). *The wisdom of crowds: Why the many are smarter than the few and how collective wisdom shapes business, economies, societies, and nations*. Doubleday & Co.

Triplett, N. (1898). The dynamogenic factors in pacemaking and competition. *The American Journal of Psychology*, *9*(4), 507–533.

Veysey, B. M., & Messner, S. F. (1999). Further testing of social disorganization theory: An elaboration of Sampson and Groves's "community structure and crime. *Journal of Research in Crime and Delinquency*, *36*(2), 156–174.

Vul, E., & Pashler, H. (2008). Measuring the crowd within: Probabilistic representations within individuals. *Psychological Science*, *19*(7), 645–647.

Watson, W. E., Johnson, L., Kumar, K., & Critelli, J. (1998). Process gain and process loss: Comparing interpersonal processes and performance of culturally diverse and non-diverse teams across time. *International Journal of Intercultural Relations*, *22*(4), 409–430.

Wells, B. M., & Skowronski, J. J. (2012). Evidence of choking under pressure on the PGA tour. *Basic and Applied Social Psychology*, *34*(2), 175–182.

Whyte, G. (1993). Escalating commitment in individual and group decision making: A prospect theory approach. *Organizational Behavior and Human Decision Processes*, *54*(3), 430–455.

Williams, K., Harkins, S., & Latane, B. (1981). Identifiability as a deterrent to social loafing: Two cheering experiments. *Journal of Personality and Social Psychology*, *40*, 303–311.

Wittenbaum, G. M., & Park, E. S. (2001). The collective preference for shared information. *Current Directions in Psychological Science*, *10*(2), 70–73.

Worchel, S., Rothgerber, H., Day, E. A., Hart, D., & Butemeyer, J. (1998). Social identity and individual productivity within groups. *British Journal of Social Psychology*, *37*(4), 389–413.

Worringham, C. J., & Messick, D. M. (1983). Social facilitation of running: An unobtrusive study. *The Journal of Social Psychology*, *121*(1), 23–29.

Zajonc, R. B., Heingartner, A., & Herman, E. M. (1969). Social enhancement and impairment of performance in the cockroach. *Journal of Personality and Social Psychology*, *13*(2), 83.

Zanbaka, C., Ulinski, A., Goolkasian, P., & Hodges, L. F. (2004, November). Effects of virtual human presence on task performance. In *Proceedings of the International conference on artificial reality and telexistence 2004* (pp. 174–181).

Zhong, C. B., Bohns, V. K., & Gino, F. (2010). Good lamps are the best police: Darkness increases dishonesty and self-interested behavior. *Psychological Science*, *21*(3), 311–314.

Zhong, C. B., & Leonardelli, G. J. (2008). Cold and lonely: Does social exclusion literally feel cold? *Psychological Science*, *19*(9), 838–842.

Chapter 10

Guest Chapter: How does collective violence spread?

John Drury

'Contagion' – the notion that behaviour spreads between people simply by exposure – is one of the most popular ideas in the social and behavioural sciences. Put the word into Google Scholar and you will find over 700 academic publications with the word in the title in 2022 alone. Despite the origins of the term 'contagion' in the study of infectious diseases, the vast majority of these publications are about behaviour not catching illnesses. The concept of contagion has been employed in diverse disciplines, including marketing, public opinion research, sociology, economics, and public health – as well as in psychology. It has been applied to both simple behaviours – yawning, itching, smiling, clapping, anxiety, and excitement – as well as to complex social phenomena – including suicide, obesity, and market 'panic'. One topic where the concept of 'contagion' has been extensively applied is that of the spread of collective violence. Civil unrest or rioting often seems to occur in waves, with multiple riot events following each other. 'Contagion' has been one account of how that spread happens.

This chapter will examine the question of how collective violence spreads between people and locations. I will argue that the concept of 'contagion' conceals more than it reveals about the psychology of spread. The evidence suggests that we need a different way of talking and thinking about the spread of collective violence. I will begin by telling the story of how those researching the spread of collective violence came to apply the concept of 'contagion'. I'll then present some of the evidence on how simple behaviours (emotion, scratching, and yawning) spread between individuals. In the last section, I will use the example of the 2011 English riots to show how the social identity approach makes better sense of the evidence than 'contagion'.

DOI: 10.4324/9781003396208-10

THE STORY OF 'CONTAGION'

In the period 1964–1968, the United States recorded around 500 riots, and a huge programme of research was initiated to understand them (Waddington, 1992). One feature of the events was that the riots occurred in clusters rather than singly. Different explanations were offered for this clustering.

First, it was noted that the riots tended to be concentrated in the summer months, so it was suggested that the heat affected people's brains, causing them to riot. This 'brain-boil' explanation overlooked a more obvious cause of street violence in the summer months, however. In the warm weather, young people are more likely to be outside and gather on street corners, which means that they are more likely to encounter the police. Indeed, relations with police was a second explanation: perhaps the locations that saw rioting were those where the local community already had poor relations with police? Third, deprivation was suggested as an explanation – after all, the better-off tend not to riot.

Poor relations with police, deprivation, and 'race' (the proportion of African Americans in each city) certainly seemed to correlate with riot locations (as well as with each other). But these factors did not explain *when* rioting occurred or the temporal clusters that had been observed.

A methodological breakthrough came when sociologists applied mathematical models to the data. For example, Midlarsky (1978) looked at riot data in the period 1966–1967, using arrest figures as his measure of size of riot activity in a location. He was able to show that the number of riots that began in smaller cities after the massive disorders in the big cities of Newark and Detroit was too large to have happened independently. The best explanation was that the Newark and Detroit events influenced the occurrence of the subsequent riot events, through 'smaller cities imitating the behaviour of large ones experiencing a disorder' (p. 996).

Using a similar statistical approach, Daniel Myers (1997) analysed data on the timing and locations of US 'race' riots from 1961 to 1968. He was able to show that the more intense the riot, the greater the influence on other riots occurring; that other riots are more likely in cities closest to where the original rioting occurred; and that the influence of riots on other locations wanes over time.

In conceptualising the impact of riots on the behaviour of people in other locations, these sociologists therefore suggested the concept 'contagion', which was already being used in psychology experiments to explain how observers apparently automatically copied the aggressive behaviour of a model.

The concept of contagion already had a long history in psychology. Hippolyte Taine (1876) was one of the first people to use the term 'contagion' to describe influence between people in crowds. His history of the French Republic drew upon various concepts from medicine – including 'feverishness' and 'delirium' – to characterise the psychology of crowd behaviour. Other early crowd psychologists who came after him developed the concept further, most notably Gustave Le Bon (1895/2002) who defined 'contagion' as a process of uncritical social influence, which was enabled by the state of 'suggestibility' (similar to a hypnotic state) that he said befalls people when they become part of crowds.

At this point, it's worth thinking carefully about the word 'contagion' and its meanings. What does that word give you over other terms such as 'influence' or 'spread'? The linkage of social influence to pathology or illness by the early crowd psychologists was not accidental. The early crowd psychologists saw both disease and crowds as malign. The term 'contagion' also conveys the implication that social influence is mindless, automatic, passive, and primitive. In short, 'contagion' is a highly loaded term, not a neutral one. The choice of this term by the early crowd psychologists to describe social influence in crowds was entirely consistent with their attempt to discredit and delegitimise (working class) crowds who were seen as a threat to civilisation (Stott & Drury, 2017).

Arguably, though, the true test of the usefulness of the 'contagion' concept is empirical. Is social influence in crowds really indiscriminate, as Le Bon and others claim? Two examples where there are boundaries to social influence suggest that it may not be indiscriminate. First, Milgram and Toch (1969) pointed out that 'contagion' cannot explain why riot police are impervious to the rousing effects of a demagogue, unlike others co-present in the same crowd. There seems to be a group boundary to influence in such crowds. The second example comes from Reicher's (1984) study of the St Pauls' (Bristol) riot of 1980. This event started with a police raid on a local café. Gradually, more and more people joined in, and the police were forced to leave the local area. Reicher observed that throwing stones at the police quickly spread through the crowd. However, throwing a stone at a bus did not. Instead, others discouraged stone-throwing at the bus. Reicher explained these patterns in terms of the concept of social identity: social identity – our definition of who we are – determines group boundaries to influence and constrains what 'we' as group members regard as appropriate behaviour (Turner, 1991). In this case, the St Pauls' rioter identity was defined in terms of longstanding poor relations with the police and a loyalty to the local community.

HOW DO SIMPLE BEHAVIOURS SPREAD BETWEEN PEOPLE?

Before developing this point that social identity might be the basis of an explanation for influence in complex social phenomena, we now turn to the question of how *simple* behaviours spread between people. There are many examples in the literature that have tested experimentally the extent to which simple behaviours spread simply through exposure. In a typical paradigm for examining 'contagious' yawning, Anderson and Meno (2003) showed 77 children short videos of an adult reciting nursery rhymes and talking about animals. In one version of the video, the adult stopped speaking every ten seconds to yawn. In another version, the adult smiled instead of yawning. The children were tested individually, and were each exposed to both yawning and smiling, in a repeated measures design, with counterbalancing of the order of presentation. Afterwards, the children were asked whether they felt like yawning, and were sent back to the playroom or classroom and observed for the next five minutes.

None of the youngest (pre-school) children in the study yawned during or immediately after the video, or reported feeling like yawning. However, some of the other children yawned, including 12% of the six-year-olds and 60% of the ten-year-olds in the study. The authors concluded that contagious yawning is not reliable in children below the age of six years, and that the difference between the two age groups suggests slower development of mechanisms underlying imitative yawning, or even the involvement of different underlying psychological mechanisms. Interestingly, therefore, the supposedly highly contagious behaviour of yawning did not spread to everyone.

The 'contagion' concept has become influential in work settings, where organisations have tried to harness it to create positive mood amongst staff and between staff and customers. This matters, because positive mood in a work team is thought to contribute to productive work outcomes. Sigal Barsade's (2002) experiment on the 'ripple effect' has been an important example. Ninety-four business school students were randomly assigned to groups of two to four individuals. Each group also included a confederate, who was taking instructions from the experimenter. Participants were told that the task was a group 'managerial exercise'. Each participant had to act as a 'manager' on a salary committee negotiating the allocation of a limited sum of bonus money to their employees. Everyone had to give a short presentation about their employee. The design was 2 × 2 between subjects, with intensity of emotion expressed by the confederate (high vs low) and valence of confederate emotion (pleasant vs unpleasant) as the factors. The confederate expressed positive mood by smiling frequently (vs not smiling in the negative mood condition), and expressed intensity of that mood by making eye contact, speaking in a strong tone of voice, and speaking rapidly.

Emotional contagion was measured in two ways. First, participants completed mood ratings before and after the session. Second, the sessions were video-taped and participant behaviours coded by observers. On both types of measures, the mood of the participants appeared to be influenced by the mood of the confederate. Positive and negative moods were equally influential, as were high and low valences of mood.

According to an important model (Hatfield et al., 1992), emotional contagion, as in the Barsade example, operates as follows. When someone smiles or displays any other emotion, there is an automatic mirroring reaction in the facial musculature of whoever is viewing this smiling (or frowning) face. The automatic facial reaction sends a signal to the brain, and the emotional feeling (of happy mood, for example) is the result.

Job van der Schalk and colleagues (2011) examined whether there are social group boundaries to emotional contagion by measuring these facial responses (rather than by simply asking people to report on their emotions, for example). Participants were 42 women in a psychology course. They were shown photographs of males displaying anger, fear, and happiness. To manipulate whether the model was ingroup or outgroup to the participants, the experimenters told them that the models were either 'psychology students' (ingroup) or 'economics students' (outgroup). Emotional response activity was measured by placing electrodes on the side of participants' faces, picking up movement of the eyebrow and wrinkling of the corners of the eye. Participants were told that the purpose of the task was to examine how people recognise expressions of different groups. The results showed that anger and fear displays by models labelled as ingroup were mimicked significantly more than the same displays of an 'outgroup' (though in fact the model faces were the same). There was no difference in the 'happy' faces. These results were subsequently repeated using self-report measures.

In a review of the literature, Parkinson (2019) concludes that there is insufficient evidence to demonstrate that emotion spreads between people by contagion. The study by van der Schalk and colleagues illustrates the problem and points to an alternative explanation. A 'contagion' account would suggest that the identity of the target doesn't matter (since contagion is automatic and 'mindless'). But studies like that of van der Schalk and colleagues by contrast suggests that at some level, even for apparently automatic behaviour, people do think about identity. These findings and others like it are in line with a *social identity* explanation.

At this point, it's worth looking closely at the concept of social identity. Social identity is defined as 'that part of an individual's self-concept which derives from his [sic] knowledge of his [sic] membership of a social group (or groups) together with the emotional significance attached to that membership' (Tajfel, 1974, p. 69). Our different social identities each become relevant to us in different contexts, as a function of which (other) groups are present and how they are behaving (Turner et al., 1987) Each social identity is associated with a particular set of norms, values, interests, and emotions. For example, the norms associated with being a football fan might include loudly expressing passion at a match, whereas the norms associated with being a student at a lecture might include sitting quietly and taking notes. Therefore, when we define ourselves in terms of particular social identities we strive to enact and express the associated norms, values, interests, and emotions.

The social identity approach would suggest that, when we see other people as part of our group – as part of 'us' or 'we' – we assume that they see the world in the same way as we do. These others are therefore relevant to us as sources of information, including on how to behave.

Introducing social identity to the question of how behaviour spreads between people can help to explain some of the variability – or unreliability – of supposed 'contagion' effects, as noted earlier. Thus, if different individuals vary in their level of identification with a social group, they will also vary in their susceptibility to influence from members of that group.

Some evidence for social identity as a mediating mechanism in simple behavioural mimicry comes from some (unpublished) experiments by Fergus Neville and colleagues. A first study tested whether people would mimic an ingroup member who scratched themselves more than they would an outgroup member who did the same. The background to this was previous research suggesting that itchiness is highly 'contagious' (Schut et al., 2015). In Neville's study, participants were told that the aim of the study was to compare the accuracy of males and females in assessing emotional experience. All participants were male, and their identity as male was made salient by asking them to write down three things that they as males do often (Haslam et al., 1999). Participants then watched a short video in which someone scratched themselves eight times. In the 'ingroup' condition, the person in the video was male, and in the outgroup condition the person scratching themselves was female.

Participants' behaviour was recorded and observed, and participants also filled in questionnaire measures. The researchers found that those in the ingroup condition were more likely to scratch themselves, and scratch themselves for longer, via shared identity with the model and self-reported itchiness (see Figures 10.1 and 10.2). This relationship was only significant for those with high levels of identification with the ingroup category, again showing the importance of social identity.

A second experiment by Neville and colleagues used the same paradigm to examine the role of social identification in mimicry

■ **Figure 10.1** Yawning model.

■ **Figure 10.2** Scratching model.

of yawning, a behavioural response usually taken to be automatic and outside conscious control (e.g., Provine, 2005). This study found exactly the same pattern as for scratching. Those who saw an ingroup member yawning were more likely than those who saw an outgroup member yawning to yawn themselves and to yawn for longer, via shared identity with the model and self-reported urge to yawn. Again, this pattern was only significant for those high in social identification with the ingroup category.

HOW DO COMPLEX BEHAVIOURS SPREAD BETWEEN LOCATIONS? THE 2011 ENGLISH RIOTS

So far, then, we have shown that there is evidence that spread of behaviour is not simply a matter of exposure. If spread of behaviour was simply down to exposure, everyone exposed would exhibit the behaviour, but this doesn't seem to be the case. Some people are more likely to mimic observed behaviour than others. We've seen that social identity processes can help explain how simple behaviours spread between people, since social identification can vary between people. But what about complex behaviours? We saw earlier that there is evidence that civil unrest – rioting – can spread from one location to another. But we haven't explained the psychology of this yet.

In order to examine this question of how of rioting spreads between locations, I will focus now on research on the largest wave of civil unrest in the United Kingdom for many years: the 2011 English riots. Around 100 'disorders' took place across 66 local authority areas over Saturday 6th to Tuesday 9th August that year. Five people were killed, and over 200 police officers were injured. Nearly 2,000 incidents of criminal damage and arson were reported, and the final 'bill' for damages, loss of trade, and policing were estimated at between £250 and £500 million. Around 2,000 people were brought to court.

The precipitating incident took place when police shot dead a mixed heritage man, Mark Duggan, in Tottenham, North London. It's important to note that the rioting didn't follow immediately after this incident, however. Two days after the shooting, on Saturday 6th August, unhappy at the lack of communication from the police about Mark Duggan's death, his family and friends held a protest demonstration outside Tottenham police station demanding to speak to a senior officer. Riot police were sent into the crowd, and conflict soon developed.

The Tottenham riot included significant attacks on police and selected property. Over the following 24 hours, the rioting spread to nearby Tottenham Hale and Wood Green, where extensive looting of retail outlets took place. The next day, rioting also occurred in a large number of other districts in North and East London – including Enfield Town, Ponders End, Edmonton, Islington, Walthamstow, Waltham Cross, Dalston, and Ilford – and one location south of the river Thames (Brixton). Over the following two days there was rioting in a further 36 locations across London, with major incidents in Hackney, Croydon, Ealing, Clapham, Peckham, and Lewisham. By the third and fourth days, there were the first signs of spread outside the capital, with rioting in the West Midlands, Liverpool, Leeds, Bristol, and Nottingham. In the final days, rioting subsided in London, but there were now major disorders in the West Midlands, Merseyside, Salford, Manchester, and Nottingham, as well as more minor incidents in Slough, Watford, Gloucester, Reading, Milton Keynes, Cambridge, Leicester, and Huddersfield.

The news media reporting of the riots of 2011 certainly saw these events as influencing each other, and 'copycat behaviour' was one term used to describe this. Other commentators were more explicit that what was happening was 'contagion', as in Gary Slutkin's (2011) statement in the Guardian newspaper that 'that violence is an epidemic is not a metaphor; it is a scientific fact'.

■ **Figure 10.3** Stand-off between rioters and police, Croydon 2011. Picture courtesy of Raymond Yau.

However, the limits of this characterisation – whether metaphor or not – were obvious. Everyone in the United Kingdom heard about the rioting, but only a few thousand people actually joined in with it. Many towns and cities did not see rioting. It was a significant wave of riots, but it wasn't really a 'contagion'.

To illustrate how the social identity approach can be applied to explaining some aspects of the spread of rioting, I will concentrate here on the riots in South London in 2011. Specifically, I examine here the question of why it was that Brixton was the first location in South London to experience rioting after Tottenham, and why Croydon and Clapham did not riot until after Brixton. This selection of locations presents a good test of psychological explanations for riot spread, since there was little evidence of people travelling from Tottenham to Brixton to riot. In other words, the people rioting in South London were not those who had already rioted the day before, but were 'new' people apparently influenced to join in by the previous events.

How does one study riots? These unpredictable and dangerous events are inherently difficult to research. We'll therefore briefly consider the methodology of the English riots study at this point. Researchers are not likely to be present during the events. Therefore, they usually have to collect data afterwards. The English riots study as whole drew upon three sorts of such data (see Drury et al., 2019b).

First, the study made use of publicly available archive data. We collected over 150 newspaper sources, over 40 official reports, over 100 journal articles, over 250 videos (including both footage and interviews), a database of 2.6 million riot-related tweets, and hundreds of photographs.

Second, there we analysed data from the police. We drew upon the Home Office compilation of police figures on arrestees and criminal offences during the riots, as well as police logs and detailed data-sets from a number of individual police forces. This comprised data on over 5,000 offences and over 4,000 arrestees.

The archive and police data were used to create a detailed picture of what actually happened during the riots. But to understand rioters' motivations, perceptions, and experiences, we drew on a third sort of data: 270 interviews with rioters gathered in the weeks after the riots. These interviews were carried out by researchers at the LSE and Guardian newspaper as part of the 'Reading the Riots' project (Guardian/LSE, 2011). Local researchers used their contacts to approach rioters and ask them questions such as: what happened; what they experienced; what they did; and why they did it. The importance of this dataset was that as it was gathered very soon after the events, and interviewees were given anonymity. It provides unique insight into rioters' beliefs and behaviour.

The interview responses of riot participants from Brixton, Croydon, and Clapham had some notable similarities, but also some crucial differences (Drury et al., 2019a). In terms of similarities, hatred of police was a common theme across almost all interviewees. In terms of differences between interviewees in the three different South London locations, we first consider how Brixton people reacted psychologically to the killing of Mark Duggan and subsequent events in Tottenham. Were these events relevant to their identities?

We found that, when talking about the killing, some Brixton interviewees referred to a shared history with the Black community in Tottenham. For them, Brixton history offered a framing of the killing and rioting in Tottenham, expressed in terms of feelings of anger and injustice at the killing. Brixton, like Tottenham, had previously seen a member of the Black community shot by police and a history of community conflict with police over police brutality.

Some interviewees even said they identified with the victim:

I would've been there because I see myself as part of that same community. That could've been anyone instead of Mark Duggan that day, that could've been me, that has been me, that has been my friends.

(Brixton interviewee)

As well as describing their own anger and sense of injustice, around half of the 20 Brixton interviewees described their perception that others in their local community felt the same way. Indeed, they said that the Tottenham events led them to believe that others in their community would riot:

- I: How did you know it was going to happen?
- D: Because I got an inkling. I had it. The police had it. Everyone knew.
- I: So because there'd been riots and was a street party, everyone is expecting it to kick off. It's that what you're saying.
- D: That's exactly what I'm saying.

(Brixton interviewee)

Moreover, this meta-perception – i.e., perception of others' perception – appeared to be confirmed amongst those who attended a large street party in Brixton on the Sunday. Here, they could see the anger on others' faces and hear others express the intention that the community response in Tottenham would be repeated in Brixton.

The pattern of responses was quite different in the interviews with people from Clapham and Croydon. Here, fewer people referred to anger and injustice. More of them said that their participation in the rioting was not connected to the killing of Mark Duggan. Instead of identifying with Tottenham, what seemed to be happening in Clapham and Croydon was that different groups felt empowered by seeing a common enemy – the police – weakened across multiple locations. By the third day, rioting had taken place in North and East London and now Brixton, and the police had appeared increasingly powerless to prevent it. A common theme in the Clapham and Croydon interviews therefore was police disempowerment:

Why did it start in Clapham Junction?

Everyone saw that it could be done ... the police weren't gonna do nothin', right, the police were sort of scared. And like I said, there's enough estates to make enough of us.

(Clapham interviewee)

As with Brixton, meta-perception seemed to be important for many Clapham and Croydon interviewees. A common response was that, when the other riots happened over the following days after Tottenham, interviewees expected people in their own communities to want to join in.

In summary therefore it appears that an important reason why Brixton was the first place in South London to riot in 2011 was because of a sense of injustice in relation to what happened in Tottenham, a location they felt an affinity with. Clapham and Croydon didn't riot immediately because of relatively low levels of identification with Tottenham. Instead, they rioted only after Brixton had rioted; perceptions of increasing police vulnerability were more important as a factor determining their participation. In both cases, meta-perception – often linked to a sense of community identity – drove influence processes locally: people joined in when they believed their neighbours were angry or empowered.

Of course, many other processes were at work during the 2011 riots; these were complex events, after all. One process that seems important but for which there isn't space to go into detail with here is the actions of police. In some locations, police intervened early, to try to prevent anticipated rioting, in a way that drew in people who would not otherwise have joined in rioting. Inadvertently, some police interventions escalated conflict and contributed to the spread (Drury et al., 2022).

CONCLUSIONS

The spread of collective violence is a complex social phenomenon. This chapter has argued that the notion of 'contagion' obstructs rather than enhances understanding of how riots spread. First, the notion of 'contagion' implies that influence is inherently bad or pathological – like a disease. Second, there is evidence across both experiments and observations of group boundaries to influence. This is the case for both complex behaviours such as rioting, as well as emotions and simple behaviours such as scratching and yawning.

There is some evidence that social identity processes – in particular seeing the 'model' as ingroup to oneself – is a basis for social influence of simple behaviours between people. This explanation brings mimicry into line with contemporary explanations for conformity, minority influence, group polarisation, and leadership (Spears, 2021; Turner, 1991).

When we seek to explain complex phenomena such as the spread of collective violence, the research on the 2011 English riots suggests that, in addition to shared social identity, we also need to include reference to other concepts. In particular, the role of empowerment, meta-perception, and historical relationships between different groups are important.

A final take-away message from this chapter is that the terminology needs to change. The term 'contagion' distorts what actually happens when behaviour spreads between people and locations. We need to use a more neutral language, concentrating instead on terms such as 'social influence', 'impact', and 'spread'.

REFERENCES

Anderson, J. R., & Meno, P. (2003). Psychological influences on yawning in children. *Current Psychology Letters. Behaviour, Brain & Cognition*, *11*(2). https://doi.org/10.4000/cpl.390

Barsade, S. G. (2002). The ripple effect: Emotional contagion and its influence on group behavior. *Administrative Science Quarterly*, *47*(4), 644–675.

Drury, J., Ball, R., Neville, F., Reicher, S., & Stott, C. (2019b). *Re-reading the 2011 English riots: ESRC 'Beyond Contagion' interim report*. University of Sussex.

Drury, J., Stott, C., Ball, R., Reicher, S., Neville, F., Bell, L., Biddlestone, M., Lovell, M., Choudhury, S., & Ryan, C. (2019a). A social identity model of riot diffusion: From injustice to empowerment in the 2011 London riots. *European Journal of Social Psychology*, *50*(3), 485–720. https://doi.org/10.1002/ejsp.2650

Drury, J., Stott, C., Ball, R., Barr, D., Bell, L., Reicher, S., & Neville, F. (2022). How riots spread between cities: Introducing the police pathway. *Political Psychology*, *43*(4), 651–669. https://doi.org/10.1111/pops.12786

Guardian/LSE. (2011). *Reading the riots: Investigating England's summer of disorder*. Guardian.

Haslam, S. A., Oakes, P. J., Reynolds, K. J., & Turner, J. C. (1999). Social identity salience and the emergence of stereotype consensus. *Personality and Social Psychology Bulletin*, *25*(7), 809–818. https://doi.org/10.1177/014616729902500700

Hatfield, E., Cacioppo, J. T., & Rapson, R. L. (1992). Primitive emotional contagion. In M. S. Clark (Ed.), *Emotion and social behavior* (pp. 151–177). Sage Publications.

Le Bon, G. (2002 [1895]). *The crowd: A study of the popular mind*. Dover publications.

Midlarsky, M. I. (1978). Analyzing diffusion and contagion effects: The urban disorders of the 1960s. *American Political Science Review*, *72*(3), 996–1008.

Milgram, S., & Toch, H. (1969). Collective behavior: Crowds and social movements. In G. Lindzey & E. Aronson (Eds.), *The handbook of social psychology* (pp. 507–610). Addison.

Myers, D. J. (1997). Racial rioting in the 1960s: An event history analysis of local conditions. *American Sociological Review*, *62*(1), 94–112.

Parkinson, B. (2019). *Heart to heart*. Cambridge University Press.

Provine, R. R. (2005). Yawning: The yawn is primal, unstoppable and contagious, revealing the evolutionary and neural basis of empathy and unconscious behavior. *American Scientist*, *93*(6), 532–539.

Reicher, S. D. (1984). The St Pauls' riot: An explanation of the limits of crowd action in terms of a social identity model. *European Journal of Social Psychology*, *14*(1), 1–21.

Schut, C., Grossman, S., Gieler, U., Kupfer, J., & Yosipovitch, G. (2015). Contagious itch: What we know and what we would like to know. *Frontiers in Human Neuroscience*, *9*, 57. https://doi.org/10.3389/fnhum.2015.00057

Slutkin, G. (2011). *Rioting is a disease spread from person to person – The key is to stop the infection*. Guardian. https://www.theguardian.com/uk/2011/aug/14/rioting-disease-spread-from-person-to-person

Spears, R. (2021). Social influence and group identity. *Annual Review of Psychology*, *72*, 367–390.

Stott, C., & Drury, J. (2017). Contemporary understanding of riots: Classical crowd psychology, ideology and the social identity approach. *Public Understanding of Science*, *26*(1), 2–14.

Taine, H. (1876). *The origins of contemporary France: The ancient regime (Trans. J. Durand)*. John F. Trow & Son.

Tajfel, H. (1974). Social identity and intergroup behaviour. *Social Science Information*, *13*(2), 65–93.

Turner, J. C. (1991). *Social influence*. Open University Press.

Turner, J. C., Hogg, M. A., Oakes, P. J., Reicher, S. D., & Wetherell, M. S. (1987). *Rediscovering the social group: A self-categorization theory*. Basil Blackwell.

van der Schalk, J., Fischer, A., Doosje, B., Wigboldus, D., Hawk, S., Rotteveel, M., & Hess, U. (2011). Convergent and divergent responses to emotional displays of ingroup and outgroup. *Emotion*, *11*(2), 286.

Waddington, D. (1992). *Contemporary issues in public disorder*. Routledge.

Chapter 11

What makes a good leader?

WHAT IS LEADERSHIP?

When you think of a good leader, who comes to mind? Maybe it is a manager at work, maybe it is a head of an organisation, maybe it is a politician (yes, I know, I am pushing my luck there). When it comes to thinking about leadership, psychologists have grappled with the idea of leadership as a fixed attribute of an individual, as an adaptation to particular contexts and even as something that is specifically male! To understand some of these ideas, it is important to look at how leadership has been defined. For our purposes, we will use a definition given by Silva (2016):

> *Leadership is the process of interactive influence that occurs when, in a given context, some people accept someone as their leader to achieve common goals.*
>
> (p. 3)

It is worth remembering however, that Stogdill (1974) suggests that:

> *there are almost as many different definitions of leadership as there are persons who have attempted to define the concept.*
>
> (p. 7)

Why does it matter? According to Barrick et al. (1991), a high-performing executive leader can add in excess of 25 million dollars to the value of a company (Barrick et al. were particularly focused on Fortune 500 companies, that is a list of the 500 largest companies in the United States compiled by the Fortune magazine). Joyce et al. (2003) reported that CEOs account for about 14% of the variance in performance of a company and Collins (2001) identified companies amongst the Fortune 1000 list that had sustained performance that was significantly better than average. What distinguishes these companies? Why, a good leader of course.

LEADERS AS "GREAT PEOPLE"

So, if good leaders are what's required, how do we find them? What makes a good leader? If we look back to the time of Plato, he was suggesting that a good leader is someone who is "wise" (Takala, 1998). Em (2023) lists 28 characteristics including everything from bravery to compassion to being inspirational. Weber (1947) introduced the idea of charisma as a characteristic of a good leader that set them apart from others:

> *set apart from ordinary men and treated as endowed with supernatural, superhuman, or at least specifically exceptional powers and qualities. These are such as are not accessible to the ordinary person ...*
>
> (pp. 358–9)

The idea that certain individuals are naturally "designed" to be better leaders was encapsulated in a series of six public lectures given back in 1840 by Thomas Carlyle, a Scottish philosopher. Carlyle's lectures focused on the theme of heroes. As Spector (2016) warns us, listening to Carlyle's lectures now may not sit comfortably with us. He believed that the job of ordinary citizens was to recognise the "Great Man", to elevate this person in prominence and for us to meekly obey him (Spector, 2016). It is no accident that I use the pronoun "him" – Carlyle was assured that leadership was masculine.

Organ (1996) gives the example of Indiana University's basketball coach, Bob Knight, who gave an invited speech to a class of undergraduates on the topic of leadership. Having taken the podium, the first thing he told them was:

> *The first thing you people need to know about leadership is that most of you simply don't have it in you.*
>
> (p. 1)

Not exactly the inspirational speaker that their tutor had in mind I suspect. However, it is very much in line with the idea that good leaders are born and not made (Galton, 1892). With this in mind, Simonton (1981) conducted a study of US presidents to identify what distinguished these "leaders" from ordinary people. One hundred personal attributes were studied but only three seemed to distinguish the presidents: their height (tall is best), family size (small is best), and books published before their presidency (more is best). This doesn't really fit with the idea of a born leader.

Perhaps, then it is a constellation of traits that makes a person a good leader. Get the mix right and you're in luck. Vaughan and

Hogg (2013) list a number of traits including being above average for size, health, physical attractiveness, self-confidence, sociability, need for dominance, intelligence, and talkativeness that have all been documented in the literature. However, the message from such studies tends to be that where personality variables are correlated with leadership, these relationships tend to be variable and at best, low (e.g. Mann, 1959). Indeed, Judge et al. (2002) suggest that the results of investigations relating personality traits to leadership have been "inconsistent and disappointing". They reviewed studies trying to link the two concepts and reported that extraversion was the biggest predictor of leadership but more to the emergence of a leader rather than their effectiveness.

Yukl and Van Fleet (1992) suggest that the factor that confuses matters here is the situation. Any personality trait will have a different effect on leadership dependent on the context in which this occurs. So it is to this idea that we now turn.

LEADERS AS "SITUATIONALLY DETERMINED"

I'm going to take you back to the time of WW2, specifically to 10th May 1940. On this day, Winston Churchill became Prime Minister. Winston was known to be quite an argumentative individual. He was also known as someone who was willing to take risks and was decisive, something which Gibson and Weber (2015) advocate should characterise managers in pharmacy in modern times. During WWII, the characteristics shown by Churchill were exactly those needed in a leader. However, at the end of the war, Labour's Clement Attleee was seen as a more suitable leader for peacetime. It could be argued that the qualities shown by Winston were no longer seen as ideal (Tucker, 1977).

Carter and Nixon (1949) (Psychologists I should add not presidents of the United States!) asked children to participate in three tasks: an intellectual, a clerical, and a mechanical task. The intellectual task required individuals to plot data on a graph using tacks and string, the clerical task involved a card selection task and proofreading and the mechanical task involved building a scaffold for a dartboard to be hung from. Different leaders excelled in different tasks. Those who led in the clerical task, for example, were not the same as those who led in the mechanical task. Situational factors are important. As Haslam et al. (2020) write:

> *If character does not make the leader, perhaps context does.*

(p. 19)

■ **Figure 11.1** Was Winston Churchill a "situationally determined" leader?

They give the example of Ernest Shackleton. If you are not already familiar with Ernest's story, let me summarise: after his ship, the Endurance, was crushed by ice in the Antarctic, he led his men across 350 miles of ice, and sailed to Elephant Island. From there, he embarked on a 15-day voyage plus a further 40-mile mountainous trek, with five others to South Georgia, to get help for those left behind. All were rescued. However, as Haslam, Reicher, and Platow point out, Shackleton's leadership credentials both before and after this left a lot to be desired. He was unsuccessful both in business and in politics. It took a particular situation for him to establish himself as an effective leader.

LEADERS AS "ACTORS"

The emphasis on situations does mean that the emphasis is not so much on what leaders do but more on how they act. This is very much in line with Lewin et al.'s (1939) theory of leadership types.

Rather than one style of leadership, they suggest three leadership styles. Autocratic leaders give orders, focus on the task at hand and remain aloof. Democratic leaders ask for suggestions, discuss plans and behave like members of the group that they lead. Laissez-faire leaders largely leave groups to their own devices and intervene only when necessary (Hogg & Vaughan, 2013).

To demonstrate this, they observed the behaviour of 11-year-old boys at a school activities club. They were asked to participate in a series of activities such as carpentry or painting signs. However, the leader of each group took on a different leadership style: autocratic, democratic, or laissez-faire. Whilst 45% of the verbal statements made by the autocratic leader were orders, only 3% were for democratic leaders and 4% for laissez-faire leaders. This did not necessarily translate into better performance however. Those in the democratic leader's group produced more creative solutions, had more fun and were just as efficient as those with an autocratic leader. When the democratic leader left the room, there was virtually no difference in productivity in the group but when the autocratic leader left, productivity dropped from 52% to 16%! In the laissez-faire leader's group, productivity was consistently poor and the quality of work also was dire.

A similar idea of leaders as acting in a particular style, was put forward by Bales (1950). Leaders, he claimed, are either task specialists or socio-emotional specialists. The two are incompatible. Task specialists are concerned with getting the job done. They set clear goals, plan well, and are strong decision makers. Socio-emotional specialists are concerned with the feelings of the group members. They create a sense of social cohesion and teamwork.

Bales and Slater (2014) reported that leaders who were seen as giving guidance or contributing ideas were not necessarily the best-liked members of the group. In fact, in 70% of cases, it was someone else. However, this took time to materialise. In the first meeting, the same member was chosen as both the most liked and the "idea" contributor 64% of the time. However, subsequently, the two roles diverged until by the fourth meeting, this occurred only 10.7% of the time.

However, Sorrentino and Field (1986) disagreed that both roles are incompatible. After engaging in five weekly sessions of group problem-solving activities and discussion, those individuals who showed both task and socio-emotional attributes scored highest on leadership ratings, in leadership election and in terms of behavioural measures such as quantity of verbal participation.

LEADERS AS "CONTINGENT"

Rather than being a case of "either" task-oriented or socio-emotional-oriented leadership, perhaps these styles are "contingent" on the situation. Fiedler proposed his contingency theory in 1967. According to Fiedler, when a task is highly structured and group relations are good, different leader characteristics will be preferred compared to when a task is less well-structured and group relations are not so favourable. Fiedler was pretty determined with his theorising as he developed an inventory to assess the characteristics of a leader – the least preferred co-worker inventory. Sounds lovely doesn't it? It requires the person completing it to use rating scales to describe the person in their group that they would least like to work with. According to Fiedler, if the ratings are low, then that suggests a task-oriented leader. If high, then it suggests a relationship-oriented leader.

There is a problem for Fiedler however. Hare et al. (1998) gave the least preferred co-worker scale to 20 groups of managers in the United States. They reported that Fielder may have had his scales reversed. It is no accident that they called their paper "Wishful thinking". Stewart and Latham (1986) similarly suggested that Fielder's LPC scale lacked construct validity and Johnson and Ryan (1976) failed to find any support at all for Fiedler's theory.

One of the difficulties of the theories we have considered so far is that they focus on the qualities of the leader. However, leaders are nothing without their followers.

LEADERS AS "COLLABORATIVE"

Leaders and followers collaborate to establish a situation of mutual support according to Messick (2004). Leaders provide value that followers find beneficial whilst followers respond in ways that the leader will find beneficial. There may be rewards for the followers whilst leaders may gain in status or social approval (Hogg & Vaughan, 2013). The idea is that leadership is akin to an economic transaction. One example of this type of "transactional leadership" is Hollander's "Idiosyncrasy Credit" idea. Imagine using a credit card to purchase something you want. You have to first ensure that you have sufficient credit on the card to be able to do so. Well, according to Hollander, that analogy works well in terms of leadership. A leader has to build up sufficient credit with the group they are leading before they can do what they want to do with the group or before they can lead the group in innovative projects. Mutual benefits for followers and leaders are

■ **Figure 11.2** Leaders and followers collaborate.

maximised. A related idea was proposed in 1965 by Adams who suggested that equitable processes underlie effective leadership. Where inequity is seen to exist, then tension arises.

However, some have questioned whether effective leadership can be boiled down to simple economic terms (Burns, 1978). Leaders often have more power than followers so there is a lack of equity from the start (Haslam et al., 2020). In a book entitled "Leadership", Burns (1978) proposed a different theory, the theory of transformational leadership. According to this theory, good leadership is not just about satisfying followers' wants and needs so that they return the favour. Leadership is about inspiring followers to want to progress to new intellectual levels alongside them. This is true not just of individual followers but of the group as a whole. One example that is commonly used is that of Barack Obama. He used a slogan "Yes we can" which inspired the nation to feel they could improve as a nation (Northouse, 2017). Another example is Genghis Khan, who united different tribes to construct a huge land empire (Yates, 2002).

Bass (1985) proposed three key components of transformational leadership: consideration of individual follower's needs, ability and aspirations, intellectual stimulation, and charismatic leadership. Rather than being an alternative to transactional leadership, Bass argues that these are two different levels of leadership, ones that cause lower or higher order change in subordinates. Along with Avolio and Goodheim in 1987, Bass asked undergraduates to complete a questionnaire asking them about the leadership of world-class leaders, including military, political, and industrial personnel. World-class leaders, generally, were rated highly on measures of charisma and intellectual stimulation. They were more likely than managers to create a vision for their followers. This aligns with the work of Zaleznik (1977) who similarly pointed to the more transactional nature of leadership shown by managers compared to world-class leaders.

Whilst it may seem that we have identified a useful and reliable theory here, it is interesting to note the result of a study by Steffens et al. (2017). Let us introduce Richard Din. Richard was a bit of a whizz by any imagination. It was he that developed a vaccination to protect us all from a particular bacteria known to cause meningitis. In one condition of their study, Steffens et al. informed participants that Din had died. In another condition, no mention was made of this fact. Which group perceived Din to be most charismatic? Yes. The group that thought he had died. In a later study, Steffens et al. (2018) reported this effect for heads of state who had died between 2000 and 2013. Using over 2 million newspaper reports, they identified a pattern after their death, the number of reports that mentioned the charisma of these heads of state doubled!

As if that isn't sufficient criticism, MacNeill et al. (2018) suggest that the demarcation between transformational and transactional leadership is artificial and does not hold value in the real world of schools. Onto, our next model of leadership …

LEADERS AS PROTOTYPES

When you think of a good leader, who do you think of? What characteristics come to mind? No doubt your vision of a good leader will be based on your life experiences. Lord and Brown (2003) believe that we all hold a prototype of what a good leader is like. In their Leader Categorisation Theory, the claim is that the more an individual matches our prototype, the more positively we perceive them in a leadership role. This does, of course, allow for context as we may have a prototype for leadership in different contexts. Leadership in the sports field for example may be associated with somewhat different qualities compared to leadership in business. This suggests a role for categorisation and emphasises the way in which leadership is determined by the followers and not by the individual themselves. In a neat illustration of how this works. Nye and Forsyth (1991) asked undergraduate students to evaluate a leader who acted in either a task- or emotion-oriented manner. For those who held a prototype of a leader as someone who exudes friendliness, and is warm and positive, the socio-emotional leader was rated more positively. For those who held a prototype which did not hold these characteristics, the task-oriented leader won through. The match between the prototype and the behaviour was key.

Foti et al. (1982) conducted a similar study to explore perceptions of political leaders. Using responses to a Gallup Poll, they reported a strong correlation between leadership ratings and prototypical items on the poll. One implication, they argue, is that politicians wanting to influence potential followers may accentuate the characteristics that people typically associate with effectiveness. One additional implication is that, historically at least, these prototypes tend to see leaders as male (Brown & Geis, 1984).

LEADERS AS "MALE"

Traditionally, the prototypes of effective leaders have emphasised traits seen as stereotypically male such as unemotionality and decisiveness (Lord et al., 1986). Eagly and Karau (2002) proposed their Role Congruity Theory to explain this phenomenon. The more incongruity exists between a leadership role and our stereotype of feminine gender roles, the less likely a female will be appointed to that leadership position. Garcia-Retamero and López-Zafra (2006) asked participants to read a description of a situation in a large organisation where an employee was being considered for promotion to a managerial (leadership) position. In one condition, it was a clothing manufacturing company, in another a car manufacturer and in another, the industry was not specified. The employee was either male or female. When the organisation was unspecified or when it was labelled as a car manufacturer, the male employee was favoured. When the organisation was the clothing manufacturer, no preference was identified. Note: the female was not preferred over the male but there was no preference shown. In terms of likely performance, when the female was considered for promotion in the car manufacturing organisation, participants predicted she would perform worse than her male counterpart. Perhaps what is even more surprising is that it was female participants who were most likely to see the female candidate as less worthy of promotion! Heilman et al. (1995) suggest that these characterisations of women managers are only abated if they are described as successful managers. Generally, though, they are perceived as less competent, less active, less emotionally stable, and less rational than male leaders.

The result of this is the glass ceiling effect, a term coined by the Wall Street Journal in 1986 according to Sharma and Kaur (2014). The glass ceiling describes the invisible barrier that prevents

■ **Figure 11.3** Was Angela Merkel an example of a prototypical leader?

women from reaching higher levels of management (Kiaye & Singh, 2013). Writing in 2007, Weyer reported that only 17 of the Fortune 1000 companies documented in 2003 were led by female chief executives. Tai and Sims (2005) explored the glass ceiling effect in tech companies. Despite similar levels of education and experience, females in the company were significantly less likely to be promoted to top management positions. Males, on the other hand, experience more of a "glass escalator" (Williams, 1992).

But is it all doom and gloom for female leaders? It would appear not. There are *some* leadership positions that women are selected for more often than men. Before you whoop with joy at this fact, you might want to read on for unfortunately these leadership positions are ones that carry more risk than average.

Ryan and Haslam (2005) examined the performance of FTSE 100 companies both before and after appointing a board member. Companies who had been performing badly in the previous 5 months were more likely to appoint a female member to the board than to appoint a male. Ryan and Haslam give the example of the UK retail company W.H. Smith. Prior to the appointment of a female CEO, it had been reporting tumbling share prices with job cuts needed and falls in their net profits. The higher than expected recruitment of women leaders to failing company CEO positions is an example of what Ryan and Haslam refer to as the "glass cliff". (It is reassuring to note that Ryan and Haslam identified an increase in share price after the appointment of a woman for the companies they studied in times of economic downturn.)

Haslam and Ryan (2008) asked participants to select a leader for an organisation that was either declining or improving in terms of their profits. For half of the participants, they were told that the company was a health and beauty company whilst the other half were told it was a major design and manufacturing firm. The position advertised was financial director. In the improving performance condition, participants read about how the financial performance of the company had been increasing with consequent rises in its share value. In the declining performance condition, the reverse picture was painted. Information about three candidates was presented. Two of the three were well qualified. To the author's surprise whether the company was stereotypically feminine or masculine has no effect on rankings of suitability. However, the qualified female candidate was reliably ranked as more suitable for the leadership position when the company's performance had been declining. Haslam and Ryan point to the way in which these opportunities are presented as golden opportunities rather than poisoned chalices due to the limited number of leadership roles that women have a chance to apply for.

The prevalence of the glass cliff extends beyond CEO positions. In the 2005 general election, women in the Conservative party contested harder to win seats than men (Ryan et al., 2010). In a second study, Ryan, Haslam, and Kulich asked students in a British political science class to select a suitable candidate to contest a seat in a by-election. The only difference between conditions was that in one, the seat was described as a safe seat, that is, there was a large majority voting for their party and in the other, it was described as a risky seat. In the latter situation, the opposition party held a majority. When the seat was safe, guess what? A male candidate was chosen more often. And when the seat was risky? Why, the woman was the preferred candidate.

It does appear to be the case that our prototypes of leaders can lead us astray when it comes to gender. But all is not lost for prototypes as an idea behind leadership decisions. Van Quaquebeke et al. (2011) argue that similarity to the self also plays a role in these prototypes. The more attributes noted in our prototype match those seen in a potential leader, the more we see them as being potentially effective. However, this is strengthened still further if we see some of those qualities to be true of ourselves. The more representative people see themselves of a category, the more important the qualities and attributes of that category become for making assessments of leadership. Cue the arrival of our last theory, the social identity theory of leadership.

LEADERS AS PEOPLE LIKE US

Hogg's social identity theory (2001) proposes that the more we identify with a group, the more we look to identify a prototypical member of the group. That individual will, in our eyes, make for a more effective leader than someone who is less prototypical. They are seen to represent the values and behaviour of the group to which we belong and help to define it. Giessner and van Knippenberg (2008), for example, asked workers from 11 countries to rate a leader they had experienced in terms of both prototypicality and trustworthiness. As you may expect given Hogg's theory, the more prototypical the leader, the more trustworthy they were rated as being. Similar findings have been reported by van Dijke and De Cremer (2008). For individuals who identified strongly with a group or organisation, they claimed, high prototypicality of a leader was associated with greater fairness.

So what happens when a member of the out-group scores highly on a desirable trait that we usually associate with effective leadership? Well, we simply devalue it. Haslam et al. (2020) describe the case of the US Presidential Election of 2000. Al Gore was up against George W. Bush. When asked to rate the intelligence of each, Gore outstripped Bush. Fifty-nine percent agreed that Gore was highly intelligent. In contrast, 55% agreed that Bush was of just average intelligence. Even Bush supporters were not ignorant of this fact with 28% of them agreeing that Gore was more intelligent. To reconcile this with their presidential choice therefore, they simply minimised the importance of this attribute. Seventy-two percent of Gore supporters wanted a president who had a high level of intelligence but only 56% of Bush supporters did so.

Faced with a choice between two candidates, both of whom engage in behaviours we would consider to be stereotypical of leaders, we are more likely to see them as being able to lead effectively if they are from our in-group rather than an out-group (Hais et al (1997)). As Haslam, Reicher, and Platow state:

> ... when push comes to shove, it matters more that a leader looks like "one of us" than that he or she looks like a "typical" leader.
>
> (p. 88)

Beware the implications. As Reicher and Hopkins (2003) claim, effective leaders can be construed as "Entrepreneurs of identity". They point to deviant behaviour in a group to enhance their own prototypicality or compare themselves with out-groups that enhance their own prototypicality. They can redefine the boundaries of the group and hence lead it in new directions. Shared identity is a powerful force and by focusing on social identity, we have, I believe come full circle from where we started this volume.

REFERENCES

Bales, R. F. (1950). A set of categories for the analysis of small group interaction. *American Sociological Review*, *15*(2), 257–263.

Bales, R. F., & Slater, P. E. (2014). Role differentiation in small decision-making groups. In Talcott Parsons and R. F. Bales (eds.), *Family, Socialization and Interaction Process*. Glencoe, Illinois: The Free Press. (pp. 259–306). Routledge.

Barrick, M. R., Day, D. V., Lord, R. G., & Alexander, R. A. (1991). Assessing the utility of executive leadership. *The Leadership Quarterly*, *2*(1), 9–22.

Bass, B. M. (1985). *Leadership and performance beyond expectations*. Free Press.

Bass, B. M., Avolio, B. J., & Goodheim, L. (1987). Biography and the assessment of transformational leadership at the world-class level. *Journal of Management*, *13*(1), 7–19.

Brown, V., & Geis, F. L. (1984). Turning lead into gold: Evaluations of men and women leaders and the alchemy of social consensus. *Journal of Personality and Social Psychology*, *46*(4), 811.

Burns, J. M. (1978). *Leadership*. Harper & Row.

Carter, L. F., & Nixon, M. (1949). An investigation of the relationship between four criteria of leadership ability for three different tasks. *The Journal of Psychology*, *27*(1), 245–261.

Collins, J. (2001). *Good to great*. Harper Collins.

Eagly, A. H., & Karau, S. J. (2002). Role congruity theory of prejudice toward female leaders. *Psychological Review*, *109*(3), 573.

Em, S. (2023). A review of different ideas concerning the characteristics of a good leader and shaping new ideas of an effective 21st century leader. *Journal of General Education and Humanities*, *2*(1), 13–34.

Fiedler, F. E. (1967). *A theory of leadership effectiveness*. McGraw-Hill.

Foti, R. J., Fraser, S. L., & Lord, R. G. (1982). Effects of leadership labels and prototypes on perceptions of political leaders. *Journal of Applied Psychology*, *67*(3), 326.

Galton, F. (1892). *Finger prints (No. 57490-57492)*. Cosimo Classics.

Garcia-Retamero, R., & López-Zafra, E. (2006). Prejudice against women in male-congenial environments: Perceptions of gender role congruity in leadership. *Sex Roles*, *55*, 51–61.

Gibson, M., & Weber, R. J. (2015). Applying leadership qualities of great people to your department: Sir Winston Churchill. *Hospital Pharmacy*, *50*(1), 078–083.

Giessner, S. R., & van Knippenberg, D. (2008). "License to fail": Goal definition, leader group prototypicality, and perceptions of leadership effectiveness after leader failure. *Organizational Behavior and Human Decision Processes*, *105*(1), 14–35.

Hais, S. C., Hogg, M. A., & Duck, J. M. (1997). Self-categorization and leadership: Effects of group prototypicality and leader stereotypicality. *Personality and Social Psychology Bulletin*, *23*(10), 1087–1099.

Hains, S. C., Hogg, M. A., & Duck, J. M. (2006). Self-categorization and leadership: Effects of group prototypicality and leader stereotypicality. *Key Readings in Social Psychology*, *2*, 383.

Hare, A. P., Hare, S. E., & Blumberg, H. H. (1998). Wishful thinking: Who has the least preferred coworker? *Small Group Research*, *29*(4), 419–435.

Haslam, S. A., Reicher, S. D., & Platow, M. J. (2020). *The new psychology of leadership*. Routledge.

Haslam, S. A., & Ryan, M. K. (2008). The road to the glass cliff: Differences in the perceived suitability of men and women for leadership positions in succeeding and failing organizations. *The Leadership Quarterly*, *19*(5), 530–546.

Heilman, M. E., Block, C. J., & Martell, R. F. (1995). Sex stereotypes: Do they influence perceptions of managers? *Journal of Social Behavior and Personality*, *10*(4), 237.

Hogg, M. A. (2001). A social identity theory of leadership. *Personality and Social Psychology Review*, *5*(3), 184–200.

Hogg, M. A., & Vaughan, G. M. (2013). *Social psychology* (7th ed.). Pearson.

Johnson, R. W., & Ryan, B. J. (1976). A test of the contingency model of leadership effectiveness 1. *Journal of Applied Social Psychology*, *6*(2), 177–185.

Joyce, W., Nohria, N., Roberson, B., & Magazine, O. (2003). A formula for sustained success. *Optimize*, *15*, 69–72.

Judge, T. A., Bono, J. E., Ilies, R., & Gerhardt, M. W. (2002). Personality and leadership: A qualitative and quantitative review. *Journal of Applied Psychology*, *87*(4), 765.

Kiaye, R. E., & Singh, A. M. (2013). The glass ceiling: A perspective of women working in Durban. *Gender in Management: An International Journal*, *28*(1), 28–42.

Lewin, K., Lippitt, R., & White, R. K. (1939). Patterns of aggressive behavior in experimentally created "social climates. *The Journal of Social Psychology*, *10*(2), 269–299.

Lord, R. G., & Brown, D. J. (2003). *Leadership processes and follower self-identity*. Psychology Press.

Lord, R. G., De Vader, C. L., & Alliger, G. M. (1986). A meta-analysis of the relation between personality traits and leadership perceptions: An application of validity generalization procedures. *Journal of Applied Psychology*, *71*(3), 402.

MacNeill, N., Silcox, S., & Boyd, R. (2018). Transformational and transactional leadership: A false dichotomy of leadership in schools. *Education Today*, *11*, 10–12.

Mann, R. D. (1959). A review of the relationships between personality and performance in small groups. *Psychological Bulletin*, *56*(4), 241.

Messick, D. M. (2004). On the psychological exchange between leaders and followers. In D. M. Messick & R. M. Kramer (Eds.), *The psychology of leadership: New perspectives and research*: 81–96. Erlbaum.

Northouse, P. G. (2017). *Introduction to leadership: Concepts and practice* (4th ed.). SAGE.

Nye, J. L., & Forsyth, D. R. (1991). The effects of prototype-based biases on leadership appraisals: A test of leadership categorization theory. *Small Group Research*, *22*(3), 360–379.

Organ, D. W. (1996). Leadership: The great man theory revisited. *Business Horizons*, *39*(3), 1–4.

Reicher, S., & Hopkins, N. (2003). On the science of the art of leadership. In D. van Knippenberg & M. A. Hogg (Eds.), *Leadership and power: Identity processes in groups and organizations* (pp. 197–209). SAGE Publications. https://doi.org/10.4135/9781446216170.n15.

Ryan, M. K., & Haslam, S. A. (2005). The glass cliff: Evidence that women are over-represented in precarious leadership positions. *British Journal of Management*, *16*(2), 81–90.

Ryan, M. K., Haslam, S. A., & Kulich, C. (2010). Politics and the glass cliff: Evidence that women are preferentially selected to contest hard-to-win seats. *Psychology of Women Quarterly*, *34*(1), 56–64.

Sharma, S., & Kaur, R. (2014). Glass ceiling for women: A barrier in effective leadership. *International Journal on Leadership*, *2*(2), 35.

Silva, A. (2016). What is leadership? *Journal of Business Studies Quarterly*, *8*(1), 1.

Simonton, D. K. (1981). Presidential greatness and performance: Can we predict leadership in the White House? *Journal of Personality*, *49*(3), 306–322.

Sorrentino, R. M., & Field, N. (1986). Emergent leadership over time: The functional value of positive motivation. *Journal of Personality and Social Psychology*, *50*(6), 1091.

Spector, B. A. (2016). Carlyle, Freud, and the great man theory more fully considered. *Leadership*, *12*(2), 250–260.

Steffens, N. K., Haslam, S. A., Jetten, J., & Mols, F. (2018). Our followers are lions, theirs are sheep: How social identity shapes theories about followership and social influence. *Political Psychology*, *39*(1), 23–42.

Steffens, N. K., Peters, K., Haslam, S. A., & van Dick, R. (2017). Dying for charisma: Leaders' inspirational appeal increases post-mortem. *The Leadership Quarterly, 28*(4), 530–542.

Stewart, D. W., & Latham, D. R. (1986). On some psychometric properties of Fiedler's contingency model of leadership. *Small Group Behavior, 17*(1), 83–94.

Stogdill, R. (1974). *Handbook of Leadership, 1st Ed.* Free Press.

Tai, A. J. R., & Sims, R. L. (2005). The perception of the glass ceiling in high technology companies. *Journal of Leadership & Organizational Studies, 12*(1), 16–23.

Takala, T. (1998). Plato on leadership. *Journal of Business Ethics, 17*, 785–798.

Tucker, R. C. (1977). Personality and political leadership. *Political Science Quarterly, 92*(3), 383–393.

van Dijke, M., & De Cremer, D. (2008). How leader prototypicality affects followers' status: The role of procedural fairness. *European Journal of Work and Organizational Psychology, 17*(2), 226–250.

Van Quaquebeke, N., Van Knippenberg, D., & Brodbeck, F. C. (2011). More than meets the eye: The role of subordinates' self-perceptions in leader categorization processes. *The Leadership Quarterly, 22*(2), 367–382.

Vaughan, G. M., & Hogg, M. A. (2013). *Social psychology*. Pearson Higher Education AU.

Weber, M. (1947). *The theory of social and economic organizations*. Free Press.

Williams, C. L. (1992). The glass escalator: Hidden advantages for men in the "female" professions. *Social Problems, 39*(3), 253–267.

Yates, M. (2002) Genghis Khan:LeaderValues. Retrieved August 3, 2006 from http://www.leader-values.com/historicalleaders/

Yukl, G., & Van Fleet, D. D. (1992). Theory and research on leadership in organizations. In M. D. Dunnette & L. M. Hough (Eds.), *Handbook of industrial and organizational psychology* (pp. 147–197). Consulting Psychologists Press.

Zaleznik, A. (1977). Managers and leaders: Are they different? *Harvard Business Review, 55*(3), 67–78.

Index

Note: *Italicized* and **bold** page numbers refer to figures and tables.

Aagerup, U. 110
Abelson, R. P. 124
Abrams, D. 85, 219
Adachi, P. J. 172
addiction to love 45
adjustment bias 136–138
Adorno, T. W. 193
agentic action 61
air conditioning 150
Akerlof, G. A. 89
Albarracín, D. 118
alcoholism 35, 151–156
Alcohol Myopia 153
Alicke, M. D. 12
Allen, J. J. 27
Allen, M. 112
Allen, V. L. 190
Alley, T. R. 38
Allison, C. J. 189
Allport, G. W. 193, 194
Altman, I. 43–44
altruism 55, 65, 75; Empathy-Altruism Hypothesis 68–69
Amato, P. R. 77
American Cancer Society 117
An, S. 129
anchoring bias 136–138
Anderson, C. A. 148, 149, 166–168, 173
Anderson, J. R. 230
Anderson, J. W. 112
Andorka, M. J. 46
Andrade, M. G. 87
Andrews, K. 158
anonymity 156–157
anti-social behaviour 147, 149, 151, 154, 156–158, 161, 166, 211
Appel, M. 118
Archer, J. 160, 161
Armenti, N. P. 152
Aron, A. P. 42–44
Aronson, E. 38, 39, *39*, 108, 130, 183, 187, 215
Aronson, J. 187
Asch, S. 86, 87, 89, 91, 92, 117

Attleee, C. 245
audience inhibition 63
Auliciems, A. 148, 149
Authoritarian Personality, theory of 193
autocratic leaders 247
availability heuristic 129–132
average 36–38

Back, M. D. 27
Bales, R. F. 247
Banks, S. M. 110
Barak, A. 157
Bargh, J. A. 127
Barkley, C. 169
Baron, R. A. 123–124, 148, 150, 170
Baron, R. S. 87–88, 209
Barrick, M. R. 243
Barsade, S. G. 230–231
Bartels, A. 45
Bartholomew, K. 189
Basking In Reflected Glory (BIRG) 191
Bass, B. M. 249
Bates, E. 124
Batra, R. K. 150–151
Batson, C. D. 68, 69, 75–77
Baumeister, R. F. 4, 8, 13–15, 205
Beach, S. R. 27
beautiful day 55–56
Becker, L. A. 107
Bègue, L. 154–155
behaviour 230–234; complex, between locations 234–239
Bekafigo, M. A. 216
Bell, P. A. 150
Bellezza, S. 97
Bem, D. J. 2
be nice 32–33
Bensafi, M. 40
Bereczkei, T. 74
Berglas, S. 10–12
Berkowitz, L. 172
Berlyne, D. E. 28

Berndt, E. R. 129
Berscheid, E. 38, 43, 47
Bettencourt, B. 160, 170
better-than-average individual 12–13
BIRG *see* Basking In Reflected Glory (BIRG)
Björkqvist, K. 159, 161
Blair, T. 116
blind listening 106
Bloom, P. 199
Bond, R. 86–87
Booth, D. A. 30
Borsari, B. 95
Bossard, J. H. 27–28
Bottger, P. C. 213
Brandt, R. 5
Brannon, L. A. 133
Branscombe, N. R. 123, 192
Brauer, M. 216
Brewer, M. B. 206
Brock, T. C. 104, 107
Brooksbank, B. W. 30
Brown, D. J. 250
Brown, K. J. 159
Brown, R. 171, 172, 209, 220
Brown, W. D. 161
Bryan, J. H. 69
bullshitting 118
Burger, J. M. 34, 67
Burleson, B. R. 61
Burns, J. M.: "Leadership" 249
Burnstein, E. 74, 173
Bush, G. W. 218, 254
Bushman, B. J. 14–15, 166, 168, 173, 212
Buss, D. M. 127, 161, 163
Butz, D. A. 193
Byrne, D. 34

Cacioppo, J. T. 113
Cal, A. V. 102, 103
Calhoun, J. B. 157
Campbell, A. C. 69–70
Campbell, D. T. 116–117, 193

259

Campbell, W. K. 4
canned laughter 90–91
Carey, K. B. 95
Carlsmith, J. M. 58–59, 148
Carlyle, T. 244
Carnes, N. 135
Carpenter, C. J. 5
Carpenter, J. A. 152
Carrick, R. 92, 93
Carson, K. L. 133
Carter, L. F. 245
Cartwright, D. 205
Carver, C. S. 209
catharsis 173
Chae, J. 5
Chagnon, N. A. 165
Chaiken, S. 4, 108, 115
Chang, L. 163
charisma 244
charity donations 70
Chen, H. 217
Chen, M. 72–73
Cheney, T. 35
Choma, B. L. 192
Chorost, A. F. 46
Chou, E. Y. 110, *110*
Chu, G. C. 114
Churchill, W. 245, *246*
Cialdini, R. B. 65, 89, 117
city accommodation 77–78
Claidière, N. 85
Clendenen, V. I. 207
Coan, J. A. 24–25
cognitive misers 123, 187
Cohen, A. B. 46
Cohen, D. 164, 165
Cohen, L. E. 149
Cohn, E. G. 150
Coker, B. L. 117
Coleman, L. M. 39
collective violence 227–240
collectivist cultures 15–16
Collins, J. 243
Collins, M. E. 194
Collins, N. L. 44
Collisson, B. 10
comfort smelling 29–30
companionate love 46–47; definition of 46
conformity 85–87; outside the lab 89–90; without knowledge 92–94
Connelly, B. S. 7
"consistency" principle 117
contagion 227–233, 235, 239, 240; emotional 231

contingency theory 248
controlled processing 138–142; increasing 139–140; limits of 140–142
Cooley, C. H. 8
copycat behaviour 235
CORF *see* Cutting Off Reflected Failure (CORF)
Corman, M. D. 153
Cottrell, N. B. 208, 209
Cowley, J. J. 30
Coyne, J. C. 25
Craig, C. 147
Crandall, C. S. 135, 136
Crawford, T. J. 115–116
Crazy Bastard Hypothesis 164
Crisp, R. J. 194–195
Croes, E. A. 36
Crofton, C. 33
Cross, H. A. 26
Cross, K. P. 12
crowding 157–159
Crowley, M. 61–62
Cuddy, A. J. 184, 186
culture 86–89, 164; collectivist 15–16; role in physical attraction 45–46
Cunningham, C. 30
Cunningham, M. R. 38, 46, 55, 56
Cutting Off Reflected Failure (CORF) 190, 191

Daly, M. 161–162
Daniyal, M. 167
Darley, J. M. 43, 63, 75
Das, E. 191–192
Davies, P. 169
DeBruine, L. M. 33, 66
de Camp Wilson, T. 1
De Cremer, D. 254
De Dreu, C. K. 38
De Gail, M. A. 57
de Leeuw, R. N. 71
deliberative thinking 110
democratic leaders 247
DeSteno, D. 189
destructive feedback 170
Deutsch, M. 86, 194
DeWall, C. N. 6, 154
DiBartolo, L. 148, 149
Diekman, A. B. 131
Diener, E. 156, 212
diffusion of responsibility 63
Dijksterhuis, A. 139
Dillard, J. P. 112

Dionne, S. 127
discrimination 183, 195, 197–198
Dishion, T. J. 217
Dolinski, D. 58, 59
Dollard, J. 170–172
Donath, J. S. 34
Donohue, J. M. 129
Doob, A. N. 105, 131
Downing, L. L. 212
Drabman, R. S. 168
Dutton, D. G. 42, 43, 197

Eagly, A. H., 61–62, 107, 115, 184, 251
Eberhardt, J. L. 188
Edwards, D. 108
Edwards-Levy, A. 105
Efrat-Treister, D. 171
Eibach, R. P. 10
Eidelman, S. 135, 136
Eisenberger, N. I. 23–24
Elaboration Likelihood Model 103
Eldersveld, S. J. 116
Em, S. 244
emergency, gender and 61–62
emotional appeals 112–113
Empathy-Altruism Hypothesis 68–69
Emswiller, T. 66
Epley, N. 65
Erlandsson, A. 109–110
ESP *see* extrasensory perception (ESP)
Esses, V. M. 183
Essock-Vitale, S. M. 74
Evans, M. 3
evolution 161–163
evolutionary theory 163
excitation 173–174
excitation-transfer model 174
Exline, J. J. 9
extended contact hypothesis 194
extrasensory perception (ESP) 36

face-to-face persuasion 115–116
false consensus effect 9–10; definition of 9
false modesty 8–9
familiarity 25–28
fear 111–112
"fear-then-relief" technique 58
Felson, M. 149
Felson, R. B. 165
femininity 161
Feshbach, S. 111, 112

Fessler, D. M. 164
Festinger, L. 106, 157
Fiedler, E. R. 7
Fiedler, F. E. 248
Field, N. 247
"fight or flight" response 159
Filindra, A. 193
Fiore, A. T. 34
Fischer-Lokou, J. 57
Fisher, H. E. 23, 45
Fiske, S. T. 184
Fitz, B. 76
Flowe, H. D. 153–154
Folkes, V. S. 38
Forbes, G. B. 37
Forrester, R. L. 13
Forsyth, D. R. 14, 250
Foshay, N. N. 63
Foti, R. J. 251
Fox, C. R. 132
Freud, S. 173
Frey, B. S. 90
Friend, R. 98
Frohlich, P. F. 43
Fromkin, H. L. 96, 97
frustration 170
frustration-aggression hypothesis 171
Furnham, A. 37, 45–46

Gabrenya, W. K. Jr. 210
Gailliot, M. T. 189
Gamer, R. 104
gang delinquency 217
Garcia, S. M. 63, 64
García-Bajos, E. 125
Garcia-Retamero, R. 251
Gardner, W. L. 209
Garnham, W. A. 168–169
Gelstein, S. 31
gender 159–161; and emergency 61–62; stereotypes of 183–187
generosity 69
Genghis Khan 248
Gerard, H. B. 86
Ghandi, M. 137–138
Giancola, P. R. 153
Gibson, B. 166
Gibson, M. 245
Giessner, S. R. 254
Gifford, R. K. 189
Gilovich, T. D 6
glass ceiling effect 251–252
glass cliff metaphor 185, *185*, 253
Golder, F. 97
Goldman, M. S. 30

Goldstein, N. J. 90
Gore, A. 254–255
Gove, W. R. 158
Graber, D. A. 131
Graves, K. N. 160
Greitemeyer, T. 71, 73, 183
Griffit, W. 41, 42
Grimm, W. 169
Griskevicius, V. 98, 162
Gross, A. E. 33, 58–59
groups: bad 211–212; decision-making 212; definition of 205–206; formation, reasons for 205–206; mass of 209–210; and performance 206–207; polarisation 216, 217; risky shifts 216–218; sharing 212–213; simple task 208–209
groupthink 214–216, *214*
Grunberg, N. E. 159
Guéguen, N. 55, 57
Gupta, U. 45

Haandrikman, K. 28
Halberstadt, J. 37–38
Hamilton, D. L. 189
Hamilton, W. D. 74
hand-holding 24–25
Hansson, R. O. 77
Hanyu, K. 41
Harakeh, Z. 89
Harber, K. D. 195, 196
Hare, A. P. 248
Harkins, S. G. 210
Harmon-Jones, E. 27
Harries, K. D. 148, 150
Harris, M. B. 171
Hasher, L. 116
Haslam, S. A. 185, *185*, 245, 246, 253–255
Hassan, A. 167
Hatfield, E. 38, 46
Hawley, P. H. 160
He, D. 32
Heatherton, T. F. 15
Heilman, M. E. 184, 251
Heine, S. J. 45
helping 69–71
Hemsley, G. D. 105
Hendriks, F. 114
heuristics 123
Hogg, M. A. 245, 254
Holt-Lunstad, J. 25
Homel, R. 157
Homophily Principle 34

Hopthrow, T. 219
Horne, Z. 113
Hovland, C. I. 113, 114
Howard, D. J. 104
Hunt, J. B. 109
Huston, T. L. 46
hypermasculinity 161

ignorance, prejudice and 193–195
Ilko, S. A. 8
illusory correlation theory 188
Implicit Egotism 33
Inkeles, A. 78
introspection 1, 4, 96
Isen, A. M. 57; "Effect of feeling good on helping: Cookies and kindness" 56

Jackson, J. M. 210
Jaeger, C. M. 96
Jain, S. 113
James, H. 1
James, W. 1
Janes, L. M. 92
Janis, I. L. 111, 112, 214
Johnson, L. 215
Johnson, N. J. 25
Johnson, R. D. 212
Johnson, R. W. 248
Jones, E. E. 10–12
Jones, J. T. 33
Jones, L. M. 63
Josephs, R. A. 152, 153
Joshi, A. 184–185
Jostmann, N. B. 128–129
Joubert, C. E. 97
Joyce, W. 243
Judge, T. A. 245
Jung, H. 70–71

Kahneman, D. 130, 132–134, *133*, 134, 138
Karandashev, V. 36
Karau, S. J. 210, 251
Kaur, I. 39
Kaur, R. 251–252
Keating, C. F. 159–160
Keating, J. 218
Kellerman, J. 36
Kelley, H. H. 124–125
Kemp, E. 110–111
Kenrick, D. T. 150
Kerin, R. A. 104
Kerr, N. L. 210
Keshari, P. 113

Kiddoo, K. L. 136
Kim, H. 15–16
Kintsch, W. 124
Kirk-Smith, M. D. 30
Kitchens, J. T. 40
Kniffin, K. M. 32–33
Knight, B. 244
Knijn, T. C. 74
knowledge 87; access to 1–4, **4**
Knowles, M. L. 209
Koban, L. 89
Koenig, A. M. 61
Koestner, R. 10
Konrath, S. H. 186
Korde, R. 220
Korsakov's syndrome 126
Kowalski, R. M. 160, 161
Krawczyk, M. W. 134
Kret, M. E. 38
Kruger, J. 3
Kulik, J. A. 172
Kulkarni, S. S. 134
Kumkale, G. T. 118
Kunkel, A. W. 61
Kurz, E. 186

Lady Macbeth 60, *60*
LaFrance, M. 3
laissez-faire leaders 247
Lake, H. *70*
Lamy, L. 55
Landau, M. J. 126, 192
Lane, L. W. 142
Lang, A. R. 155
Langlois, J. H. 37
Lapidot-Lefler, N. 157
Laplace, A. C. 154
Lariscy, R. 118
Larrick, R. P. 147
Larsen, K. S. 87
Latané, B. 63–65, 210
Latham, D. R. 248
Lawrence, C. 158
Lazer, D. 218
Leader, T. 211
Leader Categorisation Theory 250
leaders: as actors 246–247;
 autocratic 247; as collaborative
 248–250; as contingent 248;
 democratic 247; as general people
 254–255; as great people 244–
 245; laissez-faire 247; as male
 251–254; as prototypes 250–251;
 as situationally determined
 245–246

leadership: definition of 243;
 styles 247; transactional 248;
 transformational 249; types,
 theory of 246
Leary, M. R. 205
Le Bon, G. 229
Lennox, V. L. 197
Leonardelli, G. J. 205
Levin, P. F. 57; "Effect of feeling
 good on helping: Cookies and
 kindness" 56
Levine, J. M. 85
Levine, M. 62, 66, 67
LeVine, R. A. 193
Levine, R. V. 62, 78
Lewandowski, G. W. 32, 43
Lewin, K. 246
Lewis, I. M. 112
Liefbroer, A. C. 74
Liersch, M. J. 142
Liljenquist, K. 59, 129
Lin, M. *128*
Lin, S. C. *128*
Lincoln, A. 147
Lindauer, M. 112
Linder, D. 38, *39*
Lobel, M. 9
López-Zafra, E. 251
Lord, C. G. 139–140
Lord, R. G. 250
Lount, R. B. Jr. 210
love: addiction to 45; companionate
 46–47
Loveland, J. M. 216
Loy, J. W. 125
Lugo, J. 169
Lykken, D. T. 217

Ma, V. 15
MacDonald, T. K. 6
MacFarlane, S. W. 150
Macintyre, S. 157
Mackinnon, S. P. 33
MacNeill, N. 250
Macrae, C. N. 141, 142
Maddux, J. E. 109
Madsen, E. A. 75
Major Histocompatibility Complex
 (MHC) 31
manhood 163
Mann, L. 156–157, 211
Marcy, C. 68, 69
Mares, D. M. 149
marital quality 25
Markey, P. M. 63

Markman, K. D. 139
Markus, H. R. 15–16
Marlatt, G. A. 155
Marmaros, D. 28
Martin, J. L. 158
Martin, R. 89–90
Maslow, A. H. 40
Mazza, M. 171
McCafferty, D. 24
McCarthyism 87
McClintock, M. K. 159
McConnell, H. K. 2
McGuire, M. T. 74
McKay-Nesbitt, J. 113
McKelvie, S. J. 131–132, **132**
McKenna, F. P. 112
media 166–169, **167**
Medvec, V. H. 138–139
Meier, B. P. 127
Meier, S. 90
Mencken, F. C. 76
Meno, P. 230
mere exposure effect 194
Merkel, A. *252*
message content: appeal to heart
 or minds 109–112; argument
 113–114; emotional appeals
 112–113
Messick, D. M. 208–209, 248
Messner, S. F. 217
Meston, C. M. 43
metaphors: use of 126–129
MHC *see* Major Histocompatibility
 Complex (MHC)
Michaels, J. W. 207–208
Midgley, C. 12
Midlarsky, M. I. 228
Migueles, M. 125
Miles-Novelo, A. 149
Milgram, S. 77, 229
Milinski, M. 31
Miller, C. B. 190–191
Miller, D. T. 138, 196–197
Miller, L. C. 44
Miller, N. 105, 116–117, 160, 170
Miller, R. S. 8
Mills, J. 108
Mims, P. R. 62
Mintz, N. L. 40
Miwa, Y. 41
Mladinic, A. 184
Moffett, K. W 149
Mojzisch, A. 213
Molloy, K. 37
Mølmen, G. N. 217

Monahan, J. L. 25
Monin, B. 10, 27, 196–197
Montoya, R. M. 28, 34
Moons, W. G. 116
Moore, S. C. 174
Mor, N. 5–6
moral credentialing 197
moral transgressions 129
Moreland, R. L. 27
Moscovici, S. 216, 219
Mrug, S. 168
Mullen, B. 209
Murnighan, J. K. 110, *110*
Murray, S. L. 13
Myers, D. G. 183, 214, 220, 228

Nakamura, G. V. 124
narcissism 4–5
National Institute of Health 106
Nawrat, R. 58, 59
Neale, M. A. 136–137
Negative Affect Escape Model 150
Neighbors, C. 95
Neville, F. 232–233
Ng, B. 158
nice games/music 71–74
Nijman, H. L. 158
Nijstad, B. A. 220
Nisbett, R. E. 1, 2, 164
Nixon, M. 245
Nolan, J. M., 93, 94
non-conformity 97
non-verbal aggression 160
Northcraft, G. B. 136–137
Norton, M. I. 10, 197–198
Nurmi, J. E. 13
Nye, J. L. 250

Obama, B. 105, 191, 218, 249
Obama Effect 195
Office for National Statistics 159
Olson, J. M. 92, 102, 103
Ones, D. S. 7
online disinhibition effect 157
Ontario Science Centre 131
Organ, D. W. 244
Osswald, S. 73
Österman, K. 159
Ostrov, J. M. 159–160
Otrachshenko, V. 151
Otta, E. 57
Ovid: "Metamorphoses" 23
Oyserman, D. 16
Ozanne, L. 112
Ozanne, M. 108–109

Padilla-Walker, L. M. 71
Page, L. A. 149
Palmer, J. K. 216
Pandey, J. 158
Paolini, S. 194
Pare, P. P. 165
Park, E. S. 213
Parkinson, B. 232
Pashler, H. 221
Pattershall, J. 135
Paulus, P. B. 220
Paunonen, S. V. 32, 33
Payne, B. K. 187
Pearson-Merkowitz, S. 193
Pehrson, S. 209, 220
Pelham, B. W. 104
Peña, J. 72–73
Pendry, L. 92, 93
perceived similarity 34–35
Pereira, C. 183
Perrett, D. I. 46
Perrin, S. 87
Perry, P. J. 28
personality traits 245
persuasion 101–118; appeal to heart or minds 109–112; emotional appeals 112–113; face-to-face 115–116; repetition, role of 116; sleeper effect 117–118; timing of 116–117
persuasive arguments theory 216
Peter, J. 74
Petrocelli, J. V. 118
Pettigrew, T. F. 194
Petty, R. E. 103
physical aggression 159, 160
physical attraction, psychology of 23–47; addiction to love 45; average 36–38; be nice 32–33; companionate love 46–47; culture, role of 45–46; familiarity 25–28; first date, scary of 42–43; gaze into each other's eyes 36; obsessed with self 33–36, *35*; place of meeting 40–42; positive person 38–39, *38*; self-disclose 43–44; smell 28–31, *29*
Piff, P. K. 67, 68
Pihl, R. O. 153
Piliavin, I. M. 65–66
Piliavin, J. A. 65–66
Pittsburgh AIDS Task Force 2
planning fallacy 3
Plant, E. A. 195
Platow, M. J. 90, 255

positive mood 56–58; effect on prosocial behaviour 56; from guilt 58–60
positive person 38–39, *38*
Postmes, T. 85
Potter, J. 108
prejudice 183, 199; and ignorance 193–195; and scarce resources 193; and threat 191–192
Priest, R. F. 28
process loss 213
Pronin, E. 96
prosocial behaviour 55, 58, *60*, 62, 63, 70, 71, 74, 78, 168; positive mood, effect of 56
provocation 169–170

Quinton, W. J. 194

Rachubik, J. 134
racial prejudice 13
Rajecki, D. W. 26–27
Randal, J. 89–90
Ransberger, V. M. 148
Ravndal, J. A. 217
'Reading the Riots' project 237
Realistic Conflict Theory 193
Rector, G. 158
Regan, D. T. 59
Reicher, S. D. 229, 255
Reidy, D. E. 160
relational aggression 160, 166
relatives 74–75
religion 75–77
Renzetti, C. M. 13
repetition 116
representativeness heuristic 133–135
Repulsion Hypothesis 35
Restrepo, P. 165
Rhodes, G. 37, 38
Rhodes, N. 87
Rhodewalt, F. 11
Richter, I. 96
Richter, T. 118
Rideout, V. J. 167
Rind, B. 56
ripple effect 230
risk aversion 219
risky shifts 216–218
Robarchek, C. A. 165
Robarchek, C. J. 165
Roberts, J. V. 131
Robinson, M. D. 126, 127
Rodin, J. 64–65

Rogers, R. W. 109
Roggman, L. A. 37
Rohrer, J. H. 85
Rohsenow, D. J. 155
Role Congruity Theory 251
Rosenbaum, M. E. 35
Rosenberg, R. S. 71–72
Rosenfield, D. 197
Ross, L. 9
Ross, M. 6
Rotton, J. 40
Routine Activity Theory 149
Ruback, R. 158
Ruddock, H. K. 207
Rushton, J. P. 69–70
Ryan, B. J. 248
Ryan, M. E. 149
Ryan, M. K. 185, *185*, 253

Sääksjärvi, M. 109
Sacerdote, B. 28
Sacks, O. 126
Sadin, M. L. 135
Salmela-Aro, K. 13
same-sex law 192
Sanders, G. S. 220
Savitsky, K. 6, 138–139
Sawyer, J. 28
scarce resources, prejudice and 193
Schachter, S. 2, 91, 174
Schadenfreude 14
Schank, R. C. 124
Scheier, M. F. 209
schemas: definition of 123–124; use of 123–126
Schimmelpfennig, C. 109
Schlenker, B. R. 8
Schmitt, M. T. 192
Schnall, S. 129
Schneider, F. W. 56
Schoeneman, T. J. 15
Schooler, J. W. 4
Schroeder, J. 210
Schubert, T. W. 126
Schultz, P. W. 94–96
Schulz-Hardt, S. 213, 215
Schwarz, N. 186
scratching model *234*
Sczesny, S. 184
Sear, R. 74
Sears, D. O. 38
Sears, J. D. 151, 152
Sedikides, C. 12
Segal, M. W. 28

self: better-than-average individual 12–13; false consensus effect 9–10; false modesty 8–9; obsessed with 4–6, *5*, 33–36, *35*; others understanding of 6–13; self-attention 209; self-awareness 212; self-bias 112; self-censorship 215; self-compensation 32; self-disclose 43–44; self-esteem 13–15, 109; self-handicapping 10–12, *11*; self-reports 6–7
Self-Handicapping Scale 11
Selfhout, M. 34
selfie-taking, on social media 5
selfish helpers 65, 78
Sentyrz, S. M. 212
sexual aggression 154
sexual harassment 3
Shackelford, T. K. 161, 163
Shackleton, E. 246
shallow gratitude 8
Sharma, S. 251–252
Sharma, V 39
Shepherd, L. 192
Sherif, M. 85, 86, 89
Shin, J. E. 28
Sieff, E. M. 2
Silke, A. 211
Silva, A. 243
Sime, J. D. 75
similarity 66–68, 90–92, 254; similarity-attraction effect 45; successful persuader 104–105
Simonton, D. K. 244
Simpatia culture 62
simple task 208–209
Sims, R. L. 252
Singer, J. 174
Singh, P. 45
Sivarajasingam, V. 174
Skowronski, J. J. 209
Slade, K. M. 77
Slater, M. D. 168
Slater, P. E. 247
sleeper effect 117–118
slime effect 39
Sluckin, W. 25–26
Slutkin, G. 235
Small, D. A. 110
smell 28–31
Smith, D. L. 163
Smith, P. B. 86–87
Smith, T. W. 6
Smithies, D. 1
Snyder, C. R. 96, 97

Snyder, M. L. 196
social anxiety 196
social cognition 123, 126, 127
social exchange theory 65–66
social identity 227, 229–230, 232–234, 236, 239, 255; definition of 232; shared 240; theory 190, 254
social loafing 210
Social Penetration Theory 44
socio-emotional specialists 247
Solomon, H. 57
Sorrentino, R. M. 247
Spencer, C. 87
Spencer, S. J. 187
spotlight effect 6
Sprecher, S. 44
Stadler, S. J. 148
Stasser, G. 213
status quo heuristic 135–136, **136**
Steele, C. M. 152, 153, 187
Steffens, N. K. 251
Steiner, I. D. 213
stereotypes 133, 139, 141, 154, 161; of gender 183–187; use of 187–190, **189**
Stern, K. 159
Stevens, H. R. 149
Stewart, A. E. 7
Stewart, D. W. 248
Stogdill, R. 243
Stoner, J. A. F. 218–219
strategic self-ignorance 13
Stroebe, W. 207
Strohmetz, D. 56
successful persuader: credible 101–103; as fast talker 105; good-looking 108–109; similarity 104–105; trustworthy 105–108
suggestibility 229
Suler, J. 157
Sunstein, C. R. 131, 219
Surowiecki, J. 212–213
Svenson, O. 12
Swami, V. 37, 45–46, 97

Tai, A. J. R. 252
Taine, H. 229
Tajfel, H. 190
Tan, R. 30
Tannenbaum, I. J. 46
task specialists 247
Tatar, M. 169
Täuber, S. 67
Tay, R. S. 112
Taylor, D. A. 43–44

Taylor, S. E. 123, 159
Taylor, S. P. 151, 152
temperature 147–151
Tenbrunsel, A. 139
Test, M. A. 69
Thomas, M. H. 168
threat, prejudice and 191–192
threatened egotism 15
Thunström, L. 13
Tiggemann, M. 97
Tinkham, A. W. 118
Titus, W. 213
Toch, H. 229
Toi, M. 68, 69
tokenism 197
Tordesillas, R. S. 4
Tormala, Z. L. 102, 103
transactional leadership 248
transformational leadership 249
transparency, illusion of 6
Tremewan, T. 37
Triplett, E. 206–207
Tropp, L. R. 194
Trump, D. 105, 116, 216
Turner, R. N. 194–195
Tversky, A. 130, 133, 134
Twain, M. 47
Twenge, J. M. 4–5, 183, 214, 220
Twenty Statements Test 15
Tylka, T. L. 46

Underwood, L. G. 47
uniqueness, theory of 96–98
Urdan, T. 12
Ušto, M. 91

Vaillancourt, T. 14
Van Baaren, R. B. 36
Vandello, J. A. 163, 164
van der Laan, C. A. 71
van der Schalk, J. 231–232
Van de Vliert, E. 150

Van Dijk, W. W. 14
van Dijke, M. 254
Van Fleet, D. D. 245
Van Knippenberg, A. D. 139
van Knippenberg, D. 254
van Leeuwen, E. 67
Van Quaquebeke, N. 254
Vargas, P. T. 73
Vaughan, G. M. 244–245
Vazire, S. 6–7
Veenvliet, S. G., 33
Veitch, R. 41, 42
verbal aggression 158, 160, 169
Veysey, B. M. 217
VNO *see* vomeronasal organ (VNO)
Vohs, K. D. 15
Voland, E. 163
Vollebergh, W. A. 89
vomeronasal organ (VNO) 29
Vonk, R. 39
Vrij, A. 149
Vul, E. 221

Wager, T. D. 89
Wagstaff, D. 37
Walker, M. B. 87
Wallbom, M. 212
Walster, E. 106
Wann, D. L. 192
"warm glow" effect 57
Warner, R. H. 136
Warnick, D. H. 220
Watson, W. E. 212–213
Weber, E. U. 130
Weber, M. 244
Weber, R. J. 245
Wedekind, C. 31
Wegner, D. M. 140–142
Wells, B. M. 209
Werner, C. M. 114, *115*
Whillans, A. V. 78
White, J. W. 160, 161

White, T. L. 30
Whiten, A. 85
Widmeyer, W. N. 125
Wiegman, O. 104
Wilder, D. A. 190
Wilk, S. L. 210
Williams, K. 210
Williams, K. D. 210
Williams, L. E. 127
Willoughby, T. 172
Wilson, D. S. 32–33
Wilson, E. O. 75
Wilson, M. 161–162
Wilson, T. D. 3, 4
Witte, K. 112
Wittenbaum, G. M. 213
Wolfson, S. 9
Wood, W. 87
Woodzicka, J. A. 3
Worchel, P. 38, 173
Worchel, S. 210
Worringham, C. J. 208–209
Wright, S. C. 194

Xu, H. 60

yawning model *233*
Yogeeswaran, K. 193
Yoon, G. 73
Yukl, G. 245

Zajonc, R. B. 112, 193–194, 207, 208
Zaleznik, A. 250
Zanbaka, C. 207
Zander, A. 205
Zavalloni, M. 216, 219
Zeichner, A. 153
Zeki, S. 45
Zhang, Y. 65
Zhong, C. B. 59, 205, 211
Zillman, D. 173, 174
Zweigenhaft, R. L. 97